THWIPIPIP!

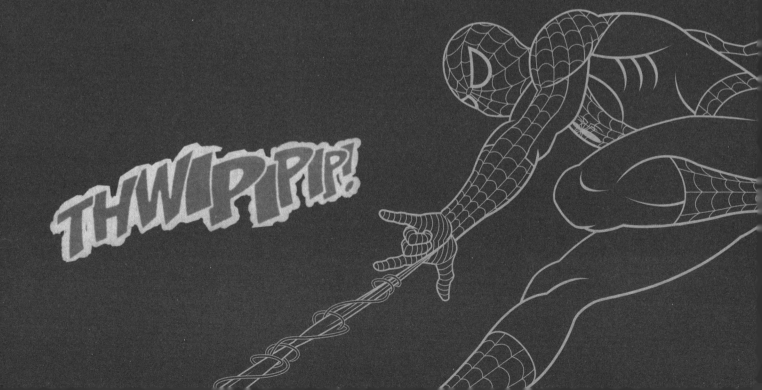

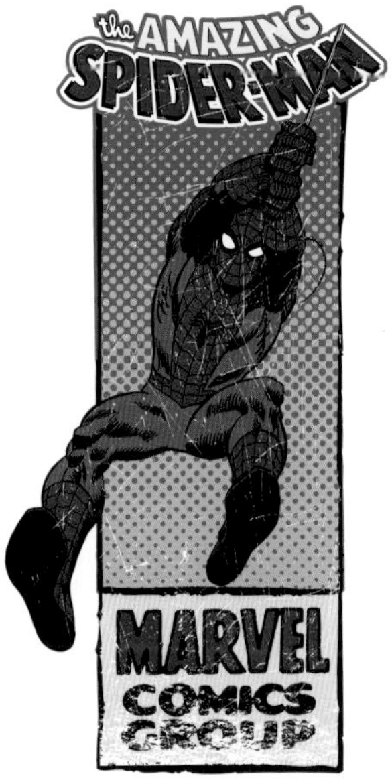
the AMAZING
SPIDER-MAN
MARVEL
COMICS
GROUP

DK

LONDON, NEW YORK, MELBOURNE,
MUNICH, AND DELHI

Senior Editors Laura Gilbert and Helen Murray
Editorial Assistant Emma Grange
Designers Owen Bennett and Lauren Rosier
Art editors Nico Alba, Akanksha Gupta, and Lisa Sodeau
Design Assistant Rhys Thomas
Senior Art Editors Guy Harvey and Rajnish Kashyap
Senior Designer and Brand Manager Robert Perry
Design Manager Ron Stobbart
Publishing Manager Catherine Saunders
Art Director Lisa Lanzarini
Publisher Simon Beecroft
Publishing Director Alex Allan
Senior Production Editors Clare McLean and Jennifer Murray
Production Controller Shabana Shakir

First published in the United States in 2012 by
DK Publishing
375 Hudson Street
New York, New York 10014

10 9 8 7 6 5 4 3 2 1
001-183356-May/12

Page design copyright © 2012 Dorling Kindersley Limited

A catalog record for this book is
available from the Library of Congress.

ISBN: 978-0-7566-9089-2

Color reproduction by Altaimage
Printed and bound in China by Hung Hing

The publisher would like to thank Shari Last for the index and
editorial assistance; Neil Kelly for editorial assistance; Anjan Dey
and Era Chawla for design assistance; Chelsea Alon, Rich Thomas,
Scott Piehl, and Lauren Kressel from Disney Publishing; Ruwan
Jayatilleke and Kelly Lamy from Marvel.

www.marvel.com

Discover more at
www.dk.com

SPIDER-MAN

INSIDE THE WORLD OF YOUR FRIENDLY NEIGHBORHOOD HERO

WRITTEN BY

MATTHEW K. MANNING

With additional text by Tom DeFalco

Contents

Foreword	6
Introducing… Spider-Man	8
The Story of Spider-Man	10
Amazing Fantasy #15	12
The Costume	14
Suit Up!	16
With Great Power…	18
The Web He Weaves	20
Peter Parker	22
Friends & Family	24
The *Daily Bugle*	26
Spider-Man of All Trades	28
Horizon Labs	29
Parker's Problems	30
When a Spider-Man Loves a Woman	32
Amazing Friends	34
Team Player	36
Spidey Team-Ups	38
Main Enemies	40
Other Enemies	44
Timeline	48
The 1960s	56
The Amazing Spider-Man #1	60
Chameleon	62
Vulture	64
Doctor Octopus	66
Sandman	68
Lizard	70
Electro	72
Mysterio	74
Green Goblin	76
Hulk vs Spider-Man	78
Kraven	80
Sinister Six	82
Scorpion	84
The Amazing Spider-Man #33	86
Rhino	88
Mary Jane	90
The 1970s	92
The Death of the Stacys	96
Spider-Man vs The Punisher	98
The New Green Goblin	100
The Amazing Spider-Man #149	102
Black Cat	104
Spider-Women	106
The 1980s	108
Hobgoblin	112
Nothing Can Stop the Juggernaut	114
The Amazing Spider-Man #248	116
The Saga of the Alien Costume	118
The Death of Jean DeWolff	120
Kraven's Last Hunt	122
The Wedding?	124
Venom	126
Venom Legacy	128
Cosmic Adventures	130
The 1990s	132
Spider-Man #1	136

Carnage	138
The Spectacular Spider-Man #200	140
Maximum Carnage	142
The Clone Saga	144
Scarlet Spider	146
The Amazing Spider-Man #400	148
Identity Crisis	150
A New Chapter	152
The 2000s	154
Ezekiel	158
Morlun	159
The New Avengers	160
The Other	162
The Iron Spider	164
Civil War	166
The Amazing Spider-Man #533	168
One More Day	170
Brand New Day	172
Brand New Threats	174
Iron Patriot	176
The Grim Hunt	178
The Amazing Spider-Man #655	180
Future Foundation	182
Alternate Realities	184
Spider Girl	186
Ultimate Spider-Man	188
Ultimate Tales	190
Amazing Artwork	192
Afterword	194
Index	196

Over the years, hundreds of artists have lent their talents to the pages of a Spider-Man comic. Each brings a new and different interpretation to the world famous wall-crawler.

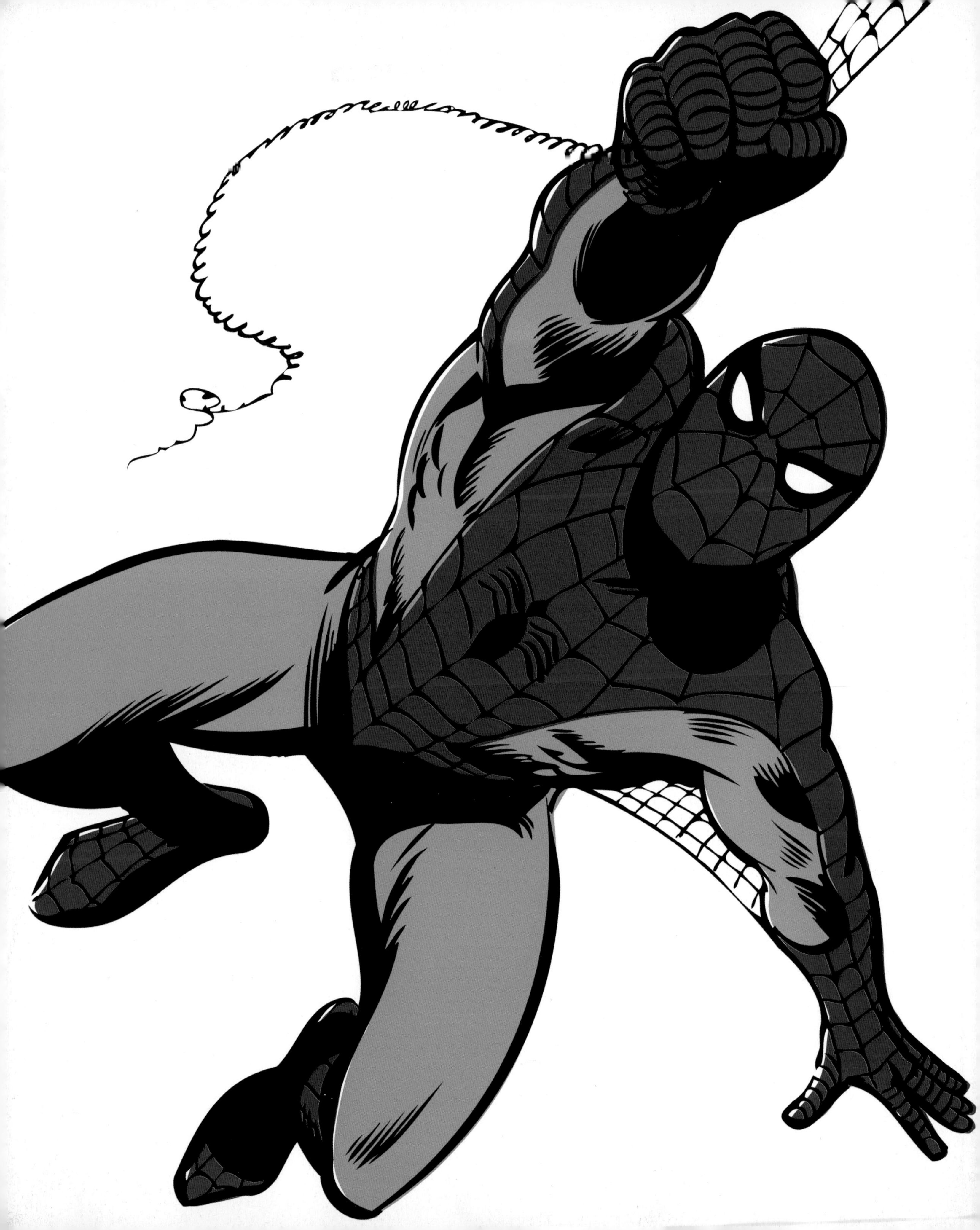

FOREWORD

LIFE IS FUNNY! (As if you didn't know). I don't mean "Ha ha funny." I mean in the sense of odd, peculiar, strange.

You're probably wondering what this has to do with Spider-Man. Well, I'm glad you asked.

You see, before coming up with the idea for everyone's favorite web-swinger, I had already created The Fantastic Four and the incredible Hulk. And, after doing Spidey, Marvel and I then generously gifted an appreciative world with such characters as the X-Men, Daredevil, Iron Man, The Avengers, and... well, you get the idea.

So here's the point. Why is it that every new person I meet usually says something like, "Hey, aren't you the one who wrote Spider-Man?" I mean, they hardly ever ask me if I wrote the Hulk, or The Silver Surfer, or even Sgt. Fury and the Howling Commandos (for those of you with really long memories)? Nope, it's always, "Aren't you the one who wrote Spider-Man?"

Now, things like that make me think. Why is Spider-Man the first character that comes to mind when people mention Marvel or me? Over the years I've come up with a theory about that and now, because of my justly famed generosity, I'd like to share it with you.

I think Spidey has made such a lasting impression because he's possibly the most realistically human of all Super Heroes. He never has enough money, he's constantly beset by personal problems, and the world doesn't exactly applaud his deeds—in fact, most people tend to suspect and distrust him. In short, he's a lot like you and me.

There's another thing about Peter and his arachnid alter ego. When his series first started, way back in 1963, Peter was just a teenager, still in school. Most of the comic-book readers were teenagers as well, so that made it really easy for them to identify with him. You see, at that time all the comic-book Super Heroes were adults. The only teenagers in comics were the heroes' sidekicks. Well, I figured, "Where is it written that teenagers can only be sidekicks?" The answer, of course, was "Nowhere!" So, Spidey was probably the first comic-book hero that teenagers themselves could identify with.

Whoa, I think I omitted another important point. You may have noticed that Peter Parker never lived in Gotham City, or Metropolis, or any place that was obviously a fictional city. Nope, his very first story planted him firmly in Forest Hills, a part of New York City. So readers could really visualize him web-swinging around the streets of New York and its environs. It was just another element that gave Spidey a feeling of reality even though he was actually part of an imaginative comic-book universe.

Finally, there was the humor. I tried to make sure that our web-headed wonder was never without some sort of wisecrack or sharp retort, no matter how tense a situation might be. That, too, was an effort to be realistic because, as you know, most young people have a flip way of speaking. They're never as proper or pedantic as so many other heroes are portrayed. In fact, just between you and me, Spidey speaks a lot like I do. Or maybe I speak like he does. After a while, it's hard to tell who's imitating whom!

And there you have it. My take on the reason Spider-Man seems to have such an unshakable hold on the minds and emotions of so many readers. Even though I'm equally proud of the many other characters the mighty Marvel bullpen and I have been associated with over the years, I now feel I can understand why our wondrous wall-crawler is the first one people think of when they talk comics to me. And I hope I've succeeded in making it clearer to you, too.

If I haven't succeeded, that's okay. It makes me resemble poor ol' Peter Parker even more. None of us ever seems to get anything totally right!

But don't waste time worrying about us. There's a lot of story waiting for you on the pages ahead. So wiggle your webs and plunge right in. You know how your friendly neighborhood Spider-Man hates to be kept waiting!

Excelsior!

One of the most iconic Super Heroes of all time, Spider-Man has leapt off the comic book page and into the mainstream. From big budget Hollywood films to action figures, from T-shirts to theme park attractions, from cartoons to a Broadway musical, Spider-Man's popularity is an indisputable fact, as is his status as Marvel's most notable creation.

INTRODUCING...

SPIDER-MAN

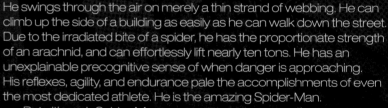

He swings through the air on merely a thin strand of webbing. He can climb up the side of a building as easily as he can walk down the street. Due to the irradiated bite of a spider, he has the proportionate strength of an arachnid, and can effortlessly lift nearly ten tons. He has an unexplainable precognitive sense of when danger is approaching. His reflexes, agility, and endurance pale the accomplishments of even the most dedicated athlete. He is the amazing Spider-Man.

But although Spider-Man possesses more power than most people could dream of, his alter ego, Peter Parker, is just a regular guy trying to make ends meet. Imbued with a strict moral code and a heightened sense of responsibility, Peter is always struggling to do the right thing, no matter the sacrifice involved. More than just the sum of his abilities, Spider-Man's strength and longevity come from the man beneath the mask, a man whose often-heard mantra dictates his every decision: "With great power there must also come—great responsibility!"

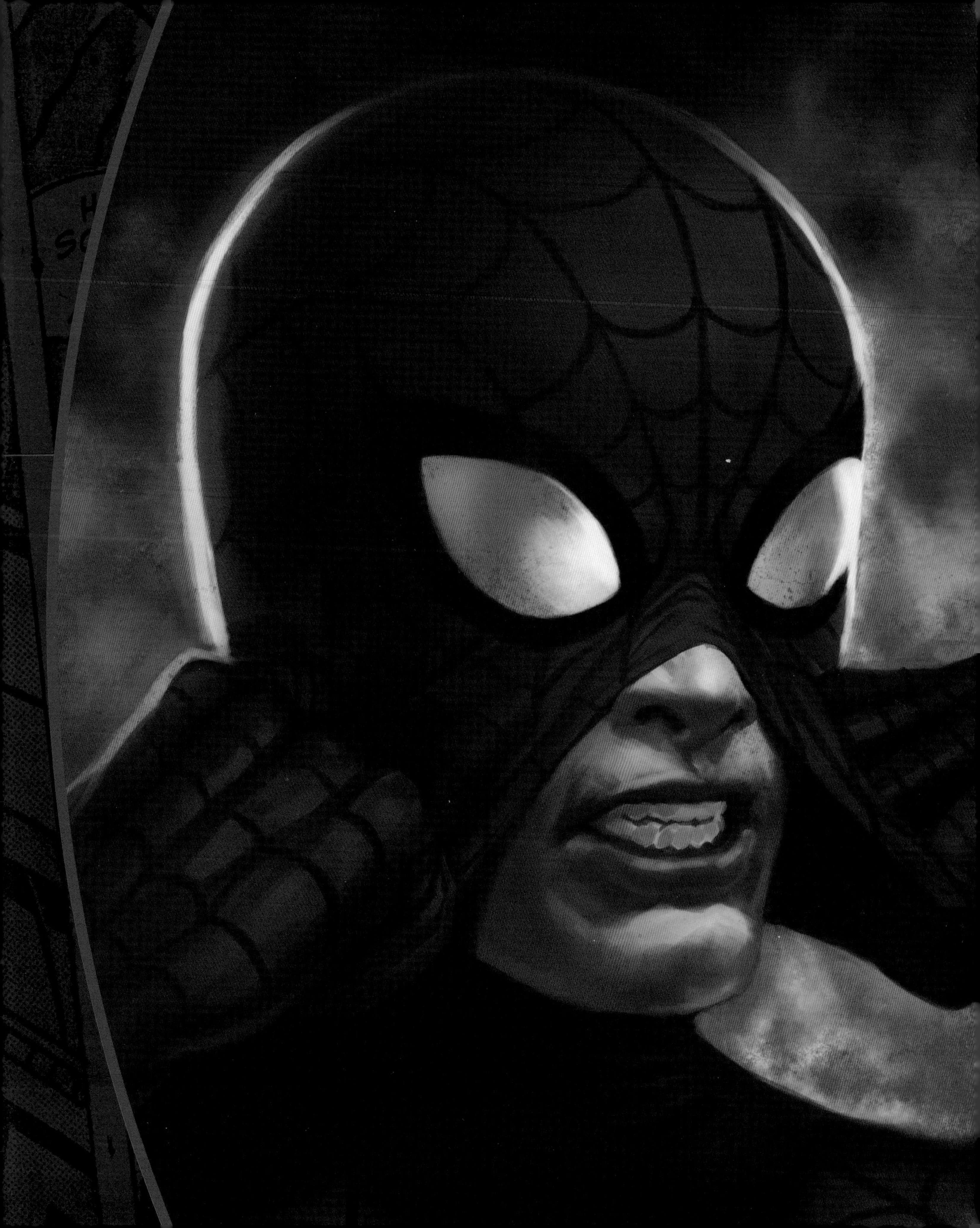

"THIS SURE BEATS WAITING FOR A BUS!"

Stan Lee was toying with the idea of leaving comics. Fed up with the stagnant Super Hero format, Lee decided that before he quit, he'd take a whack at writing comics his way. From that simple idea sprang the Marvel Age of comics, and its main attraction—Spider-Man.

Stan Lee knew that he'd chanced upon something special when he concocted the idea of the Super Hero Spider-Man and his teenage alter ego Peter Parker. Before that time, almost every teenager in comics served as a sidekick. They were meant to be a younger voice that kids could relate to in order to better enjoy the adventures of the sidekick's mentor, the comic's star. Stan never liked sidekicks, but he saw potential in the concept of having a young lead character that a newer generation could claim as their own. So Lee placed Peter Parker squarely in high school, and to go even further, he decided to make Peter a bit of a bookworm. This in turn made the hero even more relatable. Peter Parker wasn't the type of high school student to try out for the football team, he was the kind who was more comfortable sitting on the sidelines reading a good book—or comic book, as the case may be.

Knowing he had a home run on his hands, Lee put a lot of consideration into deciding which artist to pair with. Although he usually partnered with the legendary Jack Kirby, after seeing Kirby's Spider-Man artwork, Lee decided Jack was making the character too heroic, and not the underdog Lee wanted to portray. While Jack sketched the cover, Lee turned to the brilliant Steve Ditko for the interiors, and everything fell smoothly into place. With the debut of *Amazing Fantasy* #15 in August 1962, the world met the amazing Spider-Man.

THE MAN-SPIDER?
Marvel had actually toyed with the idea of a Spider-Man before. In a story drawn by Jack Kirby called "Where Will You Be, When... the Spider Strikes!" and featured in *Journey Into Mystery* #73 (October 1961), an ordinary house spider is exposed to radiation and gains the abilities of a human. This monstrous spider even shot webbing, just like Spider-Man, but he was very different to the web-slinger we know and love.

WHOP!

THE CREATORS

"AND NOW, YOU HIGH-VOLTAGE HEEL, I'LL GIVE YOU SOMETHING TO TALK ABOUT WHEN YOU WAKE UP BACK IN YOUR CELL! YOU CAN TELL THE OTHER CONS HOW IT FEELS TO BE ON THE RECEIVING END OF A KNOCKOUT PUNCH BY YOUR FRIENDLY NEIGHBORHOOD SPIDER-MAN!!"

SPIDER-MAN TO ELECTRO

August 1962

AMAZING FANTASY #15 cover — Introducing Spider-Man

AMAZING FANTASY #15

"Okay, world—better hang onto your hat! Here comes the Spider-Man!"

PETER PARKER

EDITOR-IN-CHIEF
Stan Lee

COVER ARTISTS
Jack Kirby and Steve Ditko

WRITER
Stan Lee

PENCILER
Steve Ditko

INKER
Steve Ditko

LETTERER
Art Simek

MAIN CHARACTERS: Spider-Man; Aunt May Parker; Uncle Ben Parker; The Burglar
MAIN SUPPORTING CHARACTERS: Sally; Flash Thompson; Crusher Hogan
MAIN LOCATIONS: Midtown High School; the Parker residence; Science exhibit, New York City; wrestling arena, New York City; TV studio, New York City; Acme warehouse, Queens, New York

BACKGROUND

Faced with the prospect of cancellation, the publisher of *Amazing Fantasy*, a comic packed with alien and monster stories, had nothing to lose when he agreed to let Stan Lee and Steve Ditko introduce a new and unconventional Super Hero to the world. In a mere eleven pages, writer-editor Stan Lee and artist Steve Ditko spun a tale that would take most current comic book writers around six issues to weave. It was to become the most famous story in Spider-Man's history: his origin.

Lee, together with Ditko, set the stage for Spider-Man's career by focusing on the true star, Peter Parker. Unlike many other comics of the day, which relied on super-heroics to lure in readers, Lee wanted his protagonist to be an everyman, an easily relatable high school student, who had to deal with the typical problems and troubles of adolescence outside of the hectic world of crime fighting.

And Lee and Ditko were right. Something in this tidy little piece of storytelling and artistry struck a chord with the readers, and although this was the last issue of *Amazing Fantasy*, the web-slinger proved so popular that less than a year later he was granted his own ongoing comic, *The Amazing Spider-Man*.

> "If only I had stopped him when I **could** have! But I **didn't**—and now— Uncle Ben—is dead..."
>
> **PETER PARKER**

THE STORY

When bitten by a radioactive spider at a science exhibit, bookworm Peter Parker is transformed into the mysterious teen powerhouse sensation known as the amazing Spider-Man.

His classmates called him a "professional wallflower." The girls rejected him and the boys ridiculed and berated him every chance they got. But little did the students of Midtown High realize that soon enough they'd be calling Peter Parker "amazing."

But Peter's life wasn't all bad. Back in his modest Forest Hills home, Peter Parker had a support system in the form of his elderly Uncle Ben and Aunt May (**1**). Their kindness meant the world to him, and with their guidance, he often buried himself in his schoolwork, trying his best to ignore the cruel taunts of his high school peers (**2**).

On one such day, Peter was escaping his troubles at a science exhibit in New York City on radiology. Unbeknownst to the teen, a spider dangled into an active experiment, got doused by radioactive rays, and then bit Peter Parker on his hand (**3**). Feeling strange, Peter left the exhibit and wandered into the street, not noticing a car careering toward him. As if by instinct, the young man suddenly leapt out of the way, and managed to adhere to the side of a neighboring building (**4**).

After he accidentally crunched a steel pipe in his hand as if it were paper, Peter realized that the dying spider must have gifted him with an amazing new set of abilities (**5**). This was the opportunity he'd waited his entire life for. He quickly began to take advantage of his new powers, entering himself in an open-call wrestling match against a hulking brute called Crusher Hogan (**6**). Not wanting to reveal his identity to the general public, Peter donned a cheap mask as a disguise, and then easily defeated the wrestler in true showboat fashion. The match led to the cash prize, which led to Peter nabbing a publicity agent, which in turn led to the next big chapter in his life.

Peter crafted a bright costume and used his scientific knowledge to concoct wrist shooters and a revolutionary web-like adhesive (**7**). He dubbed himself Spider-Man and it wasn't long before he was starring in his own TV special. Happily strolling backstage after the first day's filming, Peter ignored the cries for help from a nearby policeman, and allowed a fleeing burglar to run right past him, unimpeded (**8**). It was a small incident, and Peter Parker assumed that it wasn't his problem.

Instead, Peter continued his career as Spider-Man, becoming a TV star and a national sensation. However, one night, when Peter was returning home from a personal appearance as Spider-Man, he was startled to find a police car parked in front of his house. The young man soon discovered his beloved Uncle Ben had been murdered (**9**), and that the culprit was held up at the Acme warehouse at the waterfront. In a fit of rage, Peter donned his Spider-Man costume, and swung across town to the dilapidated old building. The warehouse was surrounded by police, but they were powerless—the killer had plenty of places to hide and he would be able to pick them off one by one if they charged. Realizing it was only a matter of time before darkness fell, Spider-Man sprang into action. He quickly used his powers to capture and beat the criminal (**10**), only to discover that the man was the same burglar he had let escape from the TV studio just a few days earlier.

After webbing up the criminal for the police to find, Peter Parker walked slowly into the moonlight, overwhelmed with grief and guilt (**11**) and learning the most important lesson of his life: "With great power there must also come—great responsibility!"

THE COSTUME

It was originally supposed to be just a simple stage costume. But when Spider-Man made the transition from show business to Super Hero, his famous red and blue attire soon became one of the most recognizable and celebrated costumes in the world. Peter Parker used his scientific expertise to create an ingenious costume with complex web-shooters and mask, and a belt packed with essential gadgets.

THE FIRST SPIDEY SUIT

When Peter Parker first designed his costume it wasn't for crime fighting. He essentially just needed an exciting look for his stage act. After learning that Midtown High's dance class was throwing out some old bodysuits, he slipped into the school after dark and found one that fit him. A few hours later, he had silk-screened a web pattern on the suit and made a skintight pair of gloves and boots. And Spider-Man was born.

As it turned out, Peter's knack for science was arguably rivaled by his design sense.

Peter Parker created eyepieces using one-way mirrors he found in his school's drama class's prop box. These eyepieces hide Spider-Man's identity without hindering his vision.

While a full mask hides Peter's face from the world, it also plants a seed of distrust in the minds of the general public.

THE MASK

Born out of a need to hide his true identity, Spider-Man's mask might just be the most essential part of his uniform. The mask is thin and light, composed of a synthetic stretch fabric that matches the rest of his costume. While the lightweight material may come in handy on hot summer days, it can be prone to ripping, which is a problem that Peter always has to keep at the back of his mind while battling foes. A close encounter with the Lizard's claws or Kraven the Hunter's knife could expose his identity for the world to see, and put the lives of his loved ones in jeopardy.

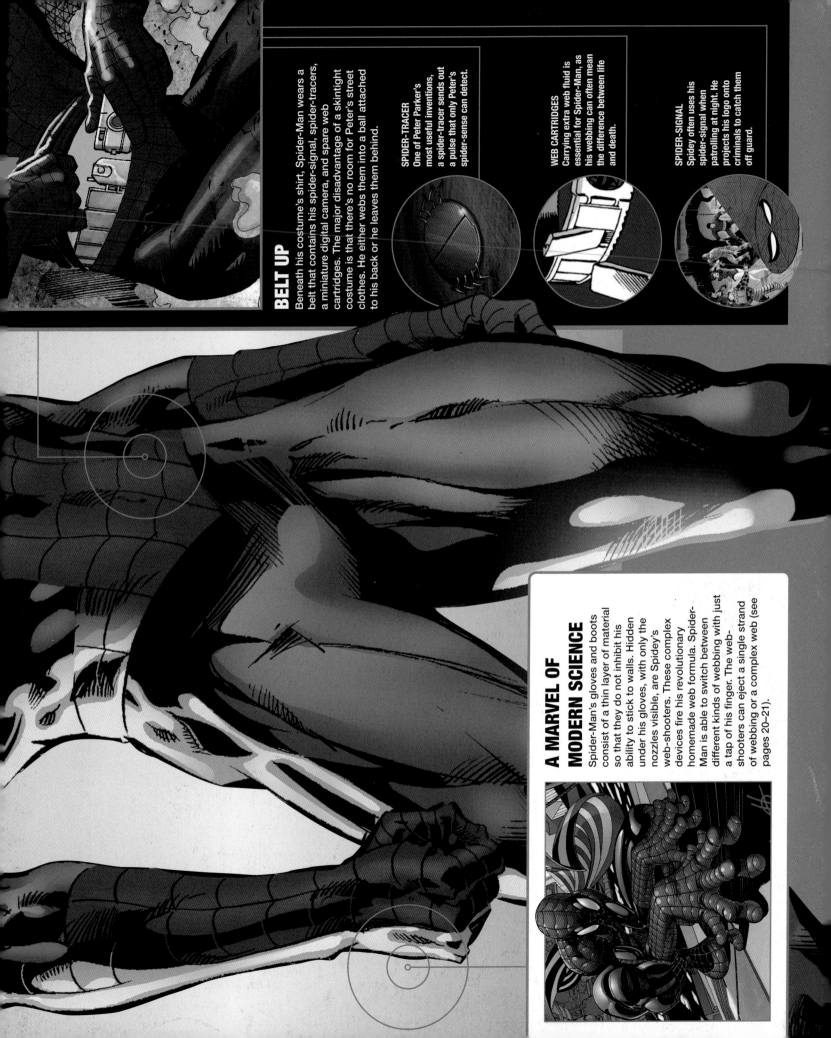

BELT UP

Beneath his costume's shirt, Spider-Man wears a belt that contains his spider-signal, spider-tracers, a miniature digital camera, and spare web cartridges. The major disadvantage of a skintight costume is that there's no room for Peter's street clothes. He either webs them into a ball attached to his back or he leaves them behind.

SPIDER-TRACER
One of Peter Parker's most useful inventions, a spider-tracer sends out a pulse that only Peter's spider-sense can detect.

WEB CARTRIDGES
Carrying extra web fluid is essential for Spider-Man, as his webbing can often mean the difference between life and death.

SPIDER-SIGNAL
Spidey often uses his spider-signal when patrolling at night. He projects his logo onto criminals to catch them off guard.

A MARVEL OF MODERN SCIENCE

Spider-Man's gloves and boots consist of a thin layer of material so that they do not inhibit his ability to stick to walls. Hidden under his gloves, with only the nozzles visible, are Spidey's web-shooters. These complex devices fire his revolutionary homemade web formula. Spider-Man is able to switch between different kinds of webbing with just a tap of his finger. The web-shooters can eject a single strand of webbing or a complex web (see pages 20–21).

SUIT UP!

With one of the most eye-catching costumes in all of Super Hero-dom, one would think Spider-Man wouldn't need to alter his uniform's iconic appearance. However, Peter Parker isn't above adopting a new suit if it will give him an advantage in a fight. From an insulated costume to protect himself from electricity, to a suit made of a living alien creature, Spider-Man's wardrobe has seen as many changes as the hero himself.

16-17

ARMORED COSTUME

Peter once donned a steel-plated version of his costume to battle a heavily armed team of villains known as the New Enforcers. The uniform was actually a pseudo-metallic composition that Peter created in the laboratories of Empire State University. But while the armor protected Spider-Man from heavy-caliber firearms, it greatly hindered his agility, and slowed him down. The suit was eventually destroyed by acid in battle.

STEALTH SUIT

Using the technology at Horizon Labs, Spider-Man developed a version of his costume that could be completely invisible by warping light and sound. The costume came equipped with lenses that allowed Spider-Man to see his own hands and feet, making movements much easier. The stealth suit was also completely impervious to sonic attacks.

BULLETPROOF COSTUME

After losing his spider-sense and getting shot with a bullet, Spider-Man used the facilities at Horizon Labs to create a bulletproof version of his costume. Flexible enough to not hinder Spider-Man's movement, the suit also employed magnetic webbing that fired out of the top of Spider-Man's wrists and blocked all radio frequencies.

FF UNIFORM

After Johnny Storm died, Spider-Man took his place as the fourth core member of the FF (the Future Foundation—the new incarnation of the Fantastic Four). Spidey was given a costume made of third generation unstable molecules, which could change design at will and had a black and white default setting. Although Spider-Man thought that the costume looked too much like the symbiote worn by his enemy Anti-Venom, being on the team meant so much to Spidey that he continued to wear the FF suit, keeping his complaints to a bare minimum.

WRESTLER COSTUME

Before Peter Parker had devised the costume and concept of Spider-Man, he first donned a mesh mask to hide his identity when he entered an open call wrestling match against hulking brute Crusher Hogan. Although the mesh mask worked as a disguise, it wouldn't cut it in the glamorous world of show business, and Peter went on to create his iconic blue and red costume.

COSMIC SPIDER-MAN

When a lab accident exposed Peter to an unknown energy source, his powers were upgraded and so was his costume. His new powers included flight, enhanced strength and senses, and the ability to shoot energy from his fingertips. In reality, the mysterious extra-dimensional entity known as the Enigma Force had bestowed upon Spider-Man its fabled Uni-Power, briefly turning Spidey into the latest in a long line of champions dubbed Captain Universe.

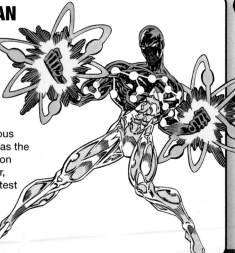

THE KNOCKOFF

On one occasion, when he was without his actual costume, Peter Parker was forced to take on the villain Overdrive while wearing a store-bought Halloween version of his famous uniform.

ALIEN COSTUME

Peter acquired his black costume while fighting on a far-off planet called Battleworld. This suit had a seemingly endless supply of webbing, and could change its appearance instantly. It seemed to respond to Peter's thoughts, and would slip over him whenever he wanted to go out web-swinging. But Peter eventually learned that the costume was an alien symbiote that wanted to form a permanent attachment to him. Even though he ultimately abandoned the alien suit, Spider-Man wore a cloth version for a time, given to him by the Black Cat.

AMAZING BAG-MAN

Stranded without clothes after discovering that his black costume was actually an alien symbiote, Peter found himself at the mercy of Human Torch. Unable to resist a joke at Spidey's expense, Johnny Storm let Spider-Man borrow a uniform that wasn't quite up to the wall-crawler's usual standards—although Johnny had a spare Fantastic Four costume, they were apparently short on masks.

SCARLET SPIDER

When Spider-Man's clone Ben Reilly returned to New York after years of travelling, he decided he couldn't escape his responsibility, and took up the identity of the Scarlet Spider. With a modified spider hoodie he'd purchased from a museum gift shop, and exterior web-shooters with a matching cartridge belt, Ben made his triumphant return to the Super Hero scene.

REILLY'S COSTUME

Peter Parker retired from costumed crime fighting for a brief time and turned over his duties to his clone Ben Reilly. Ben designed his own version of Peter's classic costume, with a much larger spider on his chest and a different design on his pants. As well as redesigning the web-shooters, he invented new weapons to add to his personal arsenal.

SIX-ARMED SPIDEY

At one point in his career, Peter's image drastically changed. In an attempt to live a normal life, Peter had developed a formula to remove his powers. Even though it hadn't been tested, he drank the liquid. When he came around, Peter felt a pain in his sides. He looked down as four extra arms burst through his costume! Peter turned to his friend Dr. Curt Connors, who helped him to develop a cure.

IRON SPIDER

In a campaign to win Peter Parker's favor, Tony Stark developed an "Iron Spider" costume made specifically for Peter's heroic needs. Able to deflect bullets, camouflage itself, and pick up radio frequencies, the suit gave Spider-Man key advantages in his war against crime, including a few extra arm-like appendages that extended out of the suit's back. While Peter eventually rejected the suit when he and Tony fell out over the Super Hero Civil War, the technology was later adapted by a group of government agents called the Scarlet Spiders.

Though Spider-Man tends to focus on his hands and feet when climbing up a wall, every part of his body has the same clinging ability.

He has the proportionate strength of a spider, the ability to adhere to nearly any surface, and an almost supernatural sense of when danger is approaching. But that's just the beginning of Spider-Man's amazing arachnid powers. His enhanced reflexes, speed, agility, and quick-healing abilities all combine to mean that Spider-Man ranks right up there with the most powerful of all the Super Heroes.

WITH GREAT POWER...

STRENGTH

Although not as strong as the Hulk, the mighty Thor, or even the Thing, your friendly neighborhood web-slinger should not be underestimated. He can bend a solid iron bar with his bare hands, lift almost 10 tons, and shatter a concrete wall with a single punch. And in a single, spider-powered spring, he can leap the height of three stories or the width of a highway.

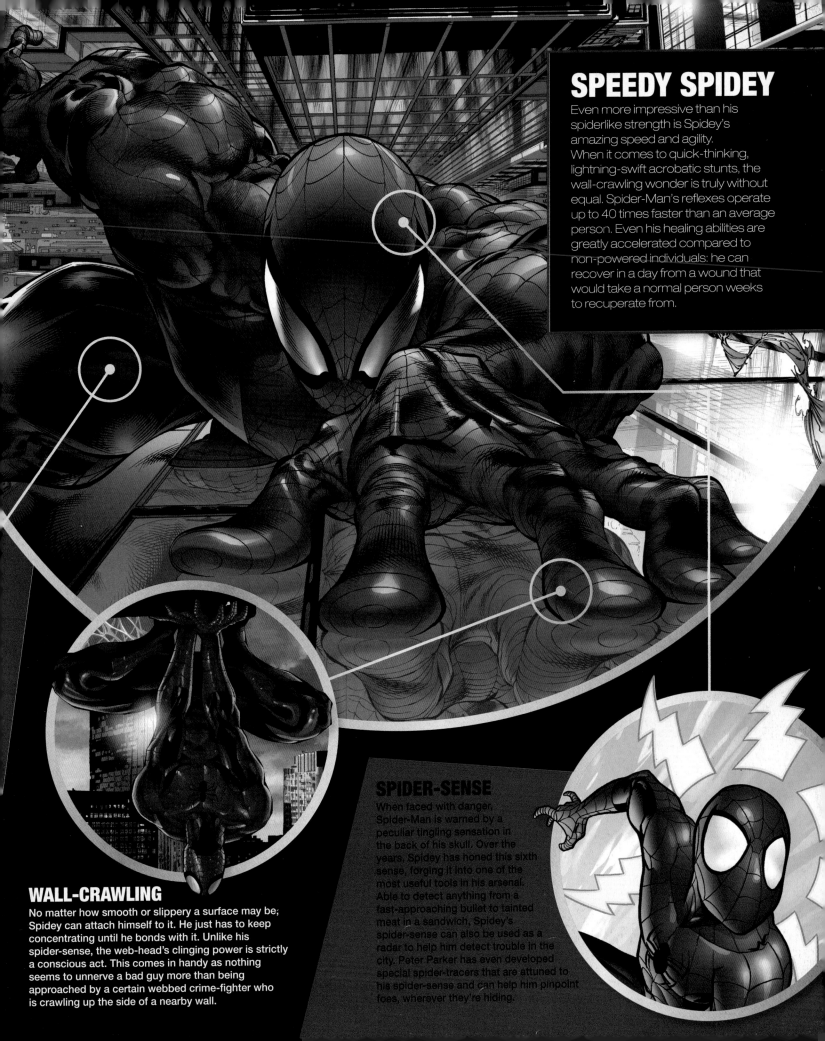

SPEEDY SPIDEY

Even more impressive than his spiderlike strength is Spidey's amazing speed and agility. When it comes to quick-thinking, lightning-swift acrobatic stunts, the wall-crawling wonder is truly without equal. Spider-Man's reflexes operate up to 40 times faster than an average person. Even his healing abilities are greatly accelerated compared to non-powered individuals: he can recover in a day from a wound that would take a normal person weeks to recuperate from.

WALL-CRAWLING

No matter how smooth or slippery a surface may be, Spidey can attach himself to it. He just has to keep concentrating until he bonds with it. Unlike his spider-sense, the web-head's clinging power is strictly a conscious act. This comes in handy as nothing seems to unnerve a bad guy more than being approached by a certain webbed crime-fighter who is crawling up the side of a nearby wall.

SPIDER-SENSE

When faced with danger, Spider-Man is warned by a peculiar tingling sensation in the back of his skull. Over the years, Spidey has honed this sixth sense, forging it into one of the most useful tools in his arsenal. Able to detect anything from a fast-approaching bullet to tainted meat in a sandwich, Spidey's spider-sense can also be used as a radar to help him detect trouble in the city. Peter Parker has even developed special spider-tracers that are attuned to his spider-sense and can help him pinpoint foes, wherever they're hiding.

THE WEB HE WEAVES

Every spider needs a web, and Spider-Man is no exception. Although the radioactive spider that bit Peter Parker granted the young man many of the natural skills and strength of arachnids, it didn't give him the ability to produce webbing. Peter had to do that the old-fashioned way, with hard work and incredible ingenuity.

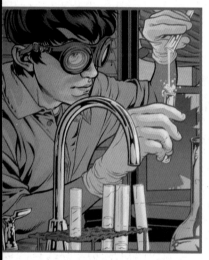

WEB FLUID

When Peter set out to create a web of his own, he used his high school's science laboratory after hours. Having studied multi-polymer compounds for a few years, he produced an adhesive fluid capable of imitating a spider's silk webbing. Extremely strong and durable, the web would dissolve after around one hour. While it would be no good as a practical adhesive to sell to chemical companies, the fluid was perfect for temporarily binding enemies of Spider-Man or swinging around the city.

WEB-SHOOTERS

While his web fluid was revolutionary and a marvel of modern chemistry, Peter didn't stop there. Without a way to fire his webs, Spider-Man was back to square one. As a solution to this problem, Peter designed two web-shooters that snap onto his wrists and can be fired by pressing his fingers to his palms. But not wanting to accidentally fire them every time he made a fist, Peter rigged the trigger so that he must tap twice in rapid succession, like a PC's mouse, to release his webbing.

The web-shooters that Peter has drafted each have nine rotating web fluid cartridges, along with the cartridge in use.

Underneath Spidey's costume is a belt that he designed to not only hold his camera and spider-signal, but also 30 extra cartridges of web fluid.

Spider-Man's web hardens upon exposure to air. Given sufficient thickness, one strand could bind the incredible Hulk and hold him prisoner, so Spidey rarely worries about it snapping under his own weight.

WEBMASTER

Always improving his technology, Spider-Man can now switch between different forms of webbing by the way he taps his trigger. With a short second tap he releases a thin cable-like strand that is perfect for web-swinging. A longer tap increases the strand's thickness for additional support, for example when binding a powerful foe like Norman Osborn. A series of brisk taps discharges many thin strands that form a fine spray, also good for blinding an opponent. If Spidey prolongs pressure on the trigger, web fluid squirts out in the form of an adhesive liquid.

ORGANIC WEBS

After a battle with the mysterious Queen, Spider-Man found himself transformed into a giant spider. While he was eventually able to change back into his old self, his brief metamorphosis was not without consequence. For some unknown reason, Spider-Man was then able to produce webbing from his own body. While it relieved some of the stress in Peter's daily life due to the fact that he no longer had to save up money to purchase the expensive chemicals needed for his webbing supply, the change was a bit off-putting for the wall-crawler, making him feel a little less human. This ability has faded away recently, however, and the details of the power loss remain a mystery.

After many hours of practice, Spidey has trained himself to use his webbing without conscious thought.

A WEB FOR ALL SEASONS

Over the years, Spider-Man has developed quite a few other uses for his webbing. He can easily use the webbing to form shapes like web-balls, bats, and bolos. Spider-Man has also been known to create more complex articles such as rafts, hang gliders, and skis. In addition, Spidey's normal webbing is also fairly heat-resistant and can easily withstand temperatures of 1,000°F (550°C). As a result, he's been known to wrap his fists in webbing as insulation to combat some of his more "hot-headed" foes. For extreme cases, he's even developed a webbing that resists temperatures of up to 10,000°F (5500°C).

"SO, THEY LAUGHED AT ME FOR BEING A BOOKWORM, EH? WELL, ONLY A SCIENCE MAJOR COULD HAVE CREATED A DEVICE LIKE THIS!"

PETER PARKER

PETER PARKER

The true face of Spider-Man, Peter Parker has seen more tragedy in his young life than most people three times his age. Racked with guilt and stress, Peter still often boasts a smile on his face, even though it's normally hidden by a skin-tight red mask.

PETER'S CHILDHOOD

Peter Parker was only a young boy when his parents, Richard and Mary Parker, died in a plane crash. He immediately moved in with his father's older brother and wife. Ben and May Parker were an elderly couple with no children of their own, and they raised Peter as if he were their son, but they rarely spoke about Peter's real parents. Peter became convinced that his parents had left him because of something he had done. Afraid of being abandoned, Peter worked hard to win his aunt and uncle's approval—though he didn't have to worry. Ben and May truly loved their nephew and would have done anything to please him.

As he grew older, Peter showed little interest in the hobbies of his peers. Although he would attend the occasional Mets game with his Uncle Ben, he never displayed any athletic prowess of his own. In fact, before he gained his spider-powers, Peter Parker had considerably less than average strength for a boy of his age. He had a fear of heights, too—even getting a book from the top shelf in the library resulted in his suffering severe symptoms of vertigo. He seemed ill-equipped for the often-harsh reality of teenage life.

When Peter's parents, Richard and Mary, were reported dead, Ben and May welcomed the orphaned child into their lives. The couple were living on a low income and had to make many sacrifices for the boy.

Peter's Uncle Ben enjoyed sharing his extensive comic collection with his nephew. Peter spent hours reading about courageous heroes and dreamed of being a costumed adventurer like Captain America, striking terror into the hearts of criminals.

MIDTOWN HIGH

In high school, Peter was an honor student, and his teachers thought very highly of him. The other students, however, had little time for a know-it-all like "Puny Parker." The girls thought he was quiet, and the boys considered him a wimp. Peter was painfully shy, and some of his fellow classmates misinterpreted his silence for snobbery. He had trouble making friends, but he never stopped trying. He often invited other students to join him at science exhibits or monster movies. But they usually responded with ridicule and almost never asked him to join them. But as he began his secret career as Spider-Man, Peter found a renewed sense of self-confidence, one his classmates slowly began to acknowledge.

> "I WISH I COULD BE A SUPER HERO. IT MUST FEEL SO GREAT TO BE ADMIRED BY THE POLICE AND THE PRESS..."
> PETER PARKER

COLLEGE STUDENT

Peter Parker graduated from Midtown High with the highest scholastic average in the school's history. He was thrilled to discover that he had won a full scholarship to Empire State University. Now secure in who he was, Peter immersed himself in his scientific studies despite web-swinging and a hectic social life. After graduating, Peter even took a job as a teaching assistant on campus to continue his postgraduate studies. Peter has never stopped learning and innovating, something that has served him incredibly well in his other life as the amazing Spider-Man.

Spider-Man ruined Peter's university graduation. In the week before the ceremony, Spidey was battling the Green Goblin and the Rocket Racer. He couldn't graduate with the rest of his class since he'd missed a required gym class.

THE MAN BEHIND THE MASK

Throughout his career as Spider-Man, Peter has always been torn between his sense of duty and the mixed feelings he has received from the public. This reception has varied from praise to outright condemnation. It has even driven him to the brink of despair, causing him to throw away his costume and renounce his alter ego. Nevertheless, his dedication to using his powers responsibly has always led to Peter donning his mask again in the hope that some day the world will learn to appreciate Spider-Man.

While Peter may have mastered the art of the quick change over the years, he finds it hard switching between his civilian and Super Hero identities, and often wishes he could just live a normal life.

FRIENDS & FAMILY

While Spider-Man has many trusted allies in his life as a hero, Peter Parker's world wouldn't be one worth fighting for without his family and circle of friends. In addition to former girlfriends turned lifelong companions, such as Betty Brant and Mary Jane Watson, Peter has had many people in his life who truly care about him. And even through difficult times, Peter has stood by those people closest to him.

UNCLE BEN PARKER

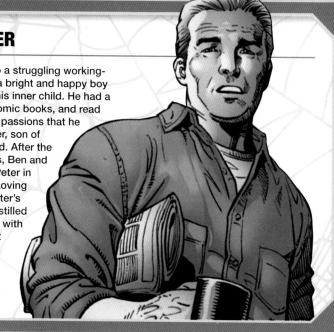

Born in Brooklyn, New York to a struggling working-class family, Ben Parker was a bright and happy boy who grew to never truly lose his inner child. He had a vivid imagination, collected comic books, and read science fiction—qualities and passions that he passed on to his nephew Peter, son of Ben's younger brother, Richard. After the tragic death of Peter's parents, Ben and his wife May took the young Peter in and raised him as their own. Loving and encouraging, Ben was Peter's best friend. It was Ben who instilled Peter with the knowledge that with great power, also comes great responsibility. And, ultimately, it was Ben's shocking death that inspired Spider-Man to become a hero.

RICHARD & MARY PARKER

Secretly operatives for the C.I.A., Peter's parents Richard and Mary Parker tried their best to give their only son as normal an upbringing as possible. But having been recruited by super spy Nick Fury, Richard had to have known that a normal life was going to be nearly impossible to accomplish. With adventures that involved fighting alongside heroes, including the man who would become known as Wolverine, Richard and Mary lived a dangerous life. And it was a life that was cut dramatically short when they died in a plane crash when Peter was just a young boy.

AUNT MAY JAMESON

May Parker didn't hesitate when she and her husband Ben were asked to take care of their nephew Peter for a few months while his parents were away on a business trip. And even more amazingly, she didn't balk at her new set of responsibilities when Peter's parents were killed and she and Ben became the boy's legal guardians. Instead she saw taking care of Peter as an opportunity to achieve her lifelong dream of becoming a parent.

But with so much death in her life, May couldn't help but be overprotective of Peter Parker. While she showered him with love every chance she had, she also worried constantly about his health and wellbeing, an almost obsessive behavior that grew even worse after Ben was murdered. These days, May has finally learned to relax, a quality she's picked up from her new husband, J. Jonah Jameson Sr.

RANDY ROBERTSON

Peter Parker met Randy Robertson during his days as a college student at Empire State University. Introduced by Randy's father and Peter's employer Joe Robertson of the *Daily Bugle*, Randy and Peter hit it off and began a friendship that continues to this day. Originally a political activist and avid protestor, Randy's personality has mellowed over the years, and he has gone from a career in social work to that of an actor. Lately, Randy has been dating one of Peter's friends at the *Daily Bugle*, Norah Winters.

VIN GONZALES

Vin Gonzales, a tough New York City cop, was Peter Parker's roommate. But he is not a fan of Spider-Man. While Peter's and Vin's friendship was a bit rocky from the start due to Peter's secret escapades as Spider-Man, it got worse when Vin was discovered as part of a conspiracy to frame the wall-crawler. Vin was sentenced to jail time and Peter began dating the object of Vin's affection, Carlie Cooper. But despite their differences, Vin shares Peter's sense of responsibility, and willingly paid the price for his actions.

J. JONAH JAMESON SR.

Peter first met J. Jonah Jameson Sr. as Spider-Man when the villainous Shocker trapped the two in a subway train alongside several other innocent bystanders. Peter was impressed by the man then, and continued to be impressed with him as he stayed in Peter's life and eventually married his aunt. Always approving of Jay and May's relationship, Peter has a hard time understanding how such an honorable man like Jay Jameson could sire a child as scheming and self-centered as J. Jonah Jameson Jr., publisher of the *Daily Bugle* and Spider-Man's worst critic.

FLASH THOMPSON

Peter Parker didn't have many friends in high school, and one of the main reasons for that, was the work of his greatest adversary, Eugene "Flash" Thompson. An all-round athlete, gifted with good looks and popularity, high school bully Flash enjoyed making Peter's life miserable, ironically even as he was a staunch supporter of Spider-Man. While Peter and Flash clashed repeatedly, their animosity would blossom into friendship when they later found themselves attending the same college. While not above giving Peter a hard time on occasion, Flash is very aware of how loyal a friend Peter has become, sticking by him even through his troubles with alcohol and the terrible wartime injury that cost Flash his ability to walk.

HARRY OSBORN

When Harry Osborn first met Peter Parker at college, Peter snubbed him completely. Always lost in his own world of worry, at the time Peter was more concerned about the health of his sickly aunt than meeting classmates at his new college. But Harry gave him the benefit of the doubt and a second chance, and the two became fast friends. They later even became roommates when Harry's father, the wealthy mogul Norman Osborn, paid for the boys' luxury apartment. Peter has seen Harry through several serious problems, including a lingering drug addiction, as well as a life as the heir to the Super Villain legacy of the Green Goblin. While many people would have given up hope in their friend years ago, Peter has always done just the opposite, convinced that Harry Osborn is truly worth saving.

THE DAILY BUGLE

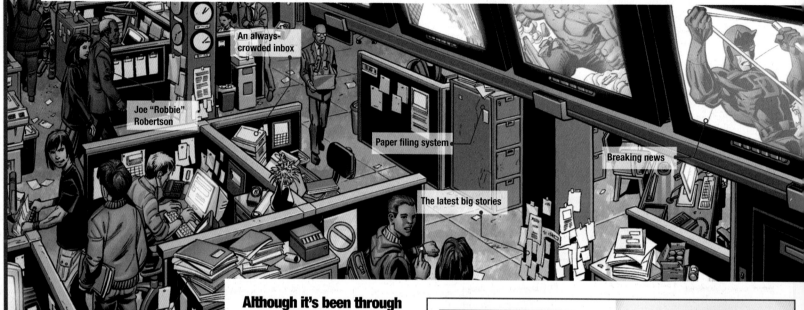

Joe "Robbie" Robertson

An always-crowded inbox

Paper filing system

Breaking news

The latest big stories

Research files

Although it's been through about as many changes as Spider-Man himself, the *Daily Bugle* is one of the world's most trusted tabloid newspapers. The newspaper has been a New York City institution since 1897, and is manned by an ever-changing staff that has included publisher J. Jonah Jameson and photographer Peter Parker.

Spider-Man takes photographs by webbing up an automatic camera in strategic locations before his fights.

— A NEW YORK ICON —

In letters 30 feet high, the original *Daily Bugle* office proudly displayed its name with a lack of subtlety that could only be matched by the passion of its editorial page and the flamboyance of its publisher, J. Jonah Jameson. The paper itself is a picture-dominated tabloid that goes for the jugular. Its photos are often graphic and shocking, and its stories are powerful.

Recently, when Jameson suffered a near-fatal heart attack, his wife sold the *Daily Bugle* to publisher Dexter Bennett, who renamed the paper *The DB*. Many of the staff left to work at a new start-up venture, *Front Line*. While Bennett's *The DB* focused on exploitative, paparazzi-styled articles, *Front Line* continued to retain the integrity that the *Daily Bugle* had always been known for.

— PETER PARKER: — ACE PHOTOGRAPHER

J. Jonah Jameson didn't hesitate to buy photos from the teenage Peter Parker, especially since Parker seemed to have a special talent for catching Spider-Man in action. Peter's first pictures appeared in Jameson's early venture, *Now Magazine*, but Jonah soon began to feature his work in the *Daily Bugle*, helping jumpstart the teen's career. Despite Peter's consistent success in getting photos of Spider-Man, Jonah has never discovered the young man's secret.

THE STAFF

J.J. JAMESON

He may appear to be a grouchy, self-centered old skinflint on the outside, but peel away his protective layers and you will discover that the real J. Jonah Jameson is actually even worse. The *Daily Bugle* publisher and staunch anti-Spider-Man activist never tires of hearing his own voice, and he'll gladly give you the opinions he thinks you ought to have. Although he no longer works at the *Daily Bugle,* Jameson will undoubtedly be back in the paper business before too long.

Jameson left the newspaper business behind when he became New York City's mayor.

JOE ROBERTSON
Usually the voice of compassion and reason, Joe Robertson worked as Jameson's right-hand man and conscience, before graduating to become the paper's Editor-in-Chief.

BETTY BRANT
Peter Parker's first real girlfriend and former *Bugle* secretary, Betty is a talented reporter whose dedication to her job has sometimes cost her her friends.

NORAH WINTERS
Full of energy and determination, Norah Winters is quickly becoming one of the *Bugle*'s top reporters, and has often partnered Peter Parker.

FREDERICK FOSWELL
Although a trusted *Daily Bugle* employee, Frederick Foswell led a double life as the criminal mastermind and ringleader known as the Big Man.

THOMAS FIREHEART
Secretly the vigilante the Puma, Thomas Fireheart once purchased the *Bugle* and wrote pro-Spider-Man articles as a way of paying a perceived debt to the wall-crawler.

BEN URICH
The *Bugle*'s star reporter and the founder of rival paper, *Front Line*, Urich is an ally of both Spider-Man and Daredevil, and known for his daring stance against corruption.

NED LEEDS
One-time husband of Betty Brant, Ned Leeds served as a reporter for the *Daily Bugle* before being brainwashed into becoming Hobgoblin by the original Hobgoblin.

DEXTER BENNETT
Purchasing the *Daily Bugle* and renaming it *The DB*, Dexter Bennett seemingly had none of the integrity of his predecessor, J. Jonah Jameson.

GLORY GRANT
Formerly a secretary to J.J. Jameson and Joe Robertson at the *Daily Bugle*, Glory Grant has moved up in the world, and is now an assistant to Mayor Jameson.

LANCE BANNON
A photographic rival of Peter Parker's, Lance Bannon had a healthy career under J.J. Jameson due to his unflattering photos of Spider-Man.

PHIL URICH
Nephew of Ben Urich, Phil has been dabbling in some web reporting for the newest incarnation of the *Bugle*, while moonlighting as the villain Hobgoblin.

JACOB CONOVER
Another in the long list of corrupt *Daily Bugle* employees, reporter Jacob Conover was known in criminal circles as a ringleader named the Rose.

THE DB BUILDING

Under Dexter Bennett's watch, *The DB* building was attacked and razed by the Super Villain known as Electro. Losing all interest in the business and the expense it would take to get the paper back on its feet, Bennett sold the company back to J. Jonah Jameson. In a moment of almost uncharacteristic generosity, Jameson then gifted the name of the *Daily Bugle* to *Front Line*, instantly giving the underground paper the name recognition it needed.

Although Peter Parker is best known as a photographer, snapping pictures for the *Daily Bugle* was not really his dream profession. With a genius-level scientific intellect and a desire to pass that knowledge onto others, photography was not so much a life goal for Peter, but rather a way for him to earn money to care for his sickly Aunt May and to pay his many bills.

MR. PARKER

It seems that Peter Parker had always held the idea of being a teacher in the back of his mind. So when the opportunity arose to teach science at his old school, Midtown High, Mr. Parker decided it was the perfect opportunity to make an impact on the lives of other promising students, just as his teachers had made such a difference in his life. Although his teaching career ended sooner than he'd have liked due to the attention he received at the time of the Super Hero Civil War, Spider-Man occasionally subs at the Avengers Academy when he finds himself missing the blackboard.

THE RIGHT-HAND MAN

As a huge fan of science and its innovators, Peter had long been in awe of his fellow Super Hero and Avenger Tony Stark, also known as the Golden Avenger Iron Man. In the days preceding the controversial Super Hero Civil War, Peter served as Tony's aide of sorts, learning directly from Stark's genius as he accompanied him on trips and lived in Tony's plush Stark Tower.

Peter was shocked to learn that J.J. Jameson was able to release *Webs* without his permission, paying him a paltry $100 "gratitude fee."

THE RELUCTANT AUTHOR

Peter's career as a photojournalist peaked when a collection of his Spider-Man photographs was released in a hardbound book entitled *Webs: Spider-Man in Action*. While the book was just another money-making stunt by the *Daily Bugle* publisher J. Jonah Jameson, and didn't land Peter any real money, it did give him the opportunity to get paid for a book-signing tour and to enjoy his very own 15 minutes of fame.

Spider-Man made a surprise appearance on the book tour after chasing the jewel thief, Black Fox.

THE OVERACHIEVER

When Peter decided to continue his education, he became a teaching assistant at Empire State University. Although he often found himself extremely overworked due to juggling life as Spider-Man and also as a photographer, Peter met a lot of good friends through his co-workers and found his work with the undergrads particularly rewarding.

GLOBE TROTTER

After years of being treated like he was on the lowest rung of the ladder by J.J. Jameson at the *Daily Bugle*, Peter found the respect he deserved for a time as Chief Photographer at the *Daily Globe*. The *Bugle's* biggest rival, the *Globe* is more balanced in its reporting of Spider-Man.

HORIZON LABS

All through his life, Peter Parker was never able to live up to his full potential when not in costume as Spider-Man. But with the help of J. Jonah Jameson's wife Marla, Peter was given the opportunity to shine when she introduced him to Max Modell, the head of Horizon Labs, a research facility that creates revolutionary technology. After impressing Modell, Peter was offered a job at Horizon's coveted think tank.

Peter proved his merit on a tour of Horizon Labs and landed a job in the inner think tank.

BEYOND THE HORIZON

Peter's current employer, Horizon Labs, is a state of the art research facility. Laid out in a way to inspire its designers and engineers, the workspace has a social atrium area where its staff can mingle and swap ideas. It also houses the labs of its inner think tank where Horizon's star staffers can indulge in their most bizarre experiments to help the company—and technology—advance. As a member of this inner circle, Peter is free to design new technology for Spider-Man, as well as for the world.

MAX MODELL
The man behind Horizon Labs, Max Modell believes Peter is designing Spider-Man's technology, but doesn't know that he is actually the wall-crawler.

GRADY SCRAPS
A fellow think tank member, Grady Scraps doesn't seem like the most serious student of the sciences, although his incredible work proves otherwise.

BELLA FISHBACH
With an environmentally friendly mind and an eye towards our planet's future, Bella Fishbach is Horizon's resident green specialist, working in the inner think tank.

SAJANI JAFFREY
Another member of Horizon Labs' inner think tank, Sajani Jaffrey is the resident xenologist, specializing in alien biology, chemistry, and technology.

UATU JACKSON
All-around wonderkid Uatu Jackson graduated from high school at the age of ten before becoming the youngest member of Horizon Labs' think tank.

"THE MORE I RISK MY LIFE... THE MORE DEADLY CHANCES I TAKE... THE LESS GOOD IT SEEMS TO DO!
WITH ALL MY STRENGTH... WITH ALL MY POWERS... WHY CAN'T I EVER MAKE THINGS RIGHT?"

PETER PARKER

PARKER'S PROBLEMS

Compared to fighting Super Villains and narrowly avoiding death as Spider-Man, you would think that life as Peter Parker would be a breeze. But, truth be told, Peter's daily struggles are every bit as challenging as those of his alter ego. It seems Peter is truly cursed with the infamous "Parker Luck."

GUILT

Since the death of his parents, Peter Parker has been plagued with guilt. Despite having nothing to do with the death of Richard and Mary Parker, young Peter instinctively thought their absence was a result of his behavior. As time passed and Peter lost more of the people in his life, including his beloved Uncle Ben, to tragedies he believed he could have or should have prevented, those issues only intensified.

GIRLS

Things never seem to be going smoothly in the romance department for Peter Parker. From his early experiences of being shunned by the objects of his affection in high school, to his near marriage to Mary Jane Watson, Peter has had his share of dating troubles. As long as he continues being Spider-Man and having to make up excuses to hide his secret identity, he can only expect more problems in the future.

AUNT MAY

Having lost his parents and his Uncle Ben at such an early age, Peter has come to realize how much his Aunt May means to him. And unfortunately, May has been plagued with health problems for a good portion of Peter's life. With hospital bills often piled up alongside other accumulated debt, Peter was constantly worried about May's wellbeing, and was forced to take several jobs to help her as best he could.

SPIDER-MAN

Strangely enough, Peter's biggest problem is probably Spider-Man himself. All Peter ever really wanted was to lead a normal life and be happy. Although he has managed to carve out a lot of happiness amidst the tragedy in his world, Peter has led anything but a normal existence. Compelled to be Spider-Man for the sake of the greater  good, Peter is constantly skipping out on friends or loved ones to battle the latest Super Villain or save a family from a towering inferno. Although he loves web-swinging and helping others, Peter knows that his double life is a giant roadblock in his personal life.

When a SPIDER-MAN *Loves* a Woman

To hear Peter Parker tell it, he's never had a lucky day in his life. But for someone who sees himself to be the victim of constant bad fortune, both Peter and his alias Spider-Man have certainly had more than their fair share of romantic encounters. With so many women vying for Peter's attention, it's hard not to see Spider-Man as one of the luckiest Super Heroes in the universe.

MARCY KANE

Back when Peter Parker was a teaching assistant at Empire State University, he met and briefly dated Marcy Kane, a graduate student. What Peter wasn't aware of at the time was that Marcy was actually an alien from the planet Contraxia. She had been sent to Earth to try to find a method to save her star system.

LIZ ALLAN

Liz Allan was one of the most popular and attractive girls at Peter's school, Midtown High. She developed a crush on Peter as the shy and bookish teen slowly grew out of his shell. However, their flirtation fizzled into friendship territory, and she later went on to date and marry Peter's friend Harry Osborn, with whom she had a son, Normie.

DEBRA WHITMAN

Debra Whitman desperately wanted her relationship with her fellow graduate student Peter Parker to develop into something more than friendship, but Peter never realized how much she truly liked him. Although they went on several dates, their romance never reached the committed level that Debra was hoping for, partly due to Peter's hectic secret life as Spider-Man.

Betty Brant

Peter's first steady girlfriend Betty Brant entered his life when he was viewed as just a shy bookworm by his fellow high school classmates. Forced to drop out of high school and become a secretary at the *Daily Bugle* to support her family, Betty understood and empathized with Peter's worries. They fell in love, but Peter's dual identity took its toll on their relationship. Unhappy with the risks Peter seemed to be taking for his job as a photographer, Betty began dating reporter Ned Leeds.

Although Peter's relationship with Betty Brant ended, the two remained dedicated friends.

The one-time fiancée of Peter Parker, Mary Jane Watson will forever be "the one that got away."

Mary Jane Watson

Peter Parker certainly hit the jackpot when it came to Mary Jane Watson. The beautiful niece of Peter's neighbor and Aunt May's best friend Anna Watson, Mary Jane discovered Peter's dual identity even before they went on their first date. Hiding under the façade of a fun-loving party girl, MJ was more complicated than she'd ever let on, a fact adult Peter only discovered when they finally began their years-long romance.

SARAH RUSHMAN

Sarah Rushman, a waitress and student at Empire State University, met Peter at a party, and the two decided to go out on a date. However, their affair quickly ended when Peter discovered that Rushman was actually the violent mutant known as Marrow. She had been brainwashed into her civilian identity of Sarah Rushman by the government intelligence agency S.H.I.E.L.D.

Spidey's on-off love interest Black Cat shares his sense of adventure.

MS. MARVEL
Spider-Man's fellow Avenger Ms. Marvel was initially annoyed by team-ups with the wall-crawler. But the two became friends when Spider-Man helped her on missions, and as they've grown closer, Ms. Marvel has developed feelings for her teammate that either has yet to fully explore.

Gwen Stacy

For a time, Gwen Stacy was the love of Peter Parker's life. Peter and Gwen began a college romance that was cut much too short when the Green Goblin hurled the innocent girl off the top of the Brooklyn Bridge. Gwen's death has affected Peter profoundly, and he has tortured himself on many a sleepless night, replaying the horror in his head. He still finds himself daydreaming about their life together and what could have been.

Peter was convinced he would spend the rest of his life with his dream girl, Gwen.

Black Cat

A cat burglar by heritage, Felicia Hardy always lived a dangerous life, and her relationship with Spider-Man wasn't that different. She felt a kinship with the lone hero, but quickly became obsessed with him. Not only did she wear the black cat costume to attract Spider-Man's attention, but she also kept a shrine to his honor, and even reformed her criminal ways to stay close to the hero. The two have had an on-off relationship for years, with neither truly getting what they need out of it. Felicia had difficulty understanding Spider-Man's need to live a civilian life.

While she loves the "spider," the Black Cat isn't really that keen on the "man."

LILY HOLLISTER
Peter first met fun-loving socialite Lily Hollister through her boyfriend, Harry Osborn. Living a double life as the villain Menace, Lily once kissed Peter in order to hide her secret identity, but it was a gesture that caused Parker more grief—he felt terrible for kissing his good friend's girlfriend.

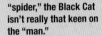

Carlie Cooper

Peter's most recent love interest Carlie Cooper is a forensic officer for the New York Police Department and Lily Hollister's friend. While it took Peter some time to fully notice and appreciate Carlie, once they finally connected, the couple realized how much they had in common, including a mutual love for science.

MICHELE GONZALES
The sister of his former roommate Vin Gonzales, Peter Parker was caught off guard when Michele Gonzales moved in with him and became his roommate. The two had a few brief affairs before realizing that they weren't a good fit for each other.

AMAZING FRIENDS

New York City is a crowded town, and no one knows that better than Spider-Man. In a city that is home to millions of people, it's no surprise that the web-slinger has met dozens of other heroes over the years. Through the course of his career, Spidey has teamed up with other Super Heroes, and he has even made a few friends from those he once considered enemies.

SILVER SABLE

Silver Sable is one of the toughest mercenaries that Spider-Man has ever come across. Having adopted her father's profession as a bounty hunter and taken it to the next level of profitability and efficiency, Silver and her team of employees—the Wild Pack—will use their expertise in combat, gymnastics, and martial arts to take down any criminal for a hefty price. Silver is usually, but not always, an ally of Spider-Man.

MORBIUS

When Dr. Michael Morbius discovered that he was dying from a rare blood disease, he attempted to treat his illness with electroshock therapy and substances found in the bodies of vampire bats. The radical treatment transformed Morbius into a living vampire of sorts with enhanced strength and bloodlust. After clashing with Spider-Man several times, the two eventually became allies.

VENOM

Peter Parker's former school bully, Eugene "Flash" Thompson has always looked up to Spider-Man. The founder of a Spider-Man fan club, Flash has never wavered in his support of the world famous wall-crawler. So when he lost his legs while serving his country, Flash didn't hesitate when the government offered him not only a chance to regain his mobility, but also to possess superpowers, by donning a living alien symbiote suit as the new Venom.

MADAME WEB

When Julia Carpenter was injected with a mysterious serum that gave her spider powers, she became known as Spider-Woman. A longtime crime fighter and ally of Spider-Man, Julia was also a member of several Super Hero teams, including the Avengers, Force Works, and Omega Flight. Having adopted many different monikers, including Arachne, she recently became known as Madame Web, after developing extra precognitive abilities.

SCARLET SPIDER

The notorious clone of Peter Parker, Ben Reilly adopted a crime-fighting identity of his own when he realized that he could not escape the responsibility that came with possessing all of the same powers and memories as the real Peter Parker. Dubbed the Scarlet Spider by the press, Ben fought valiantly alongside his "brother" and even in place of him when Spider-Man retired briefly. But Ben nobly sacrificed his own life to his cause.

PUMA

A master of martial arts with enhanced animalistic abilities, Thomas Firehart now uses his skills and powers as a contract mercenary, after conquering the world of corporate business. With his own strict moral code and a need to repay his own debts, the Puma has fought alongside Spider-Man at times. Although they often met as enemies in the past, the Puma has gained great respect for the wall-crawler.

SPIDER-WOMAN

The original Spider-Woman, Jessica Drew, has appeared on and off in Spider-Man's life, although she and the wall-crawler have spent the majority of their careers pursuing very different paths. An agent of the government peacekeeping force S.H.I.E.L.D., and later a double agent for the terrorists Hydra, Drew also joined the Avengers where she and Spider-Man are now regular partners.

TOXIN

When the serial-killing alien symbiote called Carnage gave birth to a spawn, the offspring took roost in the body of Patrick Mulligan, a New York City police officer. Although Mulligan is aware of his symbiote's corrupting influence, he has managed to keep control of the creature, and has even created an identity for himself as the crime-fighting Toxin—the first symbiote that Spider-Man considers an ally.

JACKPOT

When Jackpot first appeared, Spider-Man thought it might be Mary Jane Watson lurking under the costume. However, he soon deduced that she was Alana Jobson, a regular civilian who used Mutant Growth Hormone to give herself enhanced abilities. When Alana died, Sara Ehret adopted the Super Hero role, reluctantly realizing that her own superhuman powers were a gift she could not squander. Like Alana before her, she became an ally of Spider-Man.

ANTI-VENOM

Eddie Brock's brutal vigilante career as the villainous Venom landed him the reputation as one of Spider-Man's greatest foes. But after losing his alien symbiote suit and encountering the Super Villain Mister Negative, Eddie mysteriously manifested the rapid healing powers of Anti-Venom. Calling a truce with Spider-Man, he teamed up with the wall-crawler to battle mutual foes.

BLACK CAT

Influenced by the career of her cat burglar father, Felicia Hardy adopted the identity of the thieving Black Cat. After her adventures led her into a few conflicts with the wall-crawler, Felicia eventually changed her ways, using her "bad luck" powers to aid Spider-Man, and even becoming his girlfriend. While they're no longer romantically entangled, Spider-Man and the Black Cat still partner occasionally, something Spidey struggles to keep strictly professional.

SPIDER-GIRL

While she was reluctant to adopt the Super Hero name Spider-Girl, Anya Corazon wasn't so hesitant when it came to putting on a costume and fighting crime. The benefactor of powers from a mystical spider cult, Anya began her career as the hero Araña soon after she gained her abilities. But it wasn't until after the Kraven's Grim Hunt of spider heroes, where she had fought alongside Spider-Man, that she fully accepted the role and costume of Spider-Girl.

PROWLER

Embarking on a criminal career to prove himself after he lost his job as a window washer, Hobie Brown donned the costume of the Prowler and soon crossed paths with Spider-Man. Later reforming his illegal ways, Hobie teamed up with Silver Sable as well as several other reformed villains. He and Spider-Man have partnered on several occasions, and the Prowler even designed some new technology for one of the wall-crawler's missions.

THE FF

When the Human Torch, one of the founding members of the super-powered Fantastic Four, died, it seemed the Fantastic Four would be no more. However, one of the Human Torch's final requests was for Peter Parker to take his place on the team. Spider-Man accepted the role, only to learn that the team's patriarch, Mr. Fantastic, had decided to rebrand the team. Now called the FF (the Future Foundation), the team has become much more than a group of four crime fighters. It is a collective of young people dedicated to making the world a better place.

KEY DATA

TEAM'S FIRST APPEARANCE:
The Fantastic Four #579
(July 2010)

FOUNDER: Mr. Fantastic

ISSUE SPIDER-MAN JOINED:
FF #1 (May 2011)

BASE: The Baxter Building,
New York City, New York

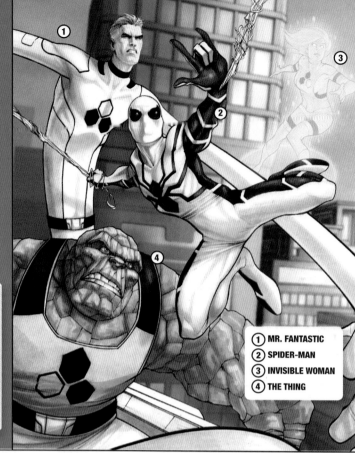

1. MR. FANTASTIC
2. SPIDER-MAN
3. INVISIBLE WOMAN
4. THE THING

THOR

SPIDER-MAN

HAWKEYE

TEAM PLAYER

Although a loner for the majority of his career, Spider-Man has recently become a major believer in the power of teamwork. He currently serves as a member of three Super Hero groups at the same time: the FF, Avengers, and New Avengers.

THE NEW FANTASTIC FOUR

Early in Spider-Man's career, the wall-crawler helped to found a new, but short-lived incarnation of the Fantastic Four. The original members of the Fantastic Four had been taken captive by an alien shape-shifting Skrull named De'Lila, who then manipulated Spider-Man, Wolverine, the Hulk, and Ghost Rider into forming a new Super Hero team.

KEY DATA

TEAM'S FIRST APPEARANCE:
The Fantastic Four #347
(December 1990)

FOUNDING MEMBERS:
Spider-Man, Hulk, Ghost Rider, Wolverine

ISSUE SPIDER-MAN JOINED:
The Fantastic Four #347

BASE: Mobile

1. GHOST RIDER
2. HULK
3. SPIDER-MAN
4. WOLVERINE

KEY DATA

TEAM'S FIRST APPEARANCE:
The Avengers #1 (September 1963)

FOUNDING MEMBERS: Thor, Iron Man, Hulk, Ant-Man, the Wasp

ISSUE SPIDER-MAN JOINED:
The Avengers (4th series) #1 (July 2010)

BASE: Avengers Tower, New York City, New York

IRON MAN

SPIDER-WOMAN

WOLVERINE

CAPTAIN AMERICA

AVENGERS

They're the world's greatest heroes. The mightiest assembly of super beings that the planet has ever known. They're the Avengers, and finding a place on their roster is the crowning achievement in any hero's career. Although Spider-Man was made a reserve Avenger years ago, he didn't achieve full membership to the ever-changing team until much later. These days, the web-crawler serves on two branches of the team, both with the icons of the Avengers as well as the heroes in the New Avengers.

1. THE THING
2. LUKE CAGE
3. MS. MARVEL
4. WOLVERINE
5. SPIDER-MAN

NEW AVENGERS

The New Avengers originally banded together after a prison breakout at the Vault, a New York maximum security penitentiary, and they were the first incarnation of the Avengers that Spider-Man joined on a full-time basis. The group faced clandestine organizations, alien threats, and mutant manifestations. But no threat tore at the team like the Super Hero Civil War, which split the New Avengers into two factions—the government-supported Mighty Avengers and the underground Secret Avengers. Spider-Man took his place with the underground faction, and has remained with the team since its rebirth under the leadership of Luke Cage.

KEY DATA

TEAM'S FIRST APPEARANCE:
New Avengers #1 (January 2005)

FOUNDING MEMBERS: Captain America, Iron Man, Luke Cage, Spider-Woman, Spider-Man

ISSUE SPIDER-MAN JOINED:
New Avengers #3 (March 2005)

BASE: Avengers Mansion, New York City, New York

SPIDEY TEAM-UPS

While it took Spider-Man years before he was recruited to an actual Super Hero team, he was partnering with other heroes almost right from the beginning of his career. From the gruff Wolverine to the welcoming Firestar, Spidey found a way to earn each hero's trust and respect.

Spider-Man had grown up reading about Captain America, so partnering with the living legend was a bit surreal.

CAPTAIN AMERICA
An icon in the world of Super Heroes, Spider-Man was more than a little intimidated by Captain America when they first teamed up. Even though Spider-Man's reputation was spotty with the police and the press, Captain America gave the fledgling hero the benefit of the doubt when they battled the Rogue Scholars, a group of time-traveling scientists, and a mutual respect was born.

WOLVERINE
On paper, they seem like an unlikely pairing. One's a natural rebel who's bucked the system for over a century—a wandering mutant with a fight-first mentality. The other's a wise-cracking bookish type whose guilt complex causes him to do the right thing above even his own personal safety. But despite their differences, Wolverine and Spider-Man have found themselves partners on many occasions. From fighting through jungles off the coast of Japan, to local Manhattan bar brawls, these two make an excellent team, something even Wolverine would admit—when Spider-Man isn't around, of course.

FIRESTAR & ICEMAN
Firestar, a former member of the Super Hero team dubbed the New Warriors, has partnered with Spidey on several occasions, most notably when she helped to curb the bloody massacre that was orchestrated by the Super Villain Carnage. Spidey and Iceman have also crossed paths a few times, both with and without Iceman's X-Men teammates. But the three found that they worked best as a trio, conquering threats like Videoman. Their teaming even led to a romance between Iceman and Firestar, but it was rather short-lived due to the two mutants' conflicting personalities.

HUMAN TORCH

Spider-Man and Johnny Storm didn't really like each other at first. Spidey always thought that the Fantastic Four's young hotshot, the Human Torch, was too arrogant. But over the years, with dozens of team-ups under their belts, the two discovered that they were actually more like brothers. So much so, that when the Human Torch died, his last wish was for Spider-Man to take his place on the Fantastic Four.

DAREDEVIL

Blind lawyer Matt Murdock, also known as Daredevil, first teamed up with Spider-Man when they took on the villainous Ringmaster and his Circus of Crime. With foes like the notorious Kingpin in common, the two crime fighters often found themselves joined in battle, and grew to become true friends. On one occasion, the pair even ended the partnership of two of their greatest respective villains: the Vulture and the Owl.

CLOAK & DAGGER

When two teen runaways were kidnapped and experimented upon with a powerful drug, they manifested bizarre powers. Now young Super Heroes, Cloak absorbs criminals into the darkness that engulfs him, while Dagger strikes them down with daggers of light. The pair met Spider-Man early in their careers and have found themselves teaming up many times since. From helping Dagger with family issues, to teaming up to defeat the Super Villain Carnage, Spider-Man and Cloak and Dagger continue to work together, and they are slowly realizing that that might not be such a bad thing.

MAIN ENEMIES

For a guy who is just trying to pay the bills and lead a modest life, Peter Parker has amassed one of the largest groups of enemies of any Super Hero. While Spider-Man is always trying to do the right thing, the criminals he comes into conflict with don't appreciate his actions, and tend to hold quite a grudge against the wall-crawler.

GREEN GOBLIN

There is probably no foe in Spider-Man's life that has struck as close to home as Norman Osborn, the original Green Goblin. He was responsible for the death of Peter Parker's longtime girlfriend, Gwen Stacy, and also corrupted his own son Harry's mind through verbal abuse, forging him into his goblin successor. Certifiably insane, but with a seemingly inexhaustable bank account and a horde of fanatical followers, the Green Goblin is one of the most powerful and dangerous men on the planet. Unfortunately for Peter Parker, it is Norman Osborn's avowed intention to destroy his wall-crawling archenemy, Spider-Man.

SANDMAN

One of the most powerful villains on Spidey's enemy list, the Sandman isn't quite as corrupt as many of the other rogues the wall-crawler battles against. Sandman has tried to reform himself, and he was even a reserve member of the Avengers at one point. Despite his attempts to change, he always falls back into his criminal ways in the end.

DOCTOR OCTOPUS

While there is certainly room for argument, Doctor Octopus just might be the greatest foe Spider-Man has ever faced. With a scientific mind that rivals that of Peter Parker, Doc Ock has challenged the web-slinger throughout Spidey's career. Between almost marrying Peter's Aunt May, carving out another criminal identity for himself as the "Master Planner," and attempting to take over all of the electronics in the entire city of Manhattan, Doctor Octopus is always brainstorming his next scheme. The thrill of the game seems to motivate Doc Ock just as much as the idea of a final victory over Spider-Man. He even saved Spider-Man's life on one occasion, just to ensure Spidey would live to fight him another day.

VULTURE

An elderly engineer with a brilliant mind, Adrian Toomes turned to a life of crime when he created a flying suit that gave him superior strength to any man half his age. As the Vulture, Toomes is corrupt and untrustworthy, and he has been known to betray other villains foolish enough to ally themselves with him. The activities of this hardened old bird are a cautionary tale for the equally gifted Peter Parker.

ELECTRO

Maxwell Dillon—the criminal known to the world as Electro—has been many things in his life: an electrical lineman, a super-powered thief, a pawn in a greater game, a voice of a political movement, and a living thunderbolt able to solidify himself into human form. But despite where his life takes him, it seems Electro will always side with the corrupt, and oppose everything Spider-Man stands for.

KRAVEN

A patient hunter who stalks his prey like a jungle cat, Kraven fought Spider-Man to prove he was the world's greatest hunter. Bested many times by Spidey, he shot and killed himself during his "last hunt." He has since reemerged by mystical means and remains in the shadows, preparing to hunt down his old foe.

VENOM

The Venom name and legacy started with a man named Eddie Brock. An unethical individual from childhood, Eddie grew up to be a lazy and untrustworthy journalist. Brock put his desire for fame and fortune above the integrity of his profession, and his lack of effort in carrying out proper research led to the downfall of his career. Blaming Spider-Man for proving his articles inaccurate, Brock's hatred attracted Spidey's former symbiote suit, and the first Venom was born out of their merging. Currently, Spidey's former bully Flash Thompson wears the symbiote suit, trying valiantly to control it's primal anger as a heroic incarnation of Venom.

CHAMELEON

The Chameleon is an expert in the field of espionage, a master criminal, and one of the first Super Villains Spider-Man faced. Using realistic masks or holographic projections, he is able to change his appearance at the drop of a hat. The Chameleon can be anyone at anytime in order to achieve his nefarious goals. Just by studying his subject for a few minutes, the Chameleon can master his victim's mannerisms, voice, and subtleties to such a degree that he can even fool those closest to his target.

MYSTERIO

Another of Spider-Man's foes to be personified by more than one criminal, Mysterio is far and away the most enigmatic of Spidey's enemies. With a vast knowledge of "movie magic" and special effects to craft a mysterious persona armed with bizarre weaponry, there is very little about Mysterio that is known for certain. Hiding behind smoke and mirrors in order to concoct elaborate traps for his prey, Mysterio has hunted Spider-Man many times, obsessed with seeking revenge for the numerous occasions that Spidey has foiled his plans.

CARNAGE

Already an unrepentant serial killer when he merged with a piece of Venom's symbiote suit, Cletus Kasady became a true monster as the Super Villain known as Carnage. Mentally imbalanced and with a sick bloodlust, Carnage has unleashed several campaigns against the innocents of New York City. He is so powerful that Spider-Man has barely been able to stop him. Even being ripped in two by the Avenger known as the Sentry wasn't enough to keep Kasady at bay, and he continues to return to Spider-Man's life to strike up his next campaign of terror.

HOBGOBLIN

Although several men have adopted the role of Hobgoblin over the years, Roderick Kingsley was the first to don the heroic costume. While his equipment was mostly pilfered from the original Green Goblin, Norman Osborn, Kingsley was much more than a cheap imitation. He represented the very real threat of a sane goblin, a cold and calculating danger in Spider-Man's life until he was dethroned and killed by the current Hobgoblin, Phil Urich.

GREEN GOBLIN II

Harry Osborn followed in his father's destructive footsteps when he took up the role of the Green Goblin. One of the most tragic cases in Spider-Man's career, Harry is possibly Peter's best friend, despite being one of Spidey's greatest enemies. Struggling with a past drug addiction and a need to contain the inner mania that the goblin has caused him, Harry is constantly attempting to rebuild his life and be the father to his children that Norman Osborn never was to him.

KINGPIN

He is the master of organized crime, and his name fits him well. Wilson Fisk is the notorious Kingpin, and he has had a hand in the corruption of New York City for many years now. A foe of both Spider-Man and the vigilante Daredevil, the Kingpin runs a tight ship and has earned the respect of even the most hardened criminals. While his reign of crime has been interrupted from time to time by other would-be crime lords and heroes seeking to bring him to justice, Fisk has always reemerged on top. A brilliant fighter despite his size, the Kingpin isn't afraid to deal with situations personally when required. However, he is smart enough to hire assassins and other immoral employees to carry out the majority of his dirty work, ensuring his place at the top of the heap.

LIZARD

Dr. Curt Connors wanted nothing more than to regrow his missing limb and help countless others in a similar situation. Unfortunately, his experiments led to him becoming the blood-craving Lizard, a creature more animal than man. Instead of making his life and the world that much better, Curt's transformation led to the death of his son, as well as that of his own humanity and many a battle with Spidey.

HYDRO-MAN

Spider-Man made another enemy for life when he accidentally knocked Morris Bench off a cargo ship and into the ocean just as an experimental generator was being tested in the water. Transformed into a being capable of turning his body into a water-like liquid at will, Hydro-Man embarked on a criminal career and has even joined an anti-Spider-Man Super Villain group called the Sinister Syndicate.

SCORPION

Private detective Mac Gargan got more than he bargained for when he allowed J. Jonah Jameson to use him as a guinea pig in his campaign against Spider-Man. Transformed into the monstrous Scorpion by scientist Dr. Farley Stillwell, Mac used his new powers to strike out against Spider-Man. While he hates the wall-crawler, Mac also developed an equal loathing for Jameson when the newspaper editor attempted to distance himself from the Scorpion's criminal ways. Although briefly interrupted by his short tenure as Venom, Gargan continues his corrupt Scorpion career to this day.

JACKAL

By all appearances, Professor Miles Warren was just another college professor at Empire State University. A closeted genius with an obsession for his former student Gwen Stacy, Warren eventually adopted the identity of the Jackal, and concocted a revolutionary cloning process. Blaming Peter Parker for the death of Gwen, the Jackal cloned Parker several times. He even convinced Peter that he wasn't the original Spider-Man, but just a genetic copy. His plan was to populate the Earth with his clones, all the while toying with Peter's life to avenge Gwen's death.

SHOCKER

Convicted burglar Herman Schultz upped his game by inventing a sonic-projection suit using the tools available to him in a prison workshop. Sending out powerful sonic waves to break out of jail, Herman created the criminal persona of the Shocker, and has been repeatedly brought to justice by Spider-Man ever since.

RHINO

Just like his animal namesake, it's nearly impossible to stop a charging Rhino, but Spider-Man has done his best to try. Stuck in a permanent suit that gives him superstrength and nearly unbreakable skin, the Rhino has often tried to deny his criminal nature. Despite volunteering for the experiment that gave him his bizarre appearance, the Rhino has sought a way to surgically remove his costume in order to return to a normal life. He recently attempted to retire from crime, but his heart is truly in the wrong place, and his corrupt nature surfaces when he's faced with tragedy or even simple desire. The Rhino is a lifelong criminal, even if he hasn't fully accepted that fact.

OTHER ENEMIES

With years of crime-fighting under his belt, Spider-Man has amassed quite an impressive rogues gallery. Spidey's clashes with these repeat offenders have become such a part of his daily routine, that even he would be hard-pressed to list every villain that has ever attempted to end his career.

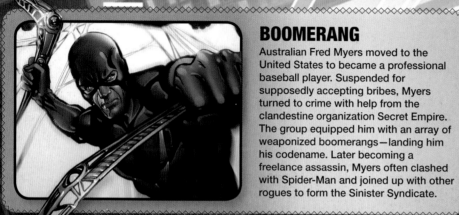

BOOMERANG

Australian Fred Myers moved to the United States to became a professional baseball player. Suspended for supposedly accepting bribes, Myers turned to crime with help from the clandestine organization Secret Empire. The group equipped him with an array of weaponized boomerangs—landing him his codename. Later becoming a freelance assassin, Myers often clashed with Spider-Man and joined up with other rogues to form the Sinister Syndicate.

GRAY GOBLIN

Norman Osborn and Gwen Stacy's illegitimate son, Gabriel Stacy suffered accelerated aging as Norman's newest project. With Norman's goblin formula flowing through his veins, Gabriel became the Gray Goblin, often attacking Spider-Man, and later took on the role of the American Son, all in an attempt to please his absent father.

MOLTEN MAN

Mark Raxton was the step-brother of Peter's longtime friend Liz Allan. He became the gilded Molten Man after an accident in which he was coated in a liquid metal derived from a meteor and developed by Spencer Smythe. With a hard frictionless skin and the ability to increase his external temperatures to over 500°F (260°C), Raxton became a formidable foe of Spidey's after turning to crime.

BEETLE

Abner Jenkins began his career in the world of Super Heroes as the Beetle, an enemy of the Human Torch. Using a technologically advanced flying suit of armor, the Beetle might have appeared cumbersome at first, but he was still a force to be reckoned with. Pursuing a life of crime led to him clashing with Spider-Man—giving the villain an arch foe that he would battle with many times as part of the Sinister Syndicate. These days, Jenkins has reformed and become a Super Hero going by the handle Mach-V.

JACK O'LANTERN

Jason Macendale debuted as the villainous Jack O'Lantern before upgrading his identity to that of a new Hobgoblin. Employing deadly flying devices, Jack O'Lantern was a haunting presence in Spidey's life, and one that several other criminals have filled since Macendale's departure from the role.

ENFORCERS

A trio of hired muscle available for the right price, the Enforcers have had a variety of employers over the years. However, it was when they were hired by the criminal known as the Big Man that they first encountered Spider-Man. Comprised of strong man Ox, the master of the lariat, Montana, and martial art expert and group leader Fancy Dan, the Enforcers often live up to their name.

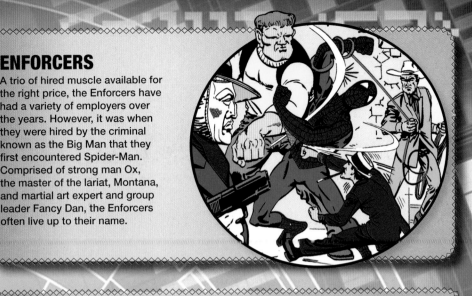

SWARM

One of Spider-Man's most bizarre foes, Swarm is the living skeleton of former Nazi scientist Fritz von Meyer. If that wasn't strange enough, Swarm's skeleton is covered in an active hive of bees that respond to his every command and are a part of his very being. Originally an enemy of the short-lived Super Hero team the Champions, a clash with Spider-Man led Swarm to adopt the wall-crawler as his arch foe.

SPIDERCIDE

One of the Jackal's Peter Parker clones, Spidercide was corrupted from the start. After being released from a cloning chamber with no memories of who or what he was, the clone wandered the streets of New York before "realizing" that he was Peter Parker. With an obsessive sense of entitlement and complete control over his molecular structure, Spidercide was willing to kill anyone who would prevent him from taking his "rightful" place as Parker.

BURGLAR

He was the first true villain in Peter Parker's life. The man known only as the Burglar first met Spider-Man when he was robbing a TV studio during Spidey's short-lived television career. At that time, Peter couldn't be bothered to stop the obvious thief—he was more concerned about his own life, and assumed that the Burglar was someone else's problem. However, when that same thief re-emerged to rob the Parker home and shoot and kill Peter's Uncle Ben, Spidey would live to regret his inaction. Although he eventually brought the Burglar to justice, Spider-Man would never forgive himself for the criminal's deeds.

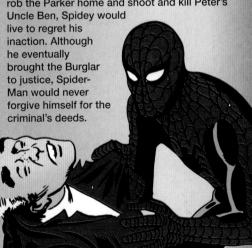

SPOT

Jonathan Ohnn was a scientist employed by the Kingpin—a thug who was attempting to recreate the powers of the Super Hero known as Cloak. Eventually succeeding in creating black disc-like portals to another dimension, Ohnn adopted the name of the Spot after his experiments caused his skin to be covered in those same black dots.

FAKE MR. AND MRS. PARKER

Peter Parker's parents had lived a fantastic life as spies for the CIA before they were killed in a sabotaged plane flight. Since Peter was a child when his parents died, he didn't have very many memories of them, so when they suddenly reappeared in his life, Peter couldn't believe his eyes. Claiming to have been held as political prisoners all these years, Peter's recently returned parents were eventually revealed to be life-like androids created by the villain Chameleon.

TINKERER

One of Spider-Man's earliest foes, Phineas Mason, aka the Tinkerer, is the modern equivalent of a mad scientist. Although he may not possess the most threatening of codenames, the Tinkerer is a brilliant inventor who has not only committed his own crimes, but has also built technology for many of Spidey's other foes.

TOMBSTONE

Hardened by a childhood as Harlem's only albino resident, Lonnie Lincoln became the whispering gangster Tombstone—a recurring presence in Spider-Man's life and one who nearly ruined the career of *Daily Bugle* mainstay, Joe Robertson.

TARANTULA

Armed with poisonous stingers built into his boots, Anton Miguel Rodriguez took his terrorist lifestyle as the Tarantula from South America to New York City. When his Super Villain career was initially cut short by a partnership between Spider-Man and the Punisher, the Tarantula's focus turned to revenge, as he now harbored a deep-seated hatred for the web-swinger.

SLYDE

Disgruntled former chemical engineer Jalome Beacher was fired from his job after inventing a frictionless chemical coating that he thought would revolutionize the frying pan industry. With no career to speak of, Jalome turned to crime, using the coating to skate over surfaces with ease and repel Spider-Man's webbing. Recently, Jalome's career was apparently ended when he was shot and seemingly killed by the criminal Underworld.

SILVERMANE

A Maggia crime lord obsessed with achieving immortality, Silvio Manfredi was dubbed Silvermane due to his prematurely white hair. Past his prime, Silvermane uses a cyborg body to stay mobile and increase his strength to superhuman proportions. He resents Spider-Man for trying to stop his quest.

SPEED DEMON

James Sanders has led a rather amazing life. Chosen by the galactic gamesman known as the Grandmaster to be one of his pawns in a grand power contest, Sanders was given super speed and originally adopted the identity of the Whizzer. After fighting the Avengers and then later the Super Hero team called the Defenders, Sanders wisely changed his name to Speed Demon to avoid confusion with a World War II era Super Hero. He then became a recurring enemy of Spider-Man's, joining up with the nefarious Sinister Syndicate.

SCORCHER

One of Norman Osborn's earliest operatives, the Scorcher—alias Steven Hudak—is an arsonist for hire, seeking revenge on Spidey for his time in prison. Using a sophisticated battle suit with built-in flamethrowers, Hudak commits crimes while remaining safely insulated.

HAMMERHEAD

When a Maggia gunman was attacked beneath a movie poster for *The Al Capone Mob*, his life was saved by disgraced surgeon Jonah Harrow. With a repaired skull made of steel alloy, he adopted the name Hammerhead and the persona of a 1920s era gangster— influenced by that landmark poster. Now he will let no one, not even Spidey, stand in his way.

SPIDER-SLAYER

Genius Inventor Spencer Smythe created the very first "Spider-Slayer," a device meant to end the career of Spider-Man. After Spencer's death, his mentally unbalanced son Alistair Smythe decided to carry on his father's legacy. Although his career got off to a rather rocky start, Alistair would later surpass the technology employed by the senior Smythe. He has since launched several campaigns against the wall-crawler, even upgrading his own body to that of a cyborg in order to become the so-called Ultimate Spider-Slayer.

CARRION

Originally a failed clone project of the Jackal, Carrion sought revenge for the assumed death of his master by lashing out at Spider-Man. Armed with a death-touch and the ability to turn his body immaterial, Carrion could make himself lighter than air, giving him a ghost-like quality that created quite a challenge for the web-slinger.

LOOTER

Experimentation on a meteorite caused would-be scientist Norton G. Fester to gain super-strength. Immediately turning to crime, Fester garbed himself in a purple and white costume and became the Looter. Reluctant to retire from his criminal ways, the Looter has battled both Peter Parker and Ben Reilly, always meeting with defeat in the end.

GRIZZLY

Maxwell Markham was a professional wrestler until the *Daily Bugle* ruined his career. After nursing his anger for eleven years, circumstances led Markham to meet the Super Villain called the Jackal. The Jackal gave the disgruntled wrestler an exo-skeleton bear costume and set Markham on the path to becoming the criminal known as the Grizzly, a fierce foe of Spidey's.

DEMOGOBLIN

When Jason Macendale made a deal with dark forces, he became a threatening presence as a demonic Hobgoblin. Later, when the demon half of his personality split off, it became Demogoblin, obsessed with killing perceived "sinners"— including Spidey.

WHITE DRAGON

The White Dragon's bid to be crime lord of Chinatown's underworld ended when he attracted Spider-Man's attention. Although he has used his skills in martial arts and gadgets, such as steel claws and a flame-throwing mask, in several grabs for power, the White Dragon has always failed, and eventually he became a pawn of Mr. Negative.

TIMELINE

- Peter Parker is born to parents Richard and Mary Parker.

- Mr. and Mrs. Parker die in a plane crash and are revealed to be spies for the CIA. Peter's Aunt May and Uncle Ben raise him as they would their own son.

- Peter attends Midtown High in Queens and excels at schoolwork, especially in the sciences. He fares much worse with his classmates, including Liz Allan and the bully Flash Thompson.

- While attending a seminar about radiation, Peter is bitten by a spider that was accidentally doused with radioactive rays. He slowly realizes that he has somehow inherited the proportionate strength and other natural abilities of a spider.

- Experimenting with his chemistry set at home, Peter develops his trademark web fluid and web-shooters. He also sneaks into school to create his first material Spider-Man costume.

- Spider-Man stars in a TV special. Backstage after the show, he lets a burglar escape past him without trying to stop him.

- Peter's Uncle Ben is killed during a botched robbery at his home.

- Peter changes into his Spider-Man costume, unaware that his neighbor's niece, Mary Jane Watson, has secretly witnessed his impressive transformation.

- Spider-Man tracks the killer to an abandoned warehouse and discovers that the criminal is none other than the same burglar he let get away back at the TV studio. He then vows to use his powers to help others, having learned that with great power there must also come great responsibility.

- *Daily Bugle* Publisher J. Jonah Jameson begins his public crusade against Spider-Man.

- Spidey saves the life of J. Jonah's son, astronaut John Jameson.

- Spider-Man petitions the Fantastic Four for membership, but reconsiders when he discovers that they don't receive salaries.

- Spider-Man battles and defeats the Chameleon for the first time.

- The Vulture and Spider-Man have their first airborne encounter.

- Peter Parker sells his first photo to J. Jonah Jameson in an effort to help his Aunt May with her money problems.

- Spider-Man fights the Tinkerer for the first time, and also unknowingly meets Mysterio who is disguised as an alien.

- Spidey develops his spider-signal belt projector to help instill fear into the hearts of criminals.

- Otto Octavius becomes Doctor Octopus and clashes with Spider-Man on their first meeting.

- The Sandman debuts and is defeated by Spider-Man.

- Spider-Man confronts the Fantastic Four's most notorious enemy, Doctor Doom.

- Heading to Florida on an assignment for the *Daily Bugle*, Spider-Man fights and defeats the Lizard for the first time.

- Spider-Man meets the Scorcher, unaware that the villain is bankrolled by Norman Osborn.

- Spider-Man meets Captain George Stacy and attempts to apply to the police force.

- Spidey helps the misunderstood Batwing after their first meeting.

- Peter Parker and Betty Brant begin to date after the Vulture returns to attack the *Daily Bugle*.

- Electro and Spider-Man clash for the first time, with Spider-Man emerging the victor.

- Spidey faces down the Enforcers and their leader, the Big Man.

- Spider-Man takes on the Headsman for the first time, another criminal under the employ of Norman Osborn.

- Peter Parker develops his first spider-tracer.

- Mysterio battles Spider-Man, the villain now garbed in his signature costume.

- Spider-Man battles the Green Goblin for the first time, but the villain gets away after leading Spidey into a fight with the Hulk.

- The Chameleon sets Kraven the Hunter on Spider-Man's trail, jumpstarting Kraven's new obsession.

- Doc Ock joins forces with Electro, Mysterio, the Vulture, Sandman, and Kraven to form the first incarnation of the Sinister Six.

- Spider-Man and Daredevil team up for the first time when they take on the Ringmaster and his Circus of Crime.

- Betty Brant's relationship with Peter begins to fizzle when she meets and dates Ned Leeds.

- J. Jonah Jameson funds Spidey's newest foe, the Scorpion.

- The Human Torch teams up with Spider-Man to battle another new member of Spidey's rogues gallery, the Beetle.

- Spencer Smythe introduces his first Spider-Slayer to J. Jonah Jameson.

- Spider-Man first crosses paths with the Crime-Master.

- Spider-Man witnesses the birth of the Molten Man, and is then forced to fight him.

- Peter graduates high school and learns of Liz Allan's crush on him.

- Peter enrolls at Empire State University alongside former bully Flash Thompson. There the two meet fellow classmates Harry Osborn and Gwen Stacy, as well as Professor Miles Warren.

- The Looter debuts and challenges Spider-Man.

- Spider-Man is faced with the robot menaces of Norman Osborn's old business partner, Mendel Stromm.

- The Green Goblin discovers Peter's dual identity and reveals himself as Norman Osborn. However, an electric charge grants Osborn with selective amnesia, and he forgets about their double lives for a time.

- The Rhino charges Spider-Man's way in their earliest encounter.

- After weeks of stalling, Peter Parker finally lets his Aunt May set him up with her friend's niece. Peter is floored when he meets the beautiful Mary Jane Watson and is instantly taken with her.

- The Avengers attempt to recruit Spider-Man, but a misunderstanding leads to Spidey sticking to his solo act.

- The Shocker sets his sights on Spidey for the first time, as does a new Vulture, Blackie Drago.

- The Kingpin makes his first play for control of New York's mobs.

- Spider-Man retires briefly before remembering the true inspiration behind his career: his Uncle Ben.

- Peter Parker meets the *Daily Bugle*'s voice of reason, Joe "Robbie" Robertson.

- Peter Parker and Gwen Stacy start dating more seriously.

- Peter meets Joe Robertson's politically active son, Randy.

- Silvermane crosses paths with both Spider-Man and the Lizard for the first time on his quest to regain his youth.

- The Prowler begins to haunt the New York night, originally clashing with Spider-Man.

- The villainous Kangaroo leaps into Spider-Man's life.

- Captain George Stacy is killed during Spider-Man's rooftop battle with Doc Ock. Spider-Man is mistaken for the killer.

- Gwen Stacy travels to Europe to deal with her loss and has a fling with Norman Osborn that results in the birth of illegitimate twins—a boy and a girl.

- Norman Osborn adopts the role of the Green Goblin again.

- Peter discovers Harry Osborn's drug addiction was due in part to Harry's failed relationship with Mary Jane Watson.

- Spider-Man grows two extra sets of arms for a time, truly appearing like his namesake. He then crosses paths with Morbius for the first time before being cured of his condition with the help of Dr. Curt Connors.

- The villainous Gibbon swings into Spider-Man's life, as does the would-be mafioso Hammerhead.

- The Green Goblin hurls Gwen Stacy, newly returned from London, from the top of the George Washington Bridge. She does not survive the fall.

- In a violent fight with Spider-Man, the Green Goblin accidentally impales himself with his glider in an incident Harry Osborn witnesses. Norman is believed to be dead.

- Peter seeks out Mary Jane Watson for comfort and sees another side to the so-called "party girl."

- John Jameson becomes the lycanthropic Man-Wolf, much to Spidey's chagrin.

- The third Vulture, Clifton Shallot, takes up the nefarious role.

- Professor Miles Warren emerges as the Jackal for the first time and hires the Punisher to fire his first shots into Spider-Man's life.

- Spider-Man takes the Spider-Mobile out for its maiden voyage.

- Spidey teams up with Ka-Zar to take on Stegron the Dinosaur Man for the first time.

- Doctor Octopus nearly marries Aunt May Parker.

- The Tarantula debuts and is instantly caught in Spidey's web.

- Harry Osborn adopts his father's identity as a new Green Goblin.

- The Grizzly rears his ugly head for the first time.

- Spider-Man moves into a new apartment and meets his neighbor Glory Grant, establishing a longtime friendship with her.

- Spider-Man not only meets the Jackal's clone of Gwen Stacy, but also his own clone doppelgänger. His clone escapes death only to leave Manhattan and adopt the identity of Ben Reilly.

- A new Mysterio, Danny Berkhart, attempts to play tricks on the wall-crawler's mind.

- Spider-Woman Jessica Drew makes a rather unorthodox debut.

- Will-O'-the-Wisp shines into Spider-Man's life.

- The heroic White Tiger and Spider-Man clash for the first time over a simple misunderstanding.

- Rocket Racer and Spider-Man meet for their initial fight.

- Harry Osborn's psychiatrist, Dr. Bart Hamilton, briefly takes over as the third Green Goblin until his untimely death.

- The White Dragon takes his first swipe at Spider-Man.

- Peter Parker graduates from Empire State University.

- Spider-Man meets the Jackal's just-as-evil clone, Carrion, as well as the sinister Fly.

- The Black Cat first crosses the wall-crawler's path.

- Peter enrolls in graduate schools at ESU and begins working as a teaching assistant for the science department.

- Spider-Man encounters a familiar new foe, the Iguana, as well as the former Champions' enemy, Swarm.

- Spider-Man has his first encounter with the mysterious and precognitive Madame Web.

- Hydro-Man wades into Spider-Man's life, followed swiftly by villains Jack O'Lantern, the Ringer, and Speed Demon.

- Spider-Man battles Cloak and Dagger, unaware that the two new vigilantes would soon become his uneasy allies.

- The killer-for-hire Boomerang focuses his attention on Spider-Man, becoming a longtime foe of the wall-crawler.

- Spidey discovers the hard way that nothing can stop the X-Men foe known as the Juggernaut—except for drying cement.

- Spidey teams up with the Frog-Man during the "hero's" debut.

- The villainous Vermin develops a new hatred for spiders after he battles the wall-crawler and Captain America.

- Spider-Man meets the criminal known as the White Rabbit during another embarrassing team-up with Frog-Man.

- The mysterious Hobgoblin begins his career by picking up where the Green Goblin left off.

- Peter Parker decides to drop out of graduate school.

- The Answer questions Spider-Man's abilities for the first time.

- Julia Carpenter adopts the role of the second Spider-Woman.

- Spider-Man returns from the Secret Wars on the alien planet Battleworld, wearing a new black symbiote alien costume.

- Spidey encounters several new rogues, including crime boss the Rose, the burglar Black Fox, and the bestial Puma.

- Spider-Man abandons his new black costume when he realizes it's alive.

- The Spot first dots the landscape of Spider-Man's life.

- Some time after marrying Harry Osborn, Liz Allan gives birth to Harry's first child, Norman Harry Osborn.

- Spider-Man meets bounty hunter Silver Sable for the first time when she is contracted to capture the Black Fox.

- The Sin-Eater viciously murders police Captain and Spider-Man ally, Jean DeWolff.

- Alistair Smythe, scientist Spencer Smythe's son and the future Ultimate Spider-Slayer, makes his less-than-impressive criminal debut, mistaking Mary Jane Watson for Spider-Man.

- A host of new criminals appear in the wall-crawler's life, including the slippery Slyde, and the deadly Chance and Foreigner.

- The Sinister Syndicate form to attempt to destroy their wall-crawling archenemy.

- Solo begins his war on terrorism, crossing paths with Spidey.

- Jason Macendale picks up the reigns as the new Hobgoblin after Ned Leeds is outed as the villain and killed.

- Long after Peter Parker realizes his true feelings for Mary Jane Watson, she finally accepts his marriage proposal.

- Peter is late to his wedding due to his adventures as Spider-Man and Mary Jane calls off the ceremony. The two soon rekindle their relationship, but marriage is now seemingly off the table forever.

- Kraven defeats Spider-Man during his "last hunt" and then commits suicide.

- Tombstone takes on the web-slinger for the first time.

- Eddie Brock becomes Venom and takes his anger out on Spidey.

- The hitmen team of Styx and Stone manifest in Spidey's life, as does the horrific Demogoblin.

- Spider-Man gains the cosmic powers and abilities of Captain Universe, as a cadre of villains stage their "Acts of Vengeance," employing the robotic Tri-Sentinel.

- Spidey is finally granted Avengers status as a reserve member.

- The Sinister Six reunite years after their original formation.

- Cardiac suits up for the first time and meets Spider-Man.

- Serial killer Cletus Kasady bonds with a part of Venom's symbiote and first unleashes Carnage.

- Spider-Man meets his ferocious six-armed Doppelgänger during the Infinity War.

- Peter Parker discovers his parents are still alive, only to later find out they were robots created in a twisted game by the Chameleon.

- Spider-Man adopts his Spider-Armor to better deal with the threat of the New Enforcers.

- Harry Osborn seemingly dies due to complications with the Goblin Formula.

- Carnage meets the disturbed Shriek, and then instigates a killing spree in Manhattan.

- Spidey faces Kraven's son, the Grim Hunter, for the first time.

- Ben Reilly returns to New York when Aunt May slips into a coma. There he accidentally confronts a confused Peter Parker.

- Judas Traveller journeys to the Ravencroft Institute for the first of his bizarre experiments on Spider-Man's mind. He is accompanied by the Scrier.

- Ben Reilly adopts the persona of the Scarlet Spider.

- Kaine rears his ugly cloned head into Peter Parker's life.

- Mary Jane reveals to Peter that she is pregnant.

- The first female Scorpion, the villainous Scorpia, debuts.

- The Jackal returns from the seeming dead, and releases another Peter Parker clone, Spidercide.

- Aunt May revives from her coma only to seemingly die a week later.

- Phil Urich debuts as a heroic Green Goblin.

- A new female Doctor Octopus challenges the Scarlet Spider.

- Peter Parker officially retires from his career as Spider-Man, allowing Ben Reilly to fill the role. Ben changes Spidey's familiar costume to better suit his style, and even dyes his hair blond.

- Mary Jane gives birth to a daughter, only to have the baby stolen from her and presumed dead.

- A very much alive original Green Goblin is revealed to be the manipulator behind the Jackal and the entire Clone Saga.

- Ben Reilly makes the ultimate sacrifice to save Peter Parker from the Green Goblin. In dying, Reilly is truly confirmed to be the clone, and Parker the original.

- Peter Parker returns in full to the role of Spider-Man.

- Spider-Man meets Kraven's other son and inheritor of his moniker, Alyosha.

- Spider-Man suffers an "identity crisis" of sorts, creating four new Super Hero personas for himself.

- Aunt May is revealed to be alive—her death a masquerade orchestrated by the Green Goblin.

TIMELINE

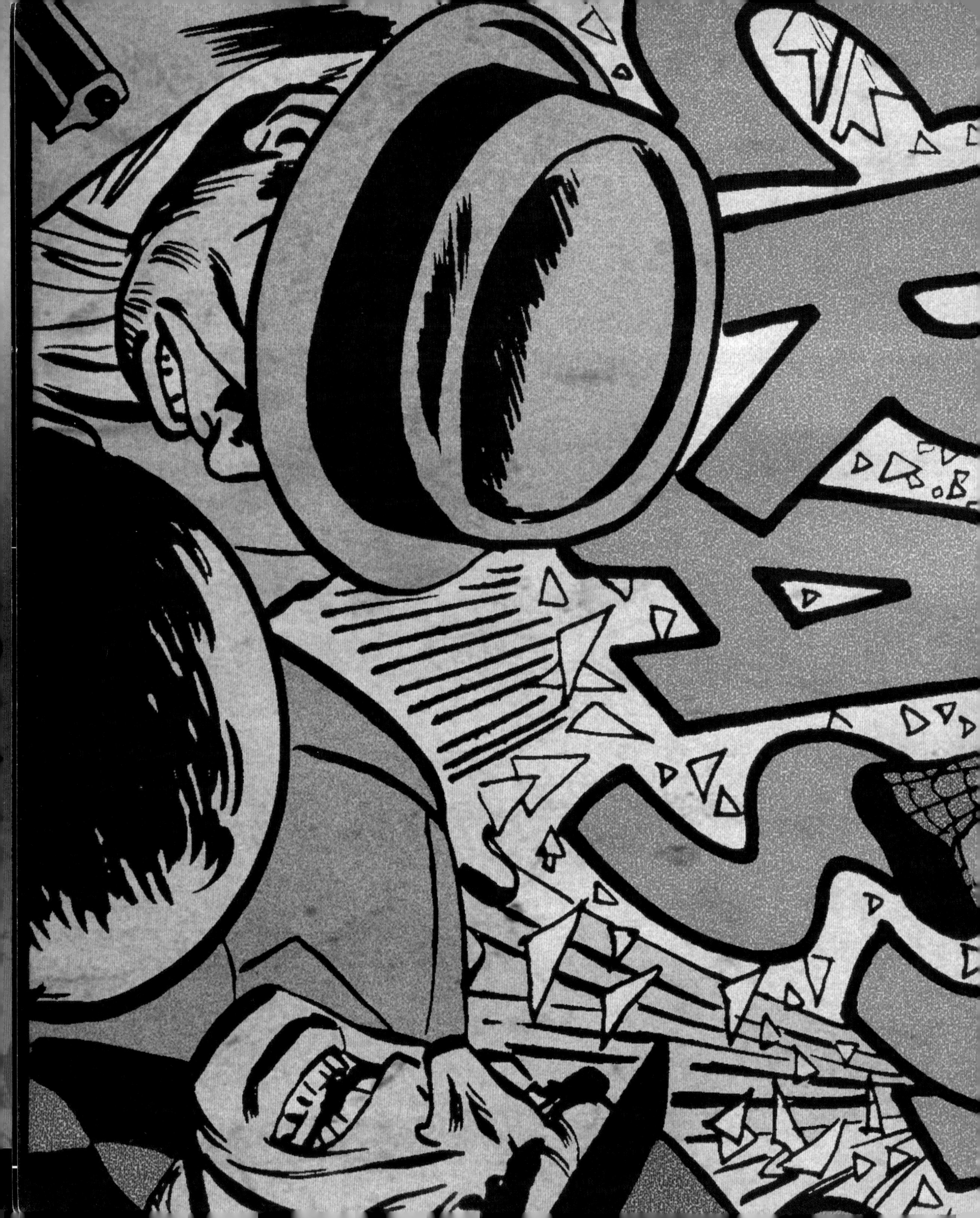

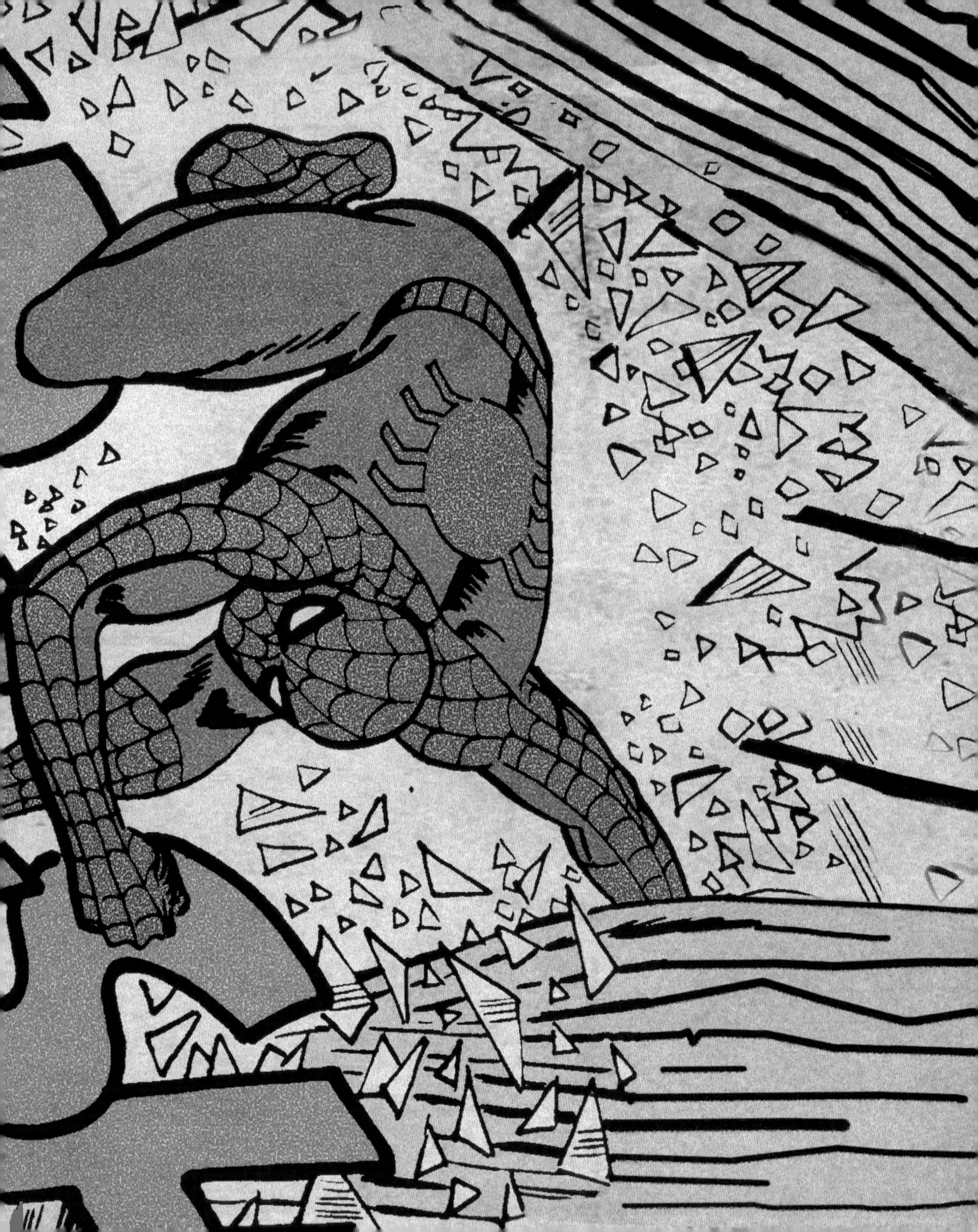

March 1963

IND. 12¢

the AMAZING SPIDER-MAN 1

APPROVED BY THE COMICS CODE AUTHORITY

MC

2 GREAT FEATURE-LENGTH SPIDER-MAN THRILLERS!

THE FANTASTIC FOUR THINK I'M TRAPPED! BUT THEY DON'T SUSPECT MY REAL POWER!

EXTRA ADDED ATTRACTION: SPIDER-MAN *MEETS* THE FANTASTIC FOUR, AS "the CHAMELEON STRIKES!"

EDITOR-IN-CHIEF
Stan Lee

COVER ARTISTS
Jack Kirby and Steve Ditko

WRITER
Stan Lee

PENCILER
Steve Ditko

INKER
Steve Ditko

LETTERERS
Johnny Dee
and John Duffi

THE AMAZING SPIDER-MAN #1

"We cannot allow that masked menace to take the law into his own hands! He is a bad influence on our youngsters!"

J. JONAH JAMESON

MAIN CHARACTERS: Spider-Man; Aunt May Parker; J. Jonah Jameson; John Jameson; the Chameleon; Mr. Fantastic; Invisible Girl; the Human Torch; the Thing
MAIN SUPPORTING CHARACTERS: The Burglar; Professor Newton
MAIN LOCATIONS: The Parker residence; unnamed rocket launch site; the Baxter Building; unnamed defence installation, New York City; the Chameleon's secret hideout; unnamed waterfront, New York City

BACKGROUND

Picking up right where they left off in *Amazing Fantasy* #15 (August 1962), writer-editor Stan Lee and artist Steve Ditko took Spider-Man out for another web-spin in the debut issue of the character's ongoing comic book series, *The Amazing Spider-Man*. The debut issue featured two self-contained stories. The lead story was a fairly standard adventure, and while it boasted the first appearance of the recurring thorn in Peter Parker's side, J. Jonah Jameson, it wasn't the reason most readers were buying the issue.

That honor fell to the second story, featuring the first-ever meeting of Spider-Man and the famous Fantastic Four. Already a hit in Stan Lee's new era of Marvel Comics, the Fantastic Four were also featured on the cover as a clever marketing strategy. Not only did their appearance solidify the fact that Spider-Man operated in the shared Marvel Universe, but it also succeeded in coaxing some of the Fantastic Four's fans to give Spider-Man a try. And if the resultant success of *The Amazing Spider-Man* is any indication, most of those fans stuck around for the long haul.

"I came up here to join up with you! I wanna be a member of the **Fantastic Four!**"

SPIDER-MAN

THE STORIES

Spider-Man saves the life of astronaut John Jameson, despite the smear campaign against the hero, orchestrated by John's father, J. Jonah Jameson. In the second story, Spidey meets the Fantastic Four for the first time before battling the enigmatic Chameleon.

Being Spider-Man was quickly proving more trouble than Peter Parker had imagined. Not only could Spider-Man not cash the checks he made for his TV appearances (he would need identification to do so), but also the publisher of the *Daily Bugle*, J. Jonah Jameson, was actively delivering lectures all over town about the supposed threat Spider-Man posed to the citizens of his city (**1**). While many believed Jameson's campaign was merely a publicity stunt to draw in new readers and promote his son, astronaut John Jameson, Spider-Man nevertheless saw his career in showbiz take a brutal nosedive.

However, while attending the launch of John Jameson's space shuttle (**2**), Peter stood by in witness as John lost control of the craft due to a technical malfunction. Realizing what had happened, the officials at ground control tried, unsuccessfully, to think of a way to save the space shuttle (**3**). But Peter Parker was no longer content to sit idly by when faced with the opportunity to help others in need. Peter changed swiftly into his Spider-Man costume (**4**), and commandeering a plane and its pilot from a nearby airfield, used a web-line to swing aboard the capsule (**5**). He attached a space guidance unit he'd been given by a military official to the capsule (**6**). With Spider-Man's help, John landed the craft safely, and Peter returned home, only to discover that J. Jonah Jameson had increased his anti-Spider-Man agenda, claiming the web-slinger had deliberately put John's mission in harm's way in order to rescue him in a public arena (**7**). It seemed Spider-Man had had his first run in with the all too infamous "Parker luck."

In the issue's second feature, Peter Parker was no closer to helping his poor aunt pay her bills. But there were other heroes who didn't seem to share Peter's financial woes. Spider-Man headed to the world-famous Baxter Building in an attempt to meet and join the fabled Fantastic Four.

Of course, one doesn't just waltz into the Fantastic Four's home and say "hello." In order to meet with the heroes, Spider-Man broke into their headquarters, bypassing their security safeguards (**8**). An alarm sounded and the Fantasic Four saw that it was Spider-Man who was breaking in (**9**). They weren't pleased that a "teenage show-off" thought he could take them by surprise. A violent clash ensued (**10**), until Spider-Man was able to plead his case. He had wanted to prove to them that he had what it takes to be a member of the Fantastic Four. Spidey's mission had been made in vain, however, as the team informed him that they didn't receive a salary for their heroics.

Meanwhile, the mysterious master of disguise and Super Villain known as the Chameleon (**11**) decided to capitalize on Spider-Man's outlaw status with the press. After devising his own artificial web-shooting gun, the Chameleon stole prized missile plans from a government installation, while wearing a replica of Spider-Man's costume (**12**). Despite the clever frame-up, Spider-Man managed to track the villain to the waterfront, and was just about to return him to the authorities (**13**) when the Chameleon disappeared. Spidey used his spider-sense to detect that the villain was disguised as one of the cops (**14**), but the real police officers refused to believe that Spider-Man wasn't the criminal. Spider-Man fled in anger, leaving the police officers to figure it out. Spider-Man may have saved the day, but he wished he had never got his superpowers. He was a loner with a tarnished reputation and a laughable bank balance.

CHAMELEON

A master of disguise who has assumed countless false identities, the Chameleon was one of the first true Super Villains Spider-Man ever faced. Filled with burning fury, he would like nothing more than to put an end to Spidey's life once and for all.

"Don't call me Dmitri. Dmitri is just one of my names."

The Chameleon

The Chameleon enlisted his half-brother Kraven in his war against Spidey. However, he feels a fierce rivalry with his sibling, as well as a desperate need for his approval.

ORIGIN

The son of an exiled Russian aristocrat and a young servant girl, Dmitri Smerdyakov was never loved as a child. His father hated the sight of him, and his mother considered him an embarrassment. Only Sergei Kravinoff, his older half-brother who later became Kraven the Hunter, acknowledged him. Obsessed with pleasing Sergei, Dmitri often put on little shows for him, acting out the various parts. Dmitri also began impersonating his classmates and neighbors, copying their physical idiosyncrasies with uncanny skill. He learned how to use makeup to modify his appearance and eventually began to create realistic facial masks and disguises.

These talents would soon come in handy for Dmitri as he embarked on a career in espionage. He began working as an industrial spy, stealing and selling commercial secrets to the highest bidder. When Spider-Man and the Chameleon first met, the former spy had just stolen secret plans and was planning to offer them to Communist countries for an immense profit. Recognizing that Spider-Man was viewed by many as a menace, the Chameleon realized that the wall-crawler would make a perfect fall guy.

Sending a message that only Spidey's special senses could detect, the Chameleon lured the unsuspecting crime-fighter into his trap. Disguising himself as the web-spinner, he attempted to frame Spidey for his own crimes. Unfortunately for Dmitri, the wall-crawler cleared his name by capturing and exposing the Chameleon, creating a fierce, all-consuming hatred for Spider-Man in the criminal's heart.

The Chameleon usually wears masks for his impersonations, but he's also been known to use holographic projections.

Aware of Peter Parker's secret identity, the Chameleon staged an elaborate fake kidnapping of Mary Jane Watson, using a holographic image to trick Spider-Man.

The Chameleon even impersonated President Barack Obama during his inauguration. Spidey helped determine which Obama was the real one by asking them both what Barack's nickname was in high school.

Although a master of disguise, the Chameleon is no match for Spidey's enhanced strength.

The Chameleon can impersonate anyone, a fact he proved when he kidnapped and took the place of J. Jonah Jameson during a plot to take over the *Daily Bugle*.

The Chameleon often captures and murders the subjects he impersonates, using a putty gun to make a mask of their face before dropping them into a chamber filled with acid.

KEY DATA

FIRST APPEARANCE: *The Amazing Spider-Man* #1 (March 1963)

REAL NAME: Dmitri Smerdyakov

AFFILIATIONS: The Sinister Six, the Sinister Twelve, the Exterminators

POWERS/ABILITIES: The Chameleon speaks dozens of languages, each with the pronunciation and subtlety of a native. He is a master of disguise, a brilliant actor, and a genius at creating lifelike masks. Thanks to years of practice and his own innate talents, the Chameleon can mimic any individual, and routinely fools even close friends and family of his target.

The Super Villain's masks are made from a synthetic material that looks and feels like human skin.

The base mask hides his identity. It is designed so other masks can be fitted quickly and securely.

The master of disguise also uses many gadgets to foil the forces of law and order, such as smoke bombs.

POWER PLAY

After years of specializing in espionage, the Chameleon decided that it was time to turn toward more profitable endeavors. Attempting to displace the Kingpin, he formed an alliance with Hammerhead and they launched a street war against Wilson Fisk. The Chameleon also kidnapped and began to impersonate J. Jonah Jameson. He planned to use the media power of the *Daily Bugle* to publicize Fisk's misdeeds and to force the authorities to mobilize against him. But when Peter Parker's spider-sense began to tingle in the presence of J. Jonah Jameson, the web-slinger began to suspect something was amiss. Spider-Man exposed the Chameleon and rescued the vitriolic publisher.

THE VULTURE LEGACY

Adrian Toomes has undoubtedly made the greatest impact as the Vulture, despite there being several other villains to claim that notorious name. The first was "Blackie" Drago, a career criminal who once shared a prison cell with Toomes and usurped the villain's technology. The second, Clifton Shallot, was a former Empire State University professor who got his hands on Adrian's invention. And while a new, savage vulture—Jimmy Natale—has reared his ugly head in Manhattan, there's little doubt that Adrian will one day return to reclaim his rightful role. Always innovating and improving his technology, Toomes is a force to be reckoned with, and should never be considered obsolete.

The Vulture can fly at a top speed of nearly 93 mph (150 kph), and can reach a maximum altitude of nearly 11,500 feet (3,500 metres).

The harness that the Vulture wears somehow increases his physical strength and endurance. He can engage in acrobatic aerial battles for hours without tiring.

KEY DATA

FIRST APPEARANCE: *The Amazing Spider-Man #2* (May 1963)

REAL NAME: Adrian Toomes

AFFILIATIONS: The Sinister Six, the Sinister Twelve

POWERS/ABILITIES: Adrian Toomes's homemade flight harness allows flight and enhanced strength and vitality. His wings are razor sharp and have been known to cut through Spider-Man's webs. Toomes has a brilliant mind that he puts to devious use.

This later version of the Vulture's black costume comes equipped with razor-sharp talons, as well as his usual flying harness.

VULTURE

Like his namesake, the Vulture is a pitiless predator. The villain preys upon the rich, the powerful, and the unwary, using an electromagnetic harness of his own invention to fly and strike on silent wings. A ferocious fighter, the Vulture attacks without mercy.

Cunning Vulture ultimately murdered Gregory Bestman, his former partner who had betrayed him.

ORIGIN

Adrian Toomes was an engineer and inventor who started an electronics firm with his best friend, Gregory Bestman. With Bestman handling the administrative side of the business, Toomes concentrated solely on his inventions. He dreamed of building an electromagnetically powered body harness that could enable an individual to fly. But Bestman was secretly plotting against Toomes and stealing his share of the profits. Soon, Bestman gained total control of the company and fired the inventor. Yet Toomes continued to work on the harness. Once the device was complete, he took his revenge by using it to terrorize his old partner and to steal from his former company. Intoxicated with the sense of power and freedom, Toomes decided to pursue a criminal career, calling himself the Vulture. As he gained confidence in his ability to fly, his crimes grew more daring, and he often issued challenges to the police to try to capture him. This led him into conflict with the fledgling Spider-Man, who was not only trying to defeat the villain, but also attempting to snap a few pictures of him to sell to the *Daily Bugle*.

Toomes's flying machine is a revolutionary piece of technology, which he usually keeps hidden beneath his Vulture costume.

After originally being defeated by the Vulture, Spider-Man developed a device that temporarily removed the villain's power of flight. Outraged by his public humiliation, the Vulture swore vengeance on Spider-Man

Although the second Vulture, "Blackie" Drago had youth on his side, the original Vulture, Toomes, was able to reclaim his mantle by using his expertise and experience, to prove he was the true Vulture.

While powerful in his Vulture costume, Adrian Toomes's most terrifying weapon is his darkly brilliant mind.

The newest Vulture, Jimmy Natale, was a former mob heavy who was unwillingly transformed into an acid-spewing bird of prey and hunter of the weak.

ALL IN THE FAMILY

Doc Ock has not only been a negative force in Spider-Man's life, but also in that of Peter Parker. While hiding out from the police, Otto once rented a room from May Parker, who never realized that he was an escaped criminal. Later, after Spider-Man forced him to leave her home, the villain learned that May was due to inherit one of the world's most sophisticated nuclear breeding reactors. In order to get his hands on the reactor, Octopus asked May to marry him, a scheme thwarted again at the very last minute by Spider-Man.

So strong is the bond with his tentacles that Doctor Octopus can control them even when they have been separated from his body.

Doc Ock's four tentacle arms are around six feet (1.8 meters) long, but they can extend to 25 feet (7.6 meters).

Each pincer can grip with enough force to crush a block of concrete.

KEY DATA

FIRST APPEARANCE: *The Amazing Spider-Man* #3 (July 1963)

REAL NAME: Otto Octavius

AFFILIATIONS: The Sinister Six, the Masters of Evil

POWERS/ABILITIES: Doctor Octopus is extremely intelligent and a gifted engineer and inventor. He controls his weaponized artificial tentacle arms with his mind. Due to his extraordinary mental capabilities, Octopus can perform several complex actions simultaneously with his arms. While each arm possesses no nerve endings, Octopus can nonetheless feel basic sensations through them.

DOCTOR OCTOPUS

Doctor Octopus possesses a genius that few people can surpass. With dozens of criminal schemes to his credit and almost as many battles with Spider-Man under his belt, Doc Ock has spent the majority of his career trying to deny the fact that Spider-Man is not only his physical superior, but his intellectual better as well.

ORIGIN

As a young boy, Otto Octavius was a shy and sensitive bookworm. A hardworking student, he didn't seem the type to grow up to become one of the world's most dangerous men. Otto's mother, Mary Lavinia Octavius, had high hopes for her son and didn't want Otto to become a manual laborer like his father. To please her, Otto decided to become a scientist, specializing in the field of nuclear research. His mother was thrilled when Otto graduated from college, since it meant that he would never have to dirty his hands like a common workingman. Otto Octavius threw himself into his career, often working 24 hours a day. He eventually became one of the nation's leading scientists. As his fame grew, Otto became arrogant, condescending, and self-absorbed. He invented a special mechanical harness that allowed him to perform dangerous experiments at a distance and also discouraged his coworkers from getting too close. However, during a freak laboratory accident, Otto Octavius was somehow physically and mentally bonded with his mechanical arms. He lashed out against the medical professionals attempting to help him and even attacked his superiors, thinking himself above moral concerns and valuing his perceived scientific triumph over human life. Moving as one with his mechanical limbs, Octavius became a monster that day. He became Doctor Octopus.

Although Doctor Octopus has fought many Super Heroes, he has become obsessed with destroying Spider-Man, believing he will never know peace until he kills the web-slinger.

Doctor Octopus's costume and look have often changed with the times. He's gone from a green jumpsuit to a white tailored suit to a wraparound trench coat, all in an attempt to have the public take him seriously.

> "… I am, indeed, a new creation. As different from them as a man to a beast."
>
> Doctor Octopus

At one point, a female scientist named Carolyn Trainer even subbed for the villain as Lady Octopus. During her dramatic debut, she challenged not just Peter Parker, but also Ben Reilly, the Scarlet Spider.

His days numbered due to exposure to radiation, Doctor Octopus decided to bestow a final "gift" to New York City by taking control of every electronic mechanism in Manhattan. But the wall-crawler tracked down Ock and defeated him, despite the villain's upgrade to eight mechanical limbs.

After an accident in his laboratory, Doctor Octopus was misdiagnosed with brain damage. In reality, his brain was creating new neuro-pathways—he could now mentally control his metal arms.

MYSTERIO

More than one man has worn the mantle of the master of illusion known as Mysterio—or that might just be another piece of brilliant misdirection. With Mysterio, nothing is as it seems. Cruel, resourceful, and always willing to hold a grudge, Mysterio has been puzzling Spidey for years.

ORIGIN

As a child, Quentin Beck dreamed of making movies. Armed with a movie camera, young Quentin built monsters out of clay, starring them in short films. While a teenager, he worked on a low-budget monster thriller, and later moved to Hollywood, where he worked as a stuntman and a special effects designer. Though his career proved fairly successful, Quentin grew tired of working behind the scenes, and sought the spotlight as an actor and director. But he didn't have the looks or talent to make it as a star, and he was much too temperamental to be a director. A comment by a friend made him realize that he could attain a different kind of fame by using his talent with special effects and illusion to become a Super Hero. And so Mysterio was born!

When the *Daily Bugle* declared Spider-Man a menace, Mysterio knew that the paper would give him the publicity he craved if he could capture the wall-crawler. There was only one problem—Spider-Man hadn't broken the law. So Mysterio disguised himself as the hero and convinced the public that Spidey was on a crime spree. He challenged the web-head to meet him, and the two fought to a draw. But Spider-Man suspected Mysterio's plot. He tracked him down and the conceited Mysterio confessed, not realizing the web-slinger was recording it all. Spidey turned Mysterio in to the police, along with the taped confession. With his dreams of being a Super Hero ruined by Spider-Man, Mysterio embarked wholeheartedly on his criminal career.

Corrupt from the start, Mysterio attempted to steal the special effects secrets of his mentor Ray Bradhaus.

Mysterio's time as a stuntman came in useful when he fought against Spider-Man on the set of an out-of-this-world movie.

Ever since Spider-Man ruined Mysterio's attempts at becoming a "hero," the criminal has plotted revenge against the wall-crawler. Unable to let go of personal grudges, the villain later adopted a hatred towards Daredevil, too.

> "...it's better to have the marks think that they're **players**... instead of the ones getting **played**."
>
> Mysterio

Mysterio's trademark is a trail of smoke, released from his gloves and boots. It can also be mixed with various toxins, acids, and hallucinogens to disorient his opponents.

A master of disguise, Mysterio first met Spider-Man when he was disguised as an alien ally of the criminal known as the Tinkerer.

When Quentin Beck seemingly died, the role of Mysterio bounced around from Beck's old friend Daniel Berkhart to teleporter Francis Klum. But eventually the original returned to reclaim his twisted mantle.

KEY DATA

FIRST APPEARANCE: (historical) *The Amazing Spider-Man* #13 (June 1964); (retcon) *The Amazing Spider-Man* #2 (May 1963)

REAL NAME: Quentin Beck

AFFILIATIONS: The Sinister Six

POWERS/ABILITIES: Although Mysterio doesn't possess superhuman powers, he is an expert at executing elaborate and believable special effects. He is armed with dozens of high-tech deadly gadgets including a smoke that can dissolve Spider-Man's webbing and magnetic spring boots to help duplicate Spider-Man's own wall-crawling abilities.

Mysterio's helmet is made of a treated glass that allows him to see out but prevents others from seeing in. It also contains a half-hour supply of oxygen.

Mysterio has his own makeshift spider-sense, courtesy of his helmet's built-in sonar device, that helps him to "see" through his smoky cloud.

THE ILLUSIONIST

With an eye toward the theatric, Mysterio has orchestrated some of the most elaborate criminal schemes that Spider-Man has ever faced, despite not possessing any actual superpowers. In order to play with his opponent's minds, Mysterio crafts scenarios in which the hero is forced to participate in bizarre adventures. From staging the bogus resurrection of Spider-Man's old friends and enemies to faking his own death, Mysterio is always making the web-slinger question himself and his own reality. Mysterio's ruses are so believable that he's been contracted to fake the deaths of other criminals who wish to go into hiding. Over the years, he's even made Spidey believe that many of his loved ones had died, including Harry Osborn and Aunt May.

A LIFE OF CRIME

Driven insane and more power-hungry than ever by the explosion in his lab, Norman Osborn decided to increase his personal fortune by turning to crime. He hired and outfitted costumed Super Villains like the Scorcher and the Headsman. But when these thieves were defeated by Spider-Man, Norman decided to take matters into his own hands. He used his company's chemical discoveries to assemble a personal armory and designed a costume for himself. All he needed was the right mask—a face to present to the world. He chose the face of the Green Goblin.

Norman based his grotesque green costume and mask on a green goblin monster from a childhood nightmare.

The Green Goblin keeps a bizarre variety of gas, smoke, and incendiary grenades in his "bag of tricks."

KEY DATA

FIRST APPEARANCE: *The Amazing Spider-Man* #14 (July 1964)

REAL NAME: Norman Osborn

AFFILIATIONS: The Sinister Twelve, the Thunderbolts, the Cabal, H.A.M.M.E.R., Dark Avengers

POWERS/ABILITIES: The Goblin Formula endows Norman Osborn with enhanced intelligence, strength, reflexes, agility, speed, and endurance, and a regenerative healing ability. He possesses a vast array of deadly, high-tech weapons, including grenade-like pumpkin bombs and his flying Goblin-Glider. He wears a chain mail tunic for extra protection in battle.

The Goblin's signature weapons are his deadly pumpkin bombs, shaped as miniature Jack-O'Lanterns.

Osborn created his ingenious Goblin-Glider, which travels at speeds of 90 mph (140 kph). Originally he flew on a rocket-like "broomstick," but soon traded that in for the razor-wings and better maneuverability of his Glider.

GREEN GOBLIN

To say Norman Osborn is simply insane is to do the criminal a great injustice. Arguably Spider-Man's most dangerous enemy, the Green Goblin has cheated death to continue his quest for power and his never-ending campaign against the web-slinger.

When Norman attempted to recreate a serum to enhance his strength and intelligence, he thought it had failed when it bubbled and exploded in his face.

"You **see**, Parker? I always knew I could defeat you anytime I **wanted...**"

Green Goblin

ORIGIN

Norman Osborn was just a child when he first became obsessed with acquiring wealth and power. His father, Amberson Osborn, was an inventor whose business failed, and he often took out his rage on his young son. Norman realized that he couldn't depend on his father for financial security, so he began working after school and saving every cent that he earned. Driven and dedicated, Norman studied chemistry, business administration, and electrical engineering in college. He became good friends with one of his teachers, Professor Mendel Stromm, and they formed a business partnership. Since Norman had put up the bulk of the financing, they called their company Osborn Chemical. Norman married his college sweetheart and they had a son, Harry, a few years later, but his wife became ill and died. After her death, Norman buried himself in his work and rarely had time for young Harry. Norman eventually learned that his business partner had embezzled money from their company so he had Stromm arrested and assumed complete control of the company. While going through Stromm's notes, Norman learned of a chemical formula that could increase a person's strength and intelligence, so he tried to recreate the experiment. But unaware that his angry son had switched a few of his chemicals, the solution turned green and exploded. After he was released from hospital following the explosion, Norman realized that the formula had worked—he was stronger and smarter than ever.

Originally, the Goblin simply wanted to establish his criminal reputation by killing Spider-Man. But with each defeat, he became more obsessed with conquering the wall-crawler.

Although Norman Osborn is a respected businessman and government official, he can't help but relapse into his Goblin persona to continue his crazed pursuit of Spider-Man.

The Green Goblin once learned Spider-Man's secret identity by exposing him to a gas that weakened his spider-sense. However, Spidey knocked the villain into a mass of live electrical wires and gave Osborn amnesia.

While the Goblin Formula increases its user's physical strength and even his intelligence, it also costs him his sanity. However, that was a small price to pay for a man as ruthless as Norman Osborn.

"YOUR SPEED WON'T SAVE YOU FOR LONG! REMEMBER— YOU'LL SOON GET TIRED—BUT THE HULK NEVER DOES!"

THE HULK

A modern case of Dr. Jekyll and Mr. Hyde, the Hulk is mild-mannered intellectual Dr. Bruce Banner when not his brutish alter ego.

Perhaps the strongest human in the universe, the Hulk is not to be trifled with.

HULK VS SPIDER-MAN

Physicist Dr. Bruce Banner shares many traits with Peter Parker, but as the gamma-irradiated behemoth known as the Hulk, he couldn't be more different from Spider-Man. The Hulk is a rampaging force of nature who thinks finesse is for sissies. He is easily irritated by Spidey's wisecracks, and has often tried to squash the wall-crawler like a bug.

THE STRONGEST ONE THERE IS

As with most people who cross the path of the incredible Hulk, Spider-Man first met the green goliath by accident. Encountering Hulk while chasing the Green Goblin in a cave in New Mexico, Spider-Man was drawn into a fight he neither wanted nor stood a chance of winning. The cave was one of the Hulk's secret hiding places and he believed Spider-Man was there to attack him. While Spidey didn't shy away from the fight, he took the first opportunity to get out of the Hulk's way. Spider-Man then manipulated the behemoth to use his brute strength to shatter a boulder, freeing Spidey from the cavern's twisted maze.

UNINTENTIONAL MONSTER

Realizing the Hulk was in a whole different weight class, Spider-Man learned to be cautious around him when they later locked horns. While on a try-out mission for the Avengers, Spidey battled the Hulk again. Realizing that the Hulk wasn't intentionally causing trouble and wanted to be left alone, Spidey did just that, abandoning his own quest for Avengers membership.

Although they have clashed many times over the years, Spider-Man put up his best showing against the Hulk when he was briefly granted cosmic powers by an extra-dimensional force. Utilizing his newly gained strength, Spidey punched the Hulk hard enough that the brute was actually sent into orbit around the planet. The Hulk thought he would die in the vacuum of space, but Spidey flew up to him and rescued him before he ran out of oxygen.

With an intimate knowledge of human and animal physiology, Kraven devised his own fighting style.

THE FIRST HUNT

When Kraven was contacted by his half-brother Dmitri, it seemed like fate to the bored hunter, who was looking for a chance to truly test his skills and abilities. Dmitri had become a villain called the Chameleon, and wanted Kraven's help in defeating his recent nemesis Spider-Man. The first meeting between Spider-Man and Kraven did not start off well for the wall-crawler. Surprised by Kraven's speed, Spider-Man had his shoulder numbed by a devastating punch—the same punch that can stop a charging rhino in its tracks. But Kraven underestimated Spider-Man and was ultimately outwitted and defeated. From that day, Kraven swore to complete his hunt and destroy Spider-Man.

Kraven's clothing reflects his years mastering the hunt. To Kraven, his outfit is not really a costume, but more of an outward display of his skill as a predator.

KEY DATA

FIRST APPEARANCE: *The Amazing Spider-Man* #15 (August 1964)

REAL NAME: Sergei Kravinoff

AFFILIATIONS: The Sinister Six

POWERS/ABILITIES: Kraven regularly ingests a potion of various jungle herbs, which gives him enhanced speed, reflexes, agility, and strength. Another effect of the potion is decelerated aging—he is nearly immortal. Even without these superhuman powers, Kraven is a brilliant hunter, fighter, athlete, and marksman. He is expert at a variety of weapons, and uses exotic potions and tranquilizers in his fights.

Thanks to the mutagenic effects of the herbal potion, Kraven can lift almost two tons and has been known to throw a full-grown gorilla from its feet.

KRAVEN

A lone hunter who has since grown into the head of a deadly pride of killers, Kraven is one of Spider-Man's most resilient foes. Only death at his own hand could cease his lifelong hunt, and even that was temporary. Kraven is more than a sportsman and expert killer—he is a force of nature.

ORIGIN

Sergei Kravinoff was born into a family of Russian aristocrats. Forced into exile during the Russian revolution, Sergei's parents eventually settled in the United Kingdom. But life was hard, and as their finances began to dwindle, Sergei's mother fell into a terrible depression. She committed suicide while Sergei was still a young child. Within a year, his father married a former servant girl, and the young Sergei became furious when he learned that his stepmother was pregnant. He accused his father of betraying his mother's memory and made the life of his half-brother Dmitri miserable. Hating his family situation, Sergei ran away. He traveled throughout Europe, Asia, and Africa, stowing away on cargo ships and trains and using his wit and cunning to survive. Eventually, he found work on a safari, where he discovered that he had a natural talent for hunting. Over the years, Sergei sharpened his hunting skills and his fame began to spread.

During his time in the jungle, Kraven stumbled upon a witch doctor who had created a potion that somehow gave him superhuman strength and speed. Now Kraven could track and kill jungle animals with ease, and he soon became desperate to find a challenge worthy of his skills.

A journalist helped cement Sergei's legend by writing articles about him. Not knowing how to spell the hunter's last name, he shortened it to Kraven.

While he has been known to employ weapons or potions to aid him in his hunt, Kraven gets a special thrill from besting his prey with his bare hands and brute strength.

Kraven has sired many children, including his now-deceased sons—Vladimir and Alyosha—and his demented daughter—Ana—who inherited her father's obsession with hunting Spider-Man.

Kraven employs knives, whips, and blowguns. He also uses poison-tipped darts to aid assaults on his enemies.

Sometimes Kraven hunts with the animals he normally fights. Much like a wild animal, Kraven asserts his dominance and then takes control of the pack.

Kraven's ultimate battle with Spider-Man culminated in Kraven burying the web-crawler alive and then committing suicide. His death would not last, though.

"It was perfect. It was a masterpiece. You took that masterpiece away from me."

Kraven

Over the course of his long life, Kraven has taken many mates, including the vindictive Sasha, who became his wife.

SINISTER SIX

Despite his superpowers, Spider-Man's one-on-one battles against his enemies are close-run victories. But when his greatest foes united to ensure his death, the heroic wall-crawler was faced with one of his deadliest challenges—the Sinister Six, a group of rogues that truly lived up to their name.

ORIGIN

After suffering three defeats at the hands of Spider-Man, Doctor Octopus realized that he needed help against the web-slinger. He got in touch with the most notorious super-powered villains who had battled Spider-Man in the past. In the end, five other super-criminals heeded Ock's call—Electro, Kraven the Hunter, Mysterio, the Sandman, and the Vulture. Others, like the Green Goblin and Dr. Doom, turned down the offer as they preferred to go their own way.

With his team formed, Doctor Octopus soon realized that he would never be able to control these Super Villains. They were incapable of working together or functioning as a well-oiled machine. Instead of trying to change this unruly bunch, Doc Ock conceived a battle plan that exploited their individual appetites for personal glory. Each member of the Sinister Six would stage a separate battle with Spider-Man at a carefully chosen location. One by one the criminals would fight him until the wall-crawler was finally destroyed. Fortunately for Spidey, the plan didn't quite work out as well as Doc Ock had planned.

Before facing these six sinister foes, Spidey suddenly lost his powers.

Hanging onto a flagpole for his very life, Spider-Man regained his abilities in the heat of battle against Electro.

With his powers restored, Spider-Man fought his way through a host of Super Villains. He was able to battle the various villains with ease.

The second incarnation of the Sinister Six appeared years after the original team's defeat. It employed Hobgoblin in place of the now-deceased Kraven.

> "I'm preparing the crowning caper of my criminal career!"
>
> Doctor Octopus

Spider-Man later faced down the army of the Sinister Twelve, which he only defeated with the help of the Fantastic Four and the Avengers.

The most recent version of the Sinister Six was once again organized by Doctor Octopus, and includes Chameleon, Mysterio, Sandman, Rhino, and Electro.

KEY DATA

FIRST APPEARANCE: *The Amazing Spider-Man Annual* #1 (January 1964)

OTHER VERSIONS: The Sinister Seven, the Sinister Twelve

KNOWN MEMBERS: Doctor Octopus, Vulture, Sandman, Mysterio, Kraven, Electro, Hobgoblin, Gog, Beetle, Scorpia, Shocker, Venom (Eddie Brock), Kraven II, Mysterio II, Chameleon, Lizard, Green Goblin, Hydro-Man, Rhino, Venom (Mac Gargan), Boomerang, Hammerhead, Tombstone

Spidey's temporary loss of powers was due to him subconsciously suppressing his powers due to his guilt about Uncle Ben's death.

Mysterio used his illusions to try to make Spider-Man believe that he was fighting the original X-Men.

Doctor Octopus instructed later Sinister Six teams to attack Spidey as a group rather than individually.

THE ORIGINALS

When the original Sinister Six put their first plan into action, they realized that Betty Brant, a secretary for the *Daily Bugle*, played an important part in Spider-Man's life. To motivate the wall-crawler, they kidnapped her, along with an innocent bystander—none other than Peter Parker's Aunt May. After facing and defeating Electro, Kraven, Mysterio, Sandman, and the Vulture, Spidey was lured into a giant fishbowl. Forced to fight his final battle underwater, Spidey faced off with Doctor Octopus, who was equipped with an air tank and mask. The Doctor tried to drown Spider-Man, but the masked teenager refused to give up. He held his breath long enough to overpower his tentacled antagonist and free Betty and Aunt May.

KEY DATA

FIRST APPEARANCE: *The Amazing Spider-Man* #25 (June 1965)

ALIAS: None

AFFILIATIONS: None

PERSONALITY TRAITS: Mary Jane is a source for calm and reason in Peter Parker's otherwise chaotic life. Although she has no special powers, she is intelligent and resourceful in times of danger, often displaying exemplary courage and tenacity. She possesses a wide range of acting skills and is trained in self-defense.

Mary Jane's career as a model has meant that her clothes are always at the height of fashion. Even her casual wear boasts impressive name brands.

Due to her tough childhood, Mary Jane is great at masking her feelings. It's a talent that has been useful for her acting career and for making up excuses for Peter's activities.

SPIDER-MAN'S GIRLFRIEND

It wasn't until Peter Parker and Mary Jane Watson began getting serious about one another that Mary Jane realized the high price that accompanied being in a relationship with Spider-Man. Danger is always present in the wall-crawler's life, and if MJ wasn't worrying about Peter coming home safely, she was worrying about her own well-being. Over the years, Mary Jane has been attacked by the likes of Tombstone and the second incarnation of the Green Goblin. However, the greatest impact on her was made by Venom. When the villain first arrived on the scene, he went straight to Mary Jane and Peter's apartment. There he confronted the model and asked her about Peter's whereabouts. MJ was so scared by Venom's visit that she persuaded Peter to move apartments.

During her relationship with Peter, Mary Jane was often the breadwinner of the household, having a much more successful career.

MARY JANE

> ## "Face it, Tiger... You just hit the jackpot!"
> Mary Jane

On the surface, Mary Jane Watson is the complete opposite of Peter Parker. Seemingly merely a fun-loving, carefree party girl with a constant smile on her face, Mary Jane proves that looks can be deceiving. There is far more to MJ than just a pretty face.

ORIGIN

Mary Jane is the daughter of Philip and Madeline Watson. Her mother was a drama student, while her father majored in American literature and wanted to be a writer. The two married as soon as they graduated from college. But as his dreams of becoming a writer faltered, Philip turned on his family, verbally abusing them and blaming them for his inability to concentrate. The relationship deteriorated to the extent that Madeline took their young children, Gayle and Mary Jane, and left Philip.

Life did not get any easier for the Watson family. Gayle married her high-school sweetheart Timothy Byrnes right after graduation. Timmy planned to be a lawyer, but the couple became pregnant. Unable to cope with the pressures of law school, and with yet another child on the way, Timmy deserted Gayle. Disaster struck again, when Mary Jane's mother died just before the birth of Gayle's second child. Gayle turned to her sister, hoping for support. But Mary Jane wasn't willing to give up her dream of becoming an actress to help her sister. Instead, she left to stay with her favorite aunt, Anna Watson, who was living in Forest Hills. During her time there, Aunt Anna introduced Mary Jane to a young man that would change her life forever. A young man named Peter Parker.

Though reluctant to let his aunt set him up on a date, when Peter finally met MJ, he couldn't believe how beautiful she was.

Mary Jane first discovered Peter's dual identity when she saw Spider-Man crawl out of Peter's bedroom on the night that Peter's Uncle Ben died. However it took her years before she revealed to Peter that she knew.

During the time Mary Jane lived with Peter, she was kidnapped by Green Goblin Harry Osborn. Although Mary Jane was terrified at first, Harry didn't want to harm his friend.

A popular model and former star of the soap opera *Secret Hospital*, Mary Jane is used to a life of glitz and glamour.

Mary Jane has had many admirers, but none were more obsessive or dangerous than her former landlord Jonathan Caesar, who even attempted to kidnap her at one point.

While they are no longer a couple, Mary Jane and Peter still have strong feelings for each other. MJ remains a true friend to Peter as one of the few people to know about his double life.

Spidey was growing up. In the tumultuous 1970s, the hero dealt with the death of loved ones and watched a friend fall victim to a drug addiction. Despite the controversy, Spidey remained as popular as ever, even earning a new monthly title in *Peter Parker, The Spectacular Spider-Man.*

THE
1970s

It was time for Spider-Man to sink or swim. In 1971, for the first time in his fictional life, the web-slinger would be forced to make his way in the Marvel Universe without the direct help of writer Stan Lee. After taking Peter Parker to the historic 100th issue of *The Amazing Spider-Man* (an issue that featured Spidey gaining four extra arms), Lee thought it best to step out from behind the writer's desk to pursue other avenues. And while he'd return to pen Spidey's adventures once or twice in the future, Lee was no longer charting the course of the hero's life.

This wasn't the first time that the creative team behind Spider-Man had shifted. Legendary artist Steve Ditko had left the title after issue #38 in 1966, and this had made way for the similarly renowned artwork of John Romita. Artist extraordinaire John Buscema had penciled a handful of issues, and the amazing Gil Kane had even taken on the task of drawing the wall-crawler a few times. But Lee leaving the book was the title's ultimate test, and one it passed with flying colors. With the groundbreaking work of future writers like Gerry Conway, *The Amazing Spider-Man* kept earning its titular adjective issue after issue.

OVERLEAF *The Amazing Spider-Man* #103 (December 1971): As if fighting villains on his home turf isn't hard enough, Spidey often travels to strange and exotic places. In the prehistoric Savage Land, he teamed up with Ka-Zar to battle the fantastical Gog.

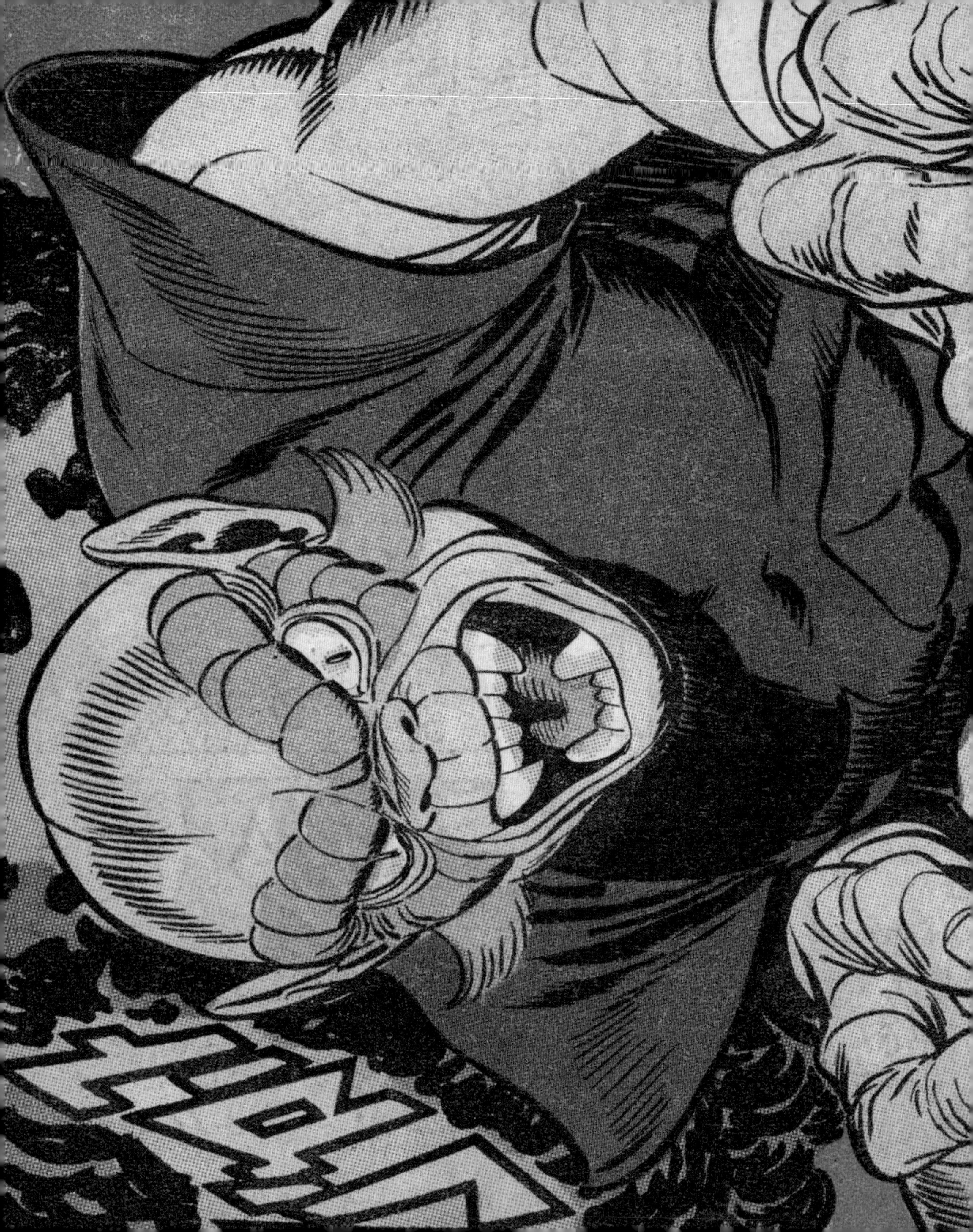

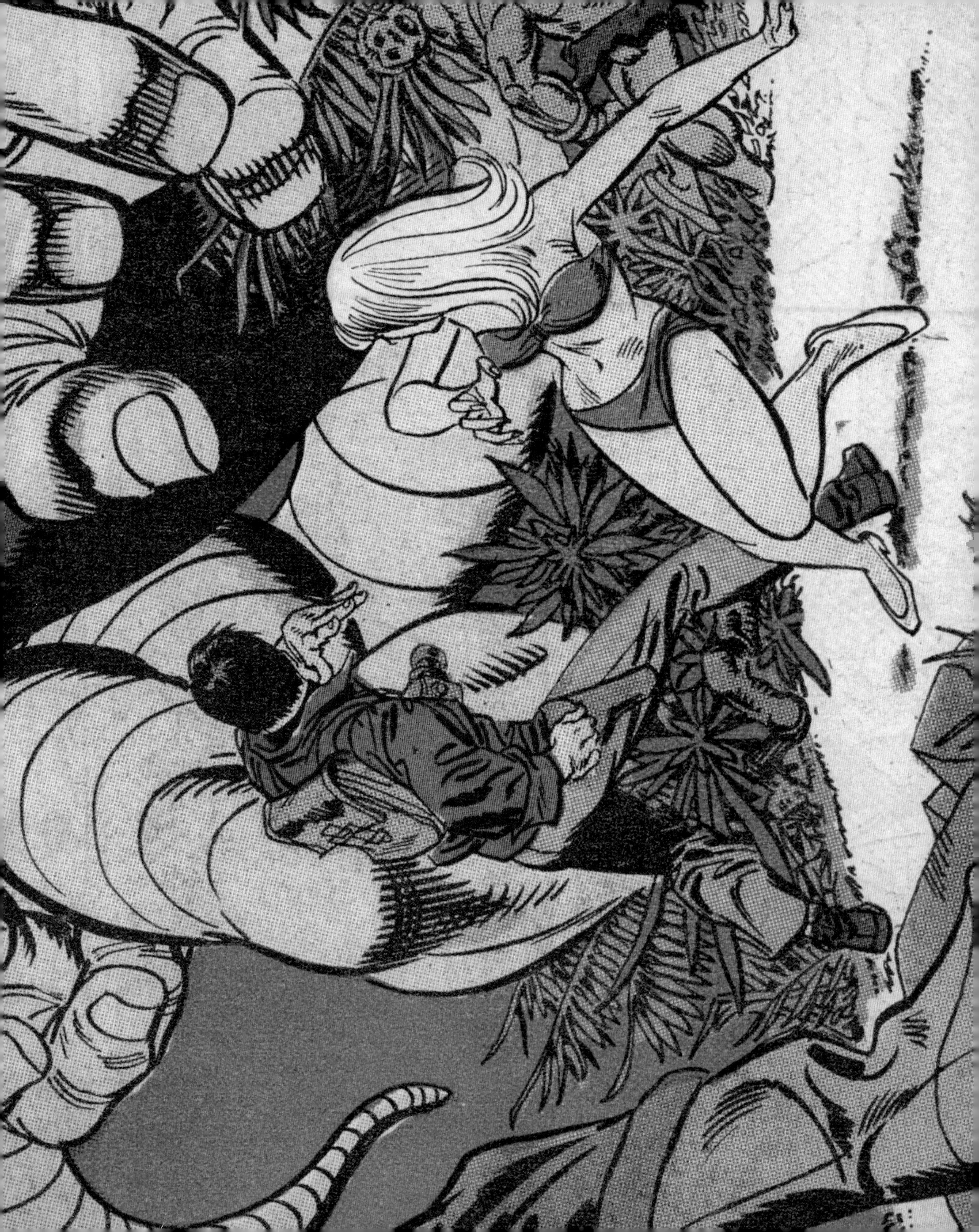

THE DEATH OF THE STACYS

Beautiful science undergrad Gwen Stacy was the first woman who truly captured the heart of Peter Parker. As their relationship blossomed, Peter grew to love her more than any of the women he had dated in the past, and wanted to spend the rest of his life with her. But fate had other plans for them.

THE BEGINNING OF THE END

After dating for some time, Gwen and Peter were becoming more serious about each other and Peter was introduced to Gwen's father, retired police captain George Stacy. Stacy was kind to Peter, and what's more, he appeared to be a Spider-Man supporter. It seemed that, like Peter, George was a hero at heart. George's heroism was proven during a rooftop battle between Spider-Man and Doctor Octopus. When stone debris hurtled toward an innocent child, George leapt into action. He put himself in harm's way and saved the child's life.

Horrified at what had happened, Spider-Man pulled his girlfriend's father from the rubble. George Stacy knew he was dying and revealed that he had deduced Spider-Man's secret identity. As he died in Peter's arms, he begged Peter to watch over Gwen and take care of her. Even though Captain Stacy accepted his fate, Peter always blamed himself for the man's death.

CALLING CARD

When Spidey returned to his apartment, the place was in a shambles and a Jack-O'Lantern, the Green Goblin's trademark weapon, rested on Gwen's purse. Realizing she had been kidnapped, Spider-Man used his spider-sense to track the Green Goblin to the top of the George Washington Bridge.

THE RETURN OF THE GREEN GOBLIN

Some time after George Stacy's death, trouble started to brew for Peter's friends. Harry Osborn began taking drugs, and the stress of dealing with this pushed his father, Norman, into insanity, leading to him resuming his role as the Green Goblin. Norman blamed Peter for Harry's condition and set out to take revenge by abducting Peter's girlfriend, Gwen Stacy.

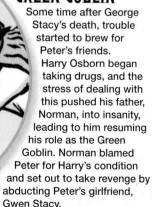

Norman Osborn had kidnapped Gwen by sneaking up on her from behind while she was distracted, worrying about the drug-addled condition of his son, Harry.

"YOU KILLED THE WOMAN I LOVE— AND FOR THAT, YOU'RE GOING TO DIE!"

SPIDER-MAN

During a furious battle with the wall-crawler atop the George Washington Bridge, the Goblin hurled Gwen over the side. Spider-Man shot out a web-line that caught the falling Gwen, but when he pulled her up, he was horrified to discover that she was already dead. While Spidey grieved, the Goblin escaped.

REVENGE

Spider-Man set out to find the Green Goblin and end his career once and for all. But, as much as he hated the Goblin, Spidey knew he couldn't take the life of another human being. He bested Osborn, and was about to take him captive when the villain mentally ordered his glider to impale Spider-Man. Warned by his spider-sense, Spidey ducked at the last moment. The glider impaled Osborn, killing him instantly—or so it seemed…

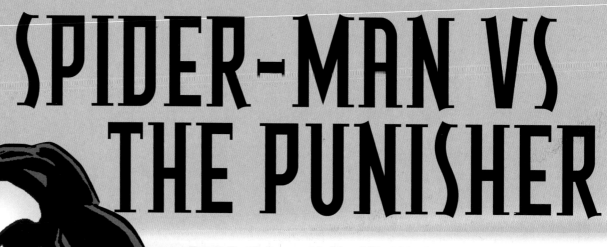

SPIDER-MAN VS THE PUNISHER

Frank Castle was a highly-skilled Marine when tragedy molded him into the deadly Punisher—a vigilante obsessed with punishing criminals beyond the reach of the law. While Spider-Man wants to defeat the Punisher to end his lethal crusade on crime, the two sometimes team up to battle dangerous foes.

THE PUNISHMENT

A proponent of deadly force and a remorseless killer, the Punisher is an enemy to the justice system, but for a good reason. The Punisher has battled Spider-Man on many occasions. He sees the web-head as an idealistic fool who lacks the stomach to use lethal force. Spider-Man thinks the Punisher is a tormented serial killer who uses unacceptable actions to achieve his own good intentions. Spider-Man has attempted to end the crazed vigilante's career several times, and has even teamed up with Wolverine and Daredevil to bring him down. But the Punisher always gets away in the end.

THE PUNISHER IS BORN
While on leave in New York, Frank Castle took his wife and two children to Central Park, where they accidentally stumbled upon a gangland killing. Fearing being identified by the Castles, the mobsters opened fire on the family, killing Frank's wife and children, although Frank somehow survived. Traumatized by the incident, Frank vowed to punish the mobsters. He deserted his career in the Marines and outfitted himself for a one-man war on crime.

TARGET: SPIDER-MAN

The Punisher first met Spider-Man when he teamed up with the Jackal, whom Frank thought was just another costumed vigilante. The Jackal manipulated the Punisher into believing that Spidey was a murderer, and Frank attempted to bring the wall-crawler to justice. But during their battle, Spider-Man proved his innocence, and the Punisher realized he had been lied to.

> "SOMETIMES I WONDER IF THAT EVIL'S RUBBED OFF ON ME... BUT I KNOW THAT DOESN'T MATTER. ALL THAT MATTERS IS THE JOB."
> THE PUNISHER

UNEASY ALLIES

Spider-Man and the Punisher constantly waver between being allies and adversaries. Circumstances often force them to work together as they both try to protect the innocent, and more often than not, the two end up partnering to stop more deadly foes. This was the case when Spidey and the Punisher worked together to track down Moses Magnum, a criminal and arms dealer who was selling an illegal gamma-radiated version of the drug MGH, Mutant Growth Hormone. However, Spider-Man recognizes that ultimately the Punisher is a killer.

The Punisher set up a sting operation to assassinate Moses Magnum. Although Spidey didn't agree with his methods, he joined forces with Magnum to capture the villain.

After Spider-Man helped him to defeat Moses Magnum, the Punisher shot Moses in the gut, forcing Spidey to take the villain to a hospital. This action left the Punisher free to escape once again.

KEY DATA

FIRST APPEARANCE: *The Amazing Spider-Man* #31 (December 1965)

REAL NAME: Harry Osborn

AFFILIATIONS: None

POWERS/ABILITIES: After using Norman Osborn's Goblin Formula, Harry gained enhanced strength, reflexes, endurance, speed, agility, and healing abilities. He also utilized and improved upon many of the original Green Goblin's weapons, including his flying Goblin Glider and trademark explosive pumpkin bombs.

Harry Osborn is constantly struggling with his past drug addiction and his own mental imbalances. He's always doing his best to keep his inner demons at bay.

Unlike his father, Harry had no interest in gaining wealth or power. He only wanted to kill Spider-Man.

HEART FAILURE

Harry Osborn was never lucky with love, a fact he took quite personally. When Harry attended Standard High School with Gwen Stacy, he had quite a crush on her, but never found the courage to ask her out. Later, when Peter introduced Harry to Mary Jane Watson, the two began to date. However, Mary Jane dumped Harry as soon as he became too possessive. This led Harry down the path of drug addiction, and helped warp his mind enough to find the idea of becoming the second Green Goblin appealing.

Harry upgraded his father's old equipment. He designed and built a newer model of the Goblin Glider, which was also later used by Phil Urich.

THE NEW GREEN GOBLIN

Harry was placed under the care of Dr. Barton Hamilton, who successfully "cured" him of his insanity. Hamilton was able to find a way to, temporarily, purge Harry's memories of ever having been the Green Goblin. But, having learnt Harry's secrets, Hamilton took advantage of Harry and became the third Green Goblin.

When the third Goblin appeared, Peter Parker assumed Harry was behind the mask, not realizing that his friend was actually Hamilton's prisoner. Harry finally escaped and battled Hamilton until the third Green Goblin was eventually killed by his own bomb.

> "I was wearing this costume long **before** you ever saw it—and I'll be wearing it long after you're **gone!**"
>
> Harry Osborn

While Harry has since retired his Green Goblin costume, he has been forced to wear it on occasion, usually to combat a lingering threat from his father's past.

At one point, Harry Osborn was presumed dead, and Phil Urich, the nephew of *Daily Bugle* reporter Ben Urich, stepped up to temporarily fill the Green Goblin role—but as a hero rather than a villain.

All throughout his adult life, Harry has wavered between stability and insanity. During the better times, he settled down and married Peter Parker's old high school friend Liz Allan. The two even had a child named Normie. During the darker times, he's relapsed to his Green Goblin persona, losing all he'd gained, focusing all his efforts on defeating Spider-Man.

Harold "Harry" Osborn met Peter Parker in college, and the two quickly became best friends. But when Harry discovered that his father Norman was the original Green Goblin and that Peter Parker was his archenemy Spider-Man, everything changed.

ORIGIN

The son of millionaire industrialist Norman Osborn, Harry had long been a troubled man. His mother died while he was a child, and his father buried himself in his work and was a domineering parent who rarely had time for his son. As a result, Harry grew up feeling inadequate. Although he resented his father, he would do almost anything to win his approval. Perceiving himself as a failure, Harry became a drug addict.

Harry secretly witnessed Spider-Man's final battle with the original Green Goblin. In horror, he watched as his father was impaled, and he wrongly blamed Spider-Man for his death. Before anyone else arrived, Harry removed the Goblin's mask and costume from his father's body. He made sure that the police couldn't link the dead industrialist with the Green Goblin. Later, Harry found a Spider-Man costume in the apartment he shared with Peter, and realized that his best friend was the man he blamed for his father's death. Turning against his longtime friend, Harry set out as the new Green Goblin, intent on destroying Peter's world and proving that he was strong enough to be his father's successor.

October 1975

THE AMAZING SPIDER-MAN #149

*"... the day I can't tell if I'm really **me**–is the day I hang up my web-shooters **forever!**"*

SPIDER-MAN (OR POSSIBLY HIS CLONE...)

EDITOR
Marv Wolfman

COVER ARTIST
Gil Kane

WRITER
Gerry Conway

PENCILER
Ross Andru

INKER
Mike Esposito

COLORIST
Janice Cohen

LETTERER
Annette Kawecki

MAIN CHARACTERS: Spider-Man; the Jackal; Gwen Stacy's clone; Spider-Man's clone

MAIN SUPPORTING CHARACTERS: Ned Leeds; the Tarantula; Anthony Serba; Mary Jane Watson; Joe Robertson; J. Jonah Jameson; Betty Brant

MAIN LOCATIONS: The Brooklyn Bridge; an abandoned tenement in lower Manhattan; Empire State University campus; the Jackal's laboratory; the *Daily Bugle* office; Shea Stadium; an unnamed cemetery, Queens; Peter Parker's apartment

BACKGROUND

It was the start of the most controversial storyline in the entire history of Spider-Man. The seeds planted in this 1975 multi-part storyline would slowly grow into the largest crossover ever to shake-up the Spidey universe—in the 1990s Clone Saga epic.

The writer Gerry Conway was no stranger to controversy. After all, just a few years earlier he had penned the death of Spider-Man's longtime love interest, Gwen Stacy, at the hands of the Green Goblin. And when Gwen seemingly returned in the months preceeding issue #149, fans were unprepared to learn she was merely a clone created by Peter Parker's teacher, Professor Miles Warren. Fans were even more shocked to learn that Warren was in fact the Super Villain named the Jackal, who had been causing most of Peter Parker's recent problems.

But no matter what the surprises in the past, fans would not be ready for the Jackal's newest clone, who leapt onto the pages of *The Amazing Spider-Man #149*. Just as they would be caught off guard nearly twenty years later when that same clone returned.

THE STORY

Faced with a bizarre challenge set by the insane Jackal, Spider-Man must defeat his own clone in order to rescue an innocent life.

There was no shortage of excitement in Spider-Man's world. He had recently faced down the new threat of the Grizzly, wrecked his Spider-Mobile due to the machinations of Mysterio, and learned of a new Super Villain out to kill him named the Jackal. And while Spider-Man's life was complicated, it couldn't hold a candle to Peter Parker's. Because just as Peter and Mary Jane Watson seemed to be taking their relationship to the next level, a familiar face popped back into Peter's life—the face of Gwen Stacy, Peter's former girlfriend whom he'd thought long dead.

Alongside Gwen's unexplained return came Peter's feelings for her. But before he could really process them, he found himself in a violent conflict with the Jackal and his accomplice, the Tarantula. While Spider-Man managed to defeat the Tarantula, the Jackal succeeded in subduing the web-crawler with his drug-tipped claws. With Spider-Man at his mercy, the Jackal revealed himself as Peter Parker's old college biology teacher, Professor Miles Warren.

While strapped to a table in the basement of an abandoned tenement building in lower Manhattan, Spider-Man had no choice but to listen to the mad ramblings of his former teacher (**1**). Even after the hero broke free of his bonds and engaged the Jackal in a brutal physical confrontation (**2**), the villain was determined to tell his bizarre story.

According to the Jackal, while he was teaching Peter's class, he'd developed quite an infatuation with Gwen Stacy. When the young girl died at the hands of the Green Goblin, Professor Warren had blamed Spider-Man for her death. He used tissue samples he had acquired from a classroom study to clone the young woman. In the process, Warren killed his lab assistant Anthony Serba, when Serba discovered what the Professor was up to. It was this traumatic event that caused Warren to truly plunge into insanity (**3**), and to develop the alter ego and split personality of the Jackal. He brought Gwen Stacey's doppelgänger to life (**4**) and vowed to defeat Spider-Man.

After relaying his tale, the Jackal then escaped, telling Spider-Man that if he ever wanted to see Gwen Stacy again, he would have to head to Shea Stadium at midnight that night. Forced to follow the madman's directions, Spider-Man arrived at the baseball field (**5**) only to once again be drugged by the villain. And when he awoke this time, Spider-Man was shocked to discover that he wasn't alone. Lying on the ground next to him was his clone, an exact double of Peter Parker, even down to the Spider-Man costume he wore.

The Jackal told the web-crawlers that only the real Peter Parker would be able to release his captive, Ned Leeds. With a ticking time bomb waiting to explode above the head of Ned, Spider-Man and his clone battled (**6**). But they realized the folly of their actions and turned their attention to the Jackal and rescuing Ned. Meanwhile, the hypnotic spell that the Jackal had cast over Gwen Stacy's clone wore off. Calling him a murderer, Gwen caused the Jackal to realize the insanity of his plan (**7**). He released Ned into the arms of Spider-Man and his clone (**8**). But the bomb was still set to explode. While Ned Leeds and Spider-Man survived the ensuing explosion, the Jackal died instantly. Caught beneath the devastation, it seemed that Spider-Man's clone had died too (**9**).

After the smoke cleared, the Gwen Stacy clone took off to explore the world, and an exhausted Peter Parker headed home (**10**). With his spider-sense tingling, Peter opened the door. But it was a welcome surprise—Mary Jane Watson was waiting for him.

*"Someday I'm going to learn to wear **ear-plugs** when I'm fighting crime."*

SPIDER-MAN

SPIDER-WOMEN

More than one super-powered woman has taken on the mantle of Spider-Woman over the years. In total, there have been four Spider-Women (although one turned out to be the creation of an evil genius), plus one Spider-Girl.

Jessica has the ability to fire bio-electric "venom blasts" from her fingertips to stun or kill opponents.

JESSICA DREW

While Jessica Drew and Peter Parker became super-powered in different ways, Jessica has become quite a fixture in Spider-Man's world these days. As Avengers teammates, the two see quite a lot of each other, despite Jessica often being annoyed by Spidey's constant need to add wisecracks and colorful commentary to every battle. Jessica gained her spider-powers while in her mother's womb when her mother was caught in a lab accident during one of her scientist father's experiments. At a young age, Jessica was trained to be a field agent of the criminal organization Hydra. But she later turned her back on the corrupt institution and carved out a name for herself as the world's first Spider-Woman, a title she holds as an active crime-fighter to this day.

Just like Spider-Man, Jessica can adhere to most surfaces. She also possesses enhanced speed, strength, and endurance.

JULIA CARPENTER

Although she is now known as the precognitive Madame Web, Julia Carpenter started off her Super Hero career as the second Spider-Woman. Having been injected with a mysterious serum that allowed her to project super-strong psionic webs with her mind, Julia adopted a black and white uniform and set out to do her best to help society. Inspiring many others over the course of her career, Julia's costume even subconsciously influenced Spider-Man to wear a black costume of his own when he first tried on his alien symbiote suit. Julia later changed her name to Arachne before accepting the role as the new Madame Web, and she passed her black and white costume to Spider-Girl, Anya Corazon. Julia has gained many friends and allies throughout her Super Hero career, serving on various Super Hero teams including the Avengers.

ANYA CORAZON

While she never called herself Spider-Woman per se, Anya has recently taken on the role of Spider-Girl, although she was more comfortable with her original hero name, Araña. The benefactor of powers from a mystical spider cult that believed in the totemistic powers of the spider, Anya became an adventurer, making the most of the powers granted to her. Her powers have faded in and out and she lost her father to an imposter incredible Hulk, but while her life has not been without tragedy, Anya tries to keep positive, even finding time to microblog about her adventures.

MATTIE FRANKLIN

During a period when Peter Parker temporarily retired as Spider-Man, Mattie Franklin stepped up to fill his role. Gaining powers during a mystical ritual meeting called the Gathering of Five, Mattie put those abilities to good use while masquerading as the original wall-crawler. When Peter returned to his heroic career, she began going by the name Spider-Woman, until her eventual downfall. Mattie's life soon sunk so low that at one point her blood was sold on the black market as the drug Mutant Growth Hormone.

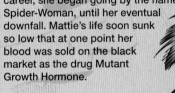

CHARLOTTE WITTER

Not all the women to adopt the name of Spider-Woman have been out to protect the world. Charlotte Witter was a tortured soul, programmed to destroy the spider-powered heroes of the world by Doctor Octopus. Witter had been a fashion designer until Octopus saw something in her and decided to kidnap her. Doc Ock used torture, starvation, and genetic experimentation to brainwash Witter into becoming his willing slave. Converted to Octopus's cause and armed with four spider-like legs, this corrupt Spider-Woman set out to prey on others with her same name. She eventually drew Spider-Man's attention after she brutally attacked fledgling heroine Mattie Franklin.

Mattie's short life came to a close when she was kidnapped by the Kraven family during their "Grim Hunt." She was stabbed in a ritualistic ceremony to raise Kraven's son, the Grim Hunter, from his grave.

Comics were growing darker, and even the lighthearted nature of Spider-Man wasn't immune to the trend. In a decade dominated by gritty violence and noir threats, Peter Parker managed to stay above it all, even if his costume did not.

THE
1980s

By the 1980s, Spider-Man's costume was iconic. The friendly wall-crawler had reached a level of comic book super-stardom usually only reserved for characters with a good 20 years of history on him. But through his hit comic, various TV spotlights, and merchandising, Spider-Man's intricate red and blue threads were known not only nationwide, but worldwide. So, Marvel decided to throw everyone for a loop and change Spidey's clothes.

In Marvel's first giant crossover blockbuster called *Marvel Super Heroes Secret Wars*, Spider-Man journeyed to a faraway planet called Battleworld, and discovered a black alien costume. He brought the suit back with him, and just like that, there was a new Spider-Man on the block.

While the alien didn't stay a permanent part of Spider-Man's wardrobe, the black look certainly did. In an era populated by comics inspired by Frank Miller's seminal gritty classic Batman: *The Dark Knight Returns* and Alan Moore's dark masterpiece *Watchmen*, it seemed only appropriate that Spider-Man should dress for the new level of disturbing threats he would face in the coming years.

OVERLEAF *Web of Spider-Man* #2 (May 1985): Spidey's original black costume was a living alien symbiote bent on bonding with him permanently. He eventually discarded it, but he liked the black look so he later wore an identical cloth costume into battle.

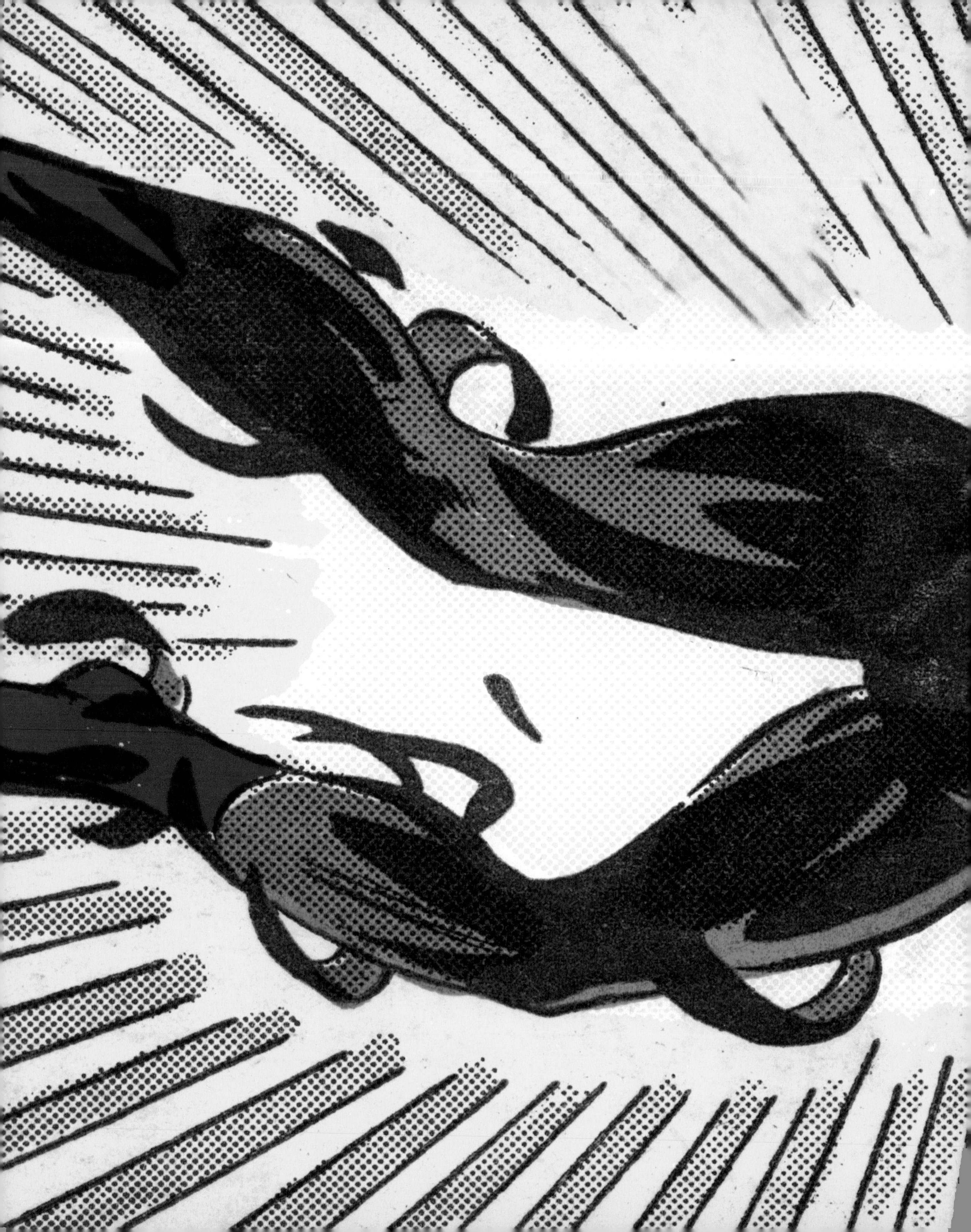

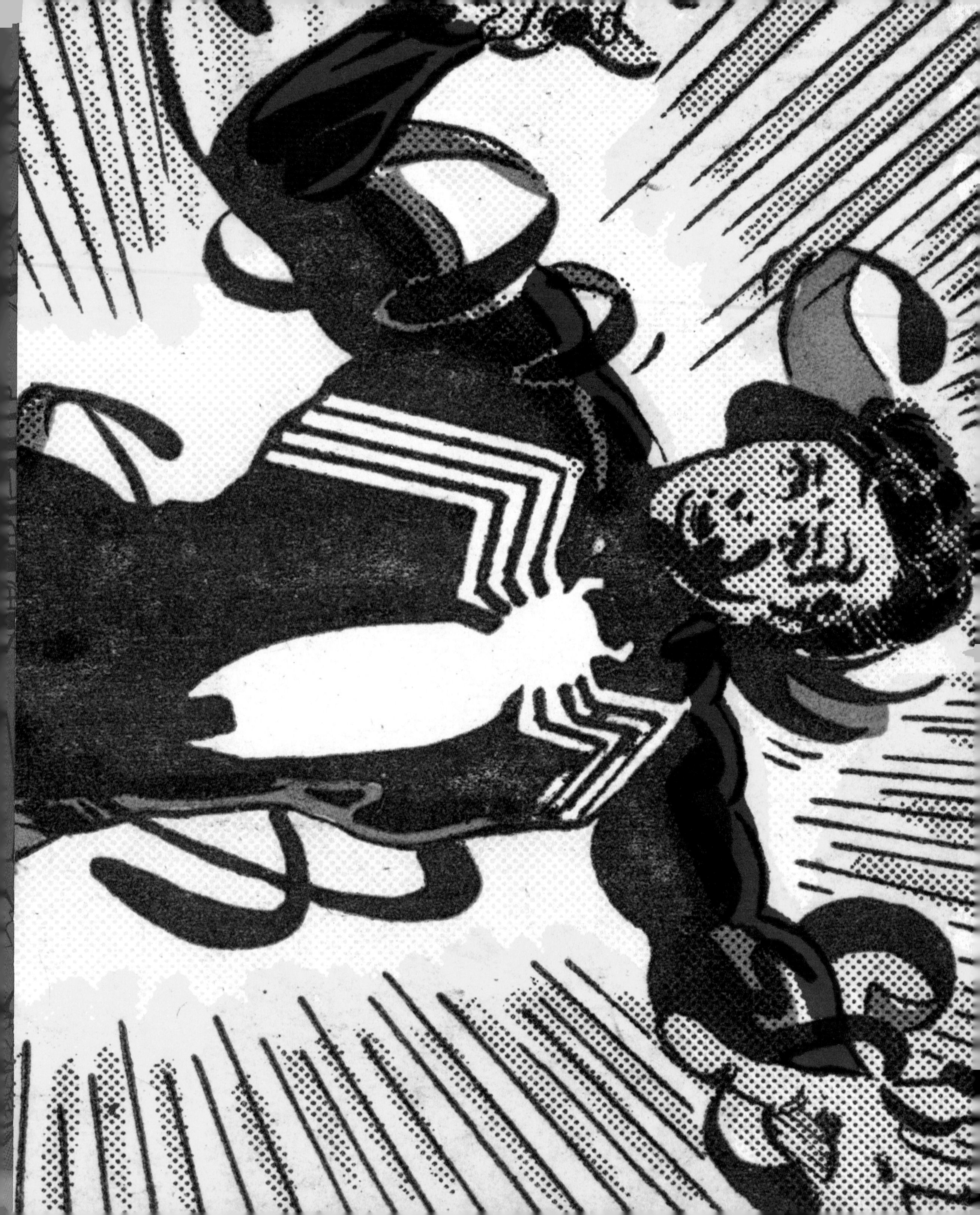

NOTHING CAN STOP THE JUGGERNAUT

When Cain Marko chanced upon a mystical ruby, he was transformed into a human Juggernaut. And when Cain came to New York City, Spider-Man discovered just how accurate the villain's moniker actually was.

MISSION: MADAME WEB

International terrorist Black Tom Cassidy learned of the existence of a psychic called Madame Web, and thought that he could use her power to help defeat the X-Men. So he sent his ally Juggernaut to kidnap the woman. Thanks to her psychic powers, Madame Web knew that the Juggernaut was coming and called Spider-Man for help. Spider-Man quickly learned that his usual tricks were useless against the Juggernaut, but at the same time, he knew he couldn't just abandon the helpless psychic.

A LOSING BATTLE

Despite his best efforts, Spidey couldn't even slow the Juggernaut. The villain captured Madame Web, but when he realized that she would die without her life-support system, he discarded her limp body, annoyed he'd gone all that way for nothing. Spidey refused to give up the fight, and the battle moved to a construction site. There he managed to trick the Juggernaut into falling into a recently poured building foundation. The Juggernaut's massive bulk dragged him to the bottom of the concrete, but thanks to the mystical properties of the ruby that gave him his powers, he did not suffocate. Spidey knew it was only a matter of time until the Juggernaut would be free again.

A FORCE OF NATURE

The Juggernaut possesses enough strength to lift over 100 tons (90 tonnes), and he can also surround himself with an impenetrable force field that protects him from all harm. When Spider-Man attacks him directly, it's little more than an annoying distraction to the villain.

A few years and several bouts after Spider-Man had lured the Juggernaut into the concrete, Spidey was in for a shock when he discovered the limp body of the Juggernaut crashing down into Central Park. It seemed something could stop the Juggernaut after all, and the wall-crawler was in no hurry to face what did.

> ## "YOU TOOK ON THE JUGGERNAUT—AND YOU GOT AN APOLOGY FROM HIM! THAT'S LIKE WINNING THE LOTTERY."
> SPIDER-MAN

CAPTAIN UNIVERSE

William Nguyen was granted the cosmic powers of Captain Universe after trying to kill himself. Blaming Juggernaut for damaging a building and costing him his job, William's first order of business was to seek out and destroy the man he felt caused his life's downward spiral. But there was more at stake than revenge. The bedrock under New York had been disturbed during Juggernaut's escape from the concrete years earlier. Nguyen's sights were set firmly on killing Juggernaut, rather than fixing the tectonic plates. Spider-Man and William stood back in amazement as the power of Captain Universe temporarily transferred to Juggernaut so the powerful villain could set right his past mistake and fix the damage to New York.

CLINGING TO LIFE

After the Juggernaut crashed down in Central Park, he was safely locked away in police custody, Spider-Man broke in to interrogate him. There he met the powerhouse behind Juggernaut's defeat, William Nguyen, the latest incarnation of Captain Universe. Universe wanted nothing less than to kill Juggernaut, but Spider-Man wasn't about to let him commit cold-blooded murder.

115

January 1984 ▶

THE AMAZING SPIDER-MAN #248

"Spider-Man wants to meet *me*?! Now I *know* I'm dreaming!"

Timothy Harrison

EDITOR-IN-CHIEF
Jim Shooter

COVER ARTIST
John Romita Jr. and Terry Austin

WRITER
Roger Stern

PENCILER
Ron Frenz

INKER
Terry Austin

LETTERER
Joe Rosen

COLORIST
Christie Scheele

MAIN CHARACTERS: Spider-Man; Timothy Harrison
MAIN SUPPORTING CHARACTERS: Jacob Conover; The Burglar; Aunt May Parker; Uncle Ben Parker
MAIN LOCATIONS: Slocum-Brewer Cancer Clinic; an unnamed TV studio, New York; the Parker residence; Acme warehouse, Queens, New York

BACKGROUND

By all appearances, *The Amazing Spider-Man* #248 looked like much of the other standard Super Hero fare of the time period. The cover boasted an action-packed image of a hero fighting a villain, and seemed to promise a fairly commonplace battle between good and evil. The first story of the issue delivered just what was expected as Spider-Man battled it out with Thunderball, a member of the villainous Wrecking Crew. But it was the issue's backup story that would elevate this comic book into something more memorable than the rest of the month's offerings. In fact, "The Kid Who Collects Spider-Man" would go on to be one of the most memorable and most loved stories of all time.

Influenced by the style of cartoonist and writer Will Eisner's comic book *The Spirit*, writer Roger Stern crafted a human-interest Spider-Man story in which neither Peter Parker nor his web-headed alter ego would be the focus of the tale. Instead, Stern used Spider-Man merely as a supporting character, yet still managed to throw in a shocking climax and a twist ending that fans still discuss to this day. This special story is regarded by many fans as one of the greatest Spider-Man yarns ever told.

> "It's our secret! Forever and ever... I promise."
>
> **Timothy Harrison**

THE STORY

Spider-Man visits his number one fan, Timothy Harrison, and makes the compassionate decision to reveal his secret identity to the young boy.

Timothy Harrison was different from most boys his age. While he enjoyed the majority of the normal pastimes of his fellow nine-year-olds, Tim had one particular interest that set him apart. Tim collected anything and everything to do with Spider-Man. So when he shut off the light in his room and prepared for an uneventful night of sleep, he was more excited than most would be when a certain wall-crawler decided to pay him a visit (**1**).

Spider-Man had first heard about Timothy from an article in the *Daily Bugle* by columnist Jacob Conover. Timothy had scrapbooks overflowing with newspaper and magazine articles about his idol, and even video footage from Spider-Man's early TV appearances. The newspaper profile on Timothy inspired Spidey to take a rare respite from crime fighting and meet his number one fan face to face. But what Spider-Man hadn't taken into consideration was that Timothy was a New Yorker, and prone to being a bit skeptical. When Spidey lifted the boy and his bed above his head with hardly an effort, Tim soon realized that he was actually in the presence of his favorite hero.

Ecstatic about meeting his idol, Tim showed off his scrapbook collection to his visitor (**2**). They flipped through newspaper articles dating back to the beginning of Spider-Man's career, and discussed exactly how Spider-Man got his powers. Spidey even gave his biggest fan a tutorial on how his web-shooters worked (**3**).

But Tim was a curious boy and wasn't about to pass up this once-in-a-lifetime opportunity. He asked Spider-Man exactly why he gave up his life of fame and fortune and began fighting crime in the first place. And surprisingly, Spider-Man was honest with the young man. He told him about the Burglar he'd failed to stop, and about how that man went on to murder someone who was very close to him. Somehow Timothy understood, and couldn't begrudge his hero for the mistakes of his past (**4**).

The conversation grew lighter then, as the two continued their trip down memory lane. Tim showed Spider-Man bullets he had dug out of a wall of a bank on one occasion after some attempted robbers fired at Spidey and missed. The two even shared a good laugh at a scrapbook Tim kept of retractions that J. Jonah Jameson had been forced to print in the *Daily Bugle* after he had been proven wrong on his assumptions about the wall-crawler (**5**).

Soon Spider-Man realized how late it was getting, so he tucked the boy in, and walked away toward the window to make his exit (**6**). But just as Spider-Man was about to leave, Tim called out one last favor of the hero. He asked Spider-Man if he would take off his mask and show him his true face. And to his surprise, Spider-Man did just that (**7**).

Spider-Man told the boy that his name was Peter Parker, that he was a photographer for the *Daily Bugle*, and that he had shot most of the photos in the articles they had just flipped through. Amazed by the trust his hero placed in him, young Tim swore himself to secrecy, and gave Spider-Man—Peter Parker—a hug before he left (**8**). Spider-Man cast a few weblines, and then departed out of the boy's window (**9**). A second later, Spider-Man paused on a nearby wall and took a moment to collect himself (**10**). And then he swung into the night away from the Slocum-Brewer Cancer Clinic (**11**).

Because Tim Harrison was different from most boys his age. Tim Harrison had been diagnosed with leukemia, and only had a few more weeks to live.

OUT WITH THE OLD

One minute, Spider-Man was on Earth, investigating a strange event in Central Park. The next, he was summoned to a faraway galaxy by a near-omnipotent being called the Beyonder. The Beyonder forced Spidey and a host of other heroes and villains into combat on a planet called Battleworld, and in the course of the many fights, Spider-Man's costume was left in tatters.

The alien costume spread over Peter Parker's form, reacting to his thoughts.

Spider-Man found a machine on Battleworld that seemingly replaced his old uniform with a new black alien version.

THE SAGA OF THE ALIEN COSTUME

When Spider-Man returned from an epic battle of Super Hero versus Super Villain on a far away planet known as Battleworld, he brought with him a souvenir of sorts: a sleek new black costume that would forever change his life.

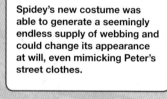

Spidey's new costume was able to generate a seemingly endless supply of webbing and could change its appearance at will, even mimicking Peter's street clothes.

IN WITH THE NEW

After defeating the villains and escaping the Beyonder, the heroes returned to Earth, and Spider-Man took his alien costume with him. Adopting it as his new uniform, Peter and his alien costume were always in some kind of psychic contact, even when physically separated. If the costume was in a different room, it came at Peter's mental summons.

NIGHT TERRORS

Each night while Peter slept, the alien costume secretly slipped over him and took the unconscious Spider-Man wall-crawling at night, craving the adrenaline that Peter's body produced. The web-swinger awoke each morning with no memory of his nocturnal adventures but utterly exhausted. He suspected something was off, but couldn't suspect the amazing truth.

Spider-Man's new costume could fire webbing from the back of his wrists, a fact the Puma discovered firsthand, much to his own regret.

IT'S ALIVE!

Feeling tired and drained, Spider-Man went to Reed Richards, alias Mr. Fantastic of the Fantastic Four, for help. After a series of tests, Mr. Fantastic made a startling pronouncement. Instead of a suit composed of an unknown extraterrestrial fabric, Spidey's new costume was a living creature. It was a sentient symbiote that had formed a mental and physical bond with the web-swinger.

A MIND OF ITS OWN

As soon as the symbiote's secret was revealed, it attempted to permanently graft itself to Spider-Man's body. Spider-Man did all he could to escape from the costume, but the symbiote tightened its grip on him, almost crushing Spidey in the process. Luckily, Reed Richards had discovered that the symbiote was vulnerable to certain sound frequencies. Using these sound waves, Richards managed to separate Spidey from the costume. At last our hero was free and the alien was imprisoned.

THE BELL TOLLS

Later, the symbiote escaped from the laboratory and pounced on the unsuspecting Spider-Man. In utter desperation, Spider-Man lured the alien to the bell tower of Our Lady Of Saints Church. He knew that the sound of the bells could free him from the symbiote. The alien, knowing that only one of them could survive the ordeal, sacrificed itself to save Peter.

THE DEATH OF JEAN DeWOLFF

She was on Spider-Man's side. She was a loyal member of the police force, dedicated to justice and doing the right thing. And like so many other of the good people Spider-Man and Peter Parker have known over the years, Jean DeWolff was cursed to die a violent death.

FAMILY BUSINESS

Jean DeWolff's father was a cop. More importantly, her beloved step-father was a cop. She grew up with the idea of life on the police force as a glamorous one, not originally aware of the job's inherent dangers. But as she rose to the rank of Captain in the NYPD, she would certainly learn those risks firsthand.

Jean shot through the ranks of the police force, receiving many commendations for her efforts and surpassing the position of the step-father she idolized.

THE ORIGINAL SIN

Jean DeWolff was shot in the chest while in her own home. To make matters worse, her body wasn't found until the neighbors noticed the smell from the hallway. It was a grisly murder mystery, and since Jean was a friend of Spider-Man's, one the wall-crawler wasn't going to simply leave for the police to solve.

Jean viewed Spider-Man as a true asset to the police force.

In order to help locate Jean's killer, Spider-Man met regularly with the sergeant in charge of her case, Stan Carter. The two formed a partnership of sorts, both supplying the other with information in order to better find Jean's killer. Carter also gave Spidey a few detective tips along the way. One that stuck with the wall-crawler was to keep an eye on the quiet suspects rather than the obvious "nuts."

ENTER DAREDEVIL

What Spider-Man didn't know was that Jean's murderer was about to become a serial killer. Clad in a ski mask and calling himself the Sin-Eater, the killer reemerged at a Manhattan courthouse. Armed with a shotgun, he killed Judge Horace Rosenthal, attracting the attention of lawyer Matt Murdock, also known as the hero Daredevil. While Daredevil did his best to pursue the murderer, Spider-Man caught up to the Sin-Eater first, facing off with him on a New York City street.

Despite Spidey's efforts, the Sin-Eater managed to escape, shooting a civilian in the process. As the villain continued his killing spree through the city, both Spider-Man and Daredevil began tracking him. Finally, when the Sin-Eater stormed the *Daily Bugle* building looking to murder J. Jonah Jameson, Peter Parker clandestinely knocked the villain out, and the Sin-Eater was arrested.

"DON'T GIVE ME SORRY! TELL IT TO THE JUDGE!... OR BETTER YET—TELL IT TO JEAN DEWOLFF!"

SPIDER-MAN

A QUIET MAN

While questioning Sin-Eater at police headquarters, Daredevil listened to the suspect's heartbeat and realized that he was lying. He and Spidey investigated the would-be criminal's apartment and discovered that the true Sin-Eater lived next door. It was Sgt. Stan Carter, the detective who had helped Spider-Man. As it turned out, Carter was a former S.H.I.E.L.D. agent who had been willingly experimented on with a drug with violent side-effects. In the end, the true Sin-Eater was exactly the kind of suspect that Sgt. Carter himself had described to Spidey.

There was a time when the world marveled at his physical prowess. A period when his courage inspired awe and his exploits drew envy. But that was before he met Spider-Man and knew failure and humiliation. It was time for Kraven the Hunter to regain his glory for one last hunt.

KRAVEN'S LAST HUNT

BURIED ALIVE

Kraven was still faster than a panther and stronger than a great ape, but he knew that he was no longer in his prime. He believed that he would never know peace unless he humbled Spider-Man. Formulating a daring plan, a deranged Kraven immersed himself in Spider-Man's essence by burying his body within a veritable mountain of spiders and by using jungle herbs and potions to expand his consciousness and prepare himself mentally. And then he took the fight straight to the spider.

Spider-Man was out web-swinging one night when he was suddenly attacked, drugged, and captured by Kraven. As the hunter advanced on his prey, Spider-Man was unconcerned. Until, that is, he saw the rifle and the look in Kraven's eyes. Aiming the rifle at Spider-Man, Kraven shot the wall-crawler in the head. After which, the villain took the wall-crawler's body back to his estate, placed him in a coffin, and buried him in the grounds.

Although Kraven had defeated his enemy, he didn't feel satiated. He still felt the need to prove his superiority.

But despite finally besting his longtime foe, Kraven wasn't satisfied. In his mind, he had to *become* his enemy to prove his superiority. So, Kraven dressed in Spider-Man's costume, and began to patrol the city, dispensing his own vicious brand of justice, killing some of the criminals he came across.

Posing as Spider-Man, Kraven even rescued Mary Jane from muggers, but she immediately saw through his disguise.

RESURRECTION

As Kraven claimed victory over Vermin, the real Spider-Man stirred—he had only been drugged by Kraven. Buried deep in the ground, Peter opened his eyes. Desperate to be reunited with Mary Jane, he broke his way free of the coffin and clawed his way to the surface. Two weeks had passed since Kraven had buried him alive.

VERMIN

A malicious face from Spider-Man's past, the incredibly strong and animalistic Vermin stalked the Manhattan streets during Kraven's tenure as Spider-Man. Kraven used his skills to track the monster through the sewers, and captured the villain.

THE CHALLENGE

After clawing his way out of the ground and reuniting with Mary Jane, Spider-Man tracked down Kraven. Filled with fury, the wall-crawler attacked the hunter, who didn't bother to resist. Kraven merely smiled. From his skewed perspective, he had won. He had allowed his old enemy to live when he could have easily killed him. Kraven had finally proven himself superior to his arch foe.

Kraven led Spider-Man to a cage where he was keeping Vermin hostage, and attempted to make the web-slinger battle the beast. When Spider-Man refused Kraven's challenge to fight Vermin, the confused monster attacked him anyway. Kraven immediately acted to save Spider-Man, his point already proven in his deranged mind.

Finally feeling satiated, Kraven released Vermin, who could not wait to be free from Kraven's daily torture.

THE FINAL KILL

Although Spider-Man was defeated by Vermin, Kraven let his foe leave to pursue the dangerous beast. Kraven finally realized that Spidey was indeed a good man, and felt the hero was no longer his concern. Having proved he could defeat Spider-Man and filled with a sense of peace, Kraven put a shotgun to his own head and committed suicide.

"THEY SAID MY MOTHER WAS INSANE."
KRAVEN

THE WEDDING?

It was the wedding of the century. Peter Parker and Mary Jane Watson finally settled down and promised themselves to each other for the rest of their lives. But sadly, their marriage wasn't built to last. In fact, it never actually happened in the first place.

Peter and Mary Jane were the perfect couple, and their union could even bring a tear to the eye of J. Jonah Jameson.

THE BIG DAY

Peter had wanted to marry his longtime girlfriend Mary Jane for some time. After rejecting Peter's first few marriage proposals due to unresolved family problems, Mary Jane finally realized that it was time to stop running away from things.

Peter originally proposed to Mary Jane by giving her a box of Cracker Jacks. The prize inside was a diamond ring.

ONE MOMENT IN TIME

Peter and Mary Jane had been happily married for many years. Like most married couples, they had gone through countless ups and downs together. But a demon named Mephisto changed all that.

Years after the day Peter and MJ said "I do," Aunt May was shot with a sniper's bullet meant for Spider-Man. While the woman who had been like a mother to him was lying on her deathbed, Peter was visited by the demon Mephisto. He promised Peter a return to health for May, but at a high cost. A demon who thrived on unhappiness, Mephisto wanted to not only end Peter and Mary Jane's relationship, but he wanted to ensure that the couple never got married in the first place. Feeling as if there was no other choice, Peter and Mary Jane agreed to the demon's terms, and everything changed.

In this new reality, Peter never made it to the church on time. His life as Spider-Man caused him to be too late for the event, and it forced Mary Jane to reexamine their relationship. She decided that they could never be married, but didn't want to end everything with Peter. So the couple stayed together, and had all the same adventures as they originally had lived, only they were never husband and wife. But this time, May survived the fatal gunshot, and in the wake of that tragedy, Mary Jane broke up with Peter, worried that her family would be put in danger again because of her relationship with Spider-Man.

Years later, Peter and Mary Jane talked about their break-up, becoming stronger friends once everything was out in the open.

Mary Jane and Peter had been the loves of each other's lives. They understood each other's weaknesses, and relied on each other's strengths.

She accepted Peter's proposal in the less-than-romantic setting of Pittsburgh airport's departure lounge.

However, as the big day approached, Peter began to have doubts. He remembered his former girlfriend Gwen Stacy, and wondered what direction his life might have taken if she hadn't died. Mary Jane also had qualms, and a number of her old boyfriends tried to dissuade her from marrying Peter.

On their wedding day, neither Peter nor Mary Jane arrived on time. Their friends feared that they both had cold feet, but the couple finally showed up, and were married by Mary Jane's uncle, Judge Spencer Watson. They were pronounced Mr. and Mrs. Parker. But that's not how it really happened...

Eddie Brock was able to release more of the symbiote's truly ferocious nature due partially to the fact that he and the creature communicated directly.

KEY DATA

FIRST APPEARANCE: *Web of Spider-Man* #18 (September 1986)

REAL NAME: Edward "Eddie" Brock

AFFILIATIONS: The Sinister Six

POWERS/ABILITIES: As Venom, Eddie Brock has enhanced strength and speed. He can stick to walls and generate and fire his own organic webbing. He can absorb small arms fire and has enhanced healing abilities. As well as possessing camouflage capabilities, he is able to bypass Spider-Man's spider-sense.

Essentially parasitic in nature, Venom's symbiote has thoughts and a mind of its own, often swaying its user to give in to his darker impulses.

Venom can use the alien symbiote to disguise himself to look like anything he can imagine. He can turn invisible by blending into the background.

LETHAL PROTECTOR

Eddie has always considered himself to be a defender of the weak and helpless. In his warped mind, he has always believed that he is the hero and that Spider-Man is the monster. After many bouts with the wall-crawler, Venom realized Spider-Man protected innocents as well, so he decided to give up his vendetta against the hero. For a time, he even temporarily moved to San Francisco, where he became the city's "lethal protector." He dispensed his own brand of justice to help those he deemed innocent and to punish those he judged guilty. However, with the symbiote's influence, he was back to his old ways in no time.

VENOM

Eddie Brock already hated Spider-Man. But when chance led to him being wrapped in a living alien symbiote that possessed an equally powerful grudge against the wall-crawler, Venom was born, and Peter Parker's world became a much more terrifying place.

Venom always had an advantage when battling Spider-Man, with his vastly superior strength and the symbiote's powers, such as the ability to camouflage itself. Eddie could also stalk Spidey without triggering the wall-crawler's spider-sense.

"You are the spider and I am your venom come back to sting you!"

Venom

Recently, Eddie Brock lost his bond with the alien symbiote, making way for several Venom successors including Flash Thompson.

As with their battle against the serial killer Carnage, Spider-Man and Venom have sometimes been forced to team up against a common foe.

Venom was able to use his symbiote to mimic Spider-Man's web-shooters and shoot organic webs from the tops of his wrists.

At one point Patricia Robertson, the sole survivor of an artic radar station disaster, became the unwilling heir to a synthetic Venom suit, and tried to kill the real Venom.

ORIGIN

Eddie Brock was once a respected reporter who worked for the *New York Globe*, a rival of the *Daily Bugle*. For a while, he was a media star, following his exposé of a man who had confessed to being the serial killer, the Sin-Eater. However, Spider-Man caught the real Sin-Eater—the man Eddie turned in was a compulsive confessor. As a result, Eddie was fired from his job and his wife left him.

With his career and personal life shattered, Eddie blamed Spider-Man for his loss. He wandered from church to church, praying for forgiveness for his hatred of Spider-Man. At Our Lady of Saints Church, Eddie's fierce emotion somehow awakened a dormant alien symbiote. The symbiote had once masqueraded as Spider-Man's costume, and it had remained in the church since its final encounter with Spider-Man. The symbiote flowed over Eddie and they joined to become Venom. Because the symbiote had once been psychically linked to Peter Parker and had learnt his most intimate secrets, Venom was stronger and more dangerous than the wall-crawler. Venom took off into the night with a renewed purpose: to destroy the life of Spider-Man.

Despite Spider-Man actually solving the Sin-Eater case for the police, Brock nevertheless blamed him for his own downfall.

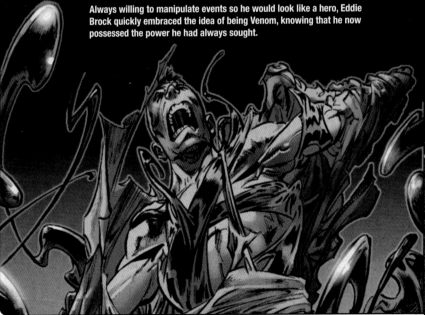

Always willing to manipulate events so he would look like a hero, Eddie Brock quickly embraced the idea of being Venom, knowing that he now possessed the power he had always sought.

VENOM LEGACY

The Venom symbiote has been passed down to many individuals during its existence. As Scorpion, Mac Gargan was one of Spider-Man's most dangerous foes. But when he adopted Eddie Brock's alien symbiote costume and became Venom, he was nearly unstoppable. And when Peter Parker's school bully Flash Thompson was given a chance to emulate Spidey, a new Venom was born.

A DEADLIER VENOM

When Eddie Brock originally donned his living alien costume, he formed a bond with the creature that was so strong, he never imagined he would give up the power and closeness the two shared as Venom. However, after years of wearing the symbiote suit, and discovering that his body was stricken with cancer, Eddie knew his time was almost up. He decided to make amends by parting with the costume. He somehow managed to separate himself from it long enough to sell it at an underground criminal auction.

Soon the suit found its way into the hands of criminal Mac Gargan, and the two beings bonded instantly. Mac abandoned his role as the Scorpion in order to upgrade to a new identity: Venom. Brutal and oftentimes cannibalistic, this new savage Venom eventually found employment with the corrupt Norman Osborn, and even tricked the world into believing he was the true Spider-Man for a time.

The symbiote recruited Mac to be his host, enjoying the criminal's angry mindset.

The high bidder at Brock's Venom auction was Don Fortunato, who gave the suit to his son Angelo. Venom rejected the weak teen in favor of Mac Gargan.

Just when Spidey thought he'd learned how to handle Eddie Brock's Venom, the alien upgraded to an even more ruthless host.

A FORCE FOR GOOD

Flash Thompson always wanted to be a hero. Growing up around Spider-Man, Flash had even tried to impersonate the wall-crawler when the need arose. As the chairman of Spider-Man's fan club, Flash learned from Spidey's heroic example, and strived to be a better person.

He took the lessons Spidey taught him to war as a soldier, and during one fateful trip, lost his legs in a successful effort to save a fellow troop member. Thinking his life of action was over, Flash was amazed when he was recruited by the military for a clandestine project that would not only see him regain his mobility, but also grant him superhuman abilities. Flash was handpicked to be the new Venom, wearing the living alien suit for covert missions. The military was aware that the symbiote would bond with its host given the opportunity. Consequently, Flash was only allowed to wear the suit for 48 hours at a time.

Flash accepted the challenge of being Venom and in doing so, fulfilled his lifelong dream of becoming a costumed hero. Whether Flash's willpower is strong enough to curb Venom's primal bloodlust is yet to be seen, but Flash intends to do his best to see that Venom stays on the side of good this time around.

The military has installed a kill switch that will destroy the user if he loses control of the symbiote.

Flash is reliant on a wheelchair, but, as Venom, he uses a pair of organic legs—as well as Venom's myriad powers.

Venom has taken a toll on Flash's civilian life. It is always on his mind, and he's been forced to lie to his girlfriend Betty Brant, in order to keep his double identity a secret.

COSMIC ADVENTURES

Spider-Man is no slouch when it comes to physical power, but he's never exactly been the strongest hero on the block. That all changed when a lab "accident" exposed Peter Parker to an unknown energy source and he was transformed into the Cosmic Spider-Man.

When saving the life of his colleague, Professor Lubisch, Peter Parker was bathed in unknown energies. While he assumed his spider-strength and endurance would save him, he never suspected the "accident" had been manufactured by a mysterious force.

WITH GREATER POWER...

Loki, the Norse God of Lies, decided it was time for a group of villains to get their act together. While all the heroes went about their daily routine, Loki gathered a core team of Super Villains for a secret attempt to defeat the heroes through various acts of vengeance. Some of the most powerful and notorious men on the planet—including Dr. Doom, the Red Skull, Magneto, Kingpin, Mandarin, and the Wizard—joined forces. The villains sent a selection of costumed criminals to fight the heroes. They hoped that since the heroes had never been attacked by these villains before, it would throw the crime-fighters off their game—and they would be defeated once and for all. But what they didn't realize was that they weren't the only schemers that day.

Across the city, Peter Parker was pursuing his graduate studies at Empire State University when he was caught in the blast of an exploding experimental generator. Almost instantly, Peter realized his powers had been magnified by some unknown force. As the coalition of villains sent their worst after Spider-Man, he bested them with ease. Peter had become Cosmic Spider-Man!

Cosmic Spidey could hear a spider crossing a window pane two blocks away and smell the fragrance of a potted plant in a distant building. With this new power, it seemed no villain could plot against him in secret.

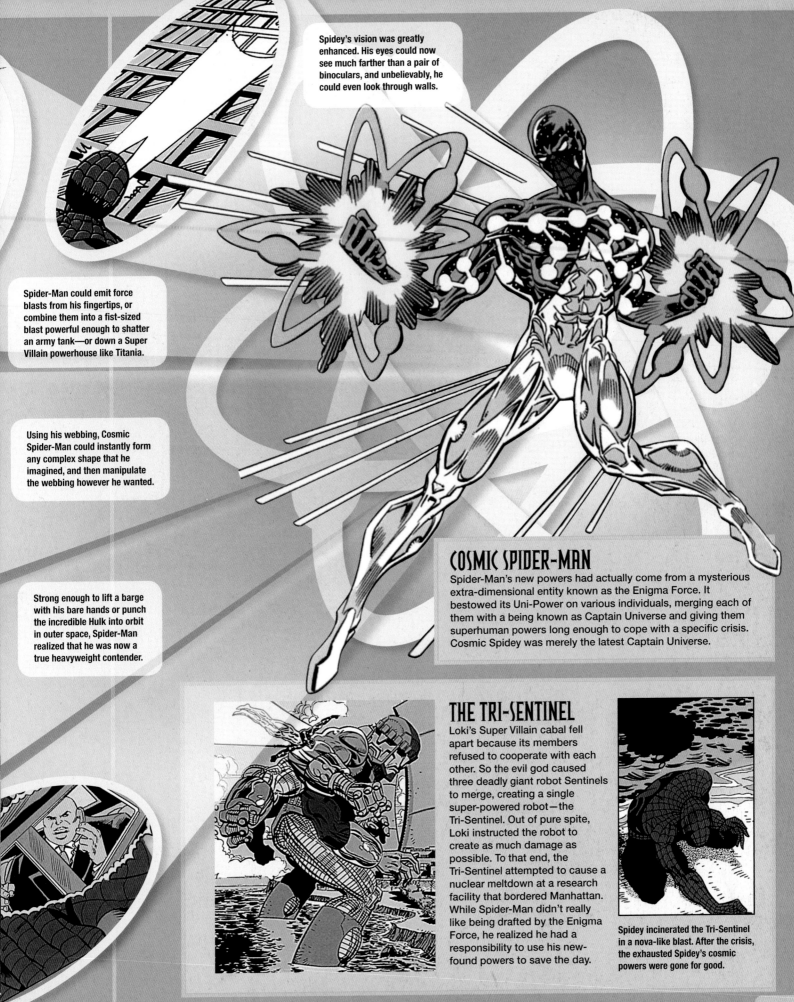

Spidey's vision was greatly enhanced. His eyes could now see much farther than a pair of binoculars, and unbelievably, he could even look through walls.

Spider-Man could emit force blasts from his fingertips, or combine them into a fist-sized blast powerful enough to shatter an army tank—or down a Super Villain powerhouse like Titania.

Using his webbing, Cosmic Spider-Man could instantly form any complex shape that he imagined, and then manipulate the webbing however he wanted.

Strong enough to lift a barge with his bare hands or punch the incredible Hulk into orbit in outer space, Spider-Man realized that he was now a true heavyweight contender.

COSMIC SPIDER-MAN

Spider-Man's new powers had actually come from a mysterious extra-dimensional entity known as the Enigma Force. It bestowed its Uni-Power on various individuals, merging each of them with a being known as Captain Universe and giving them superhuman powers long enough to cope with a specific crisis. Cosmic Spidey was merely the latest Captain Universe.

THE TRI-SENTINEL

Loki's Super Villain cabal fell apart because its members refused to cooperate with each other. So the evil god caused three deadly giant robot Sentinels to merge, creating a single super-powered robot—the Tri-Sentinel. Out of pure spite, Loki instructed the robot to create as much damage as possible. To that end, the Tri-Sentinel attempted to cause a nuclear meltdown at a research facility that bordered Manhattan. While Spider-Man didn't really like being drafted by the Enigma Force, he realized he had a responsibility to use his new-found powers to save the day.

Spidey incinerated the Tri-Sentinel in a nova-like blast. After the crisis, the exhausted Spidey's cosmic powers were gone for good.

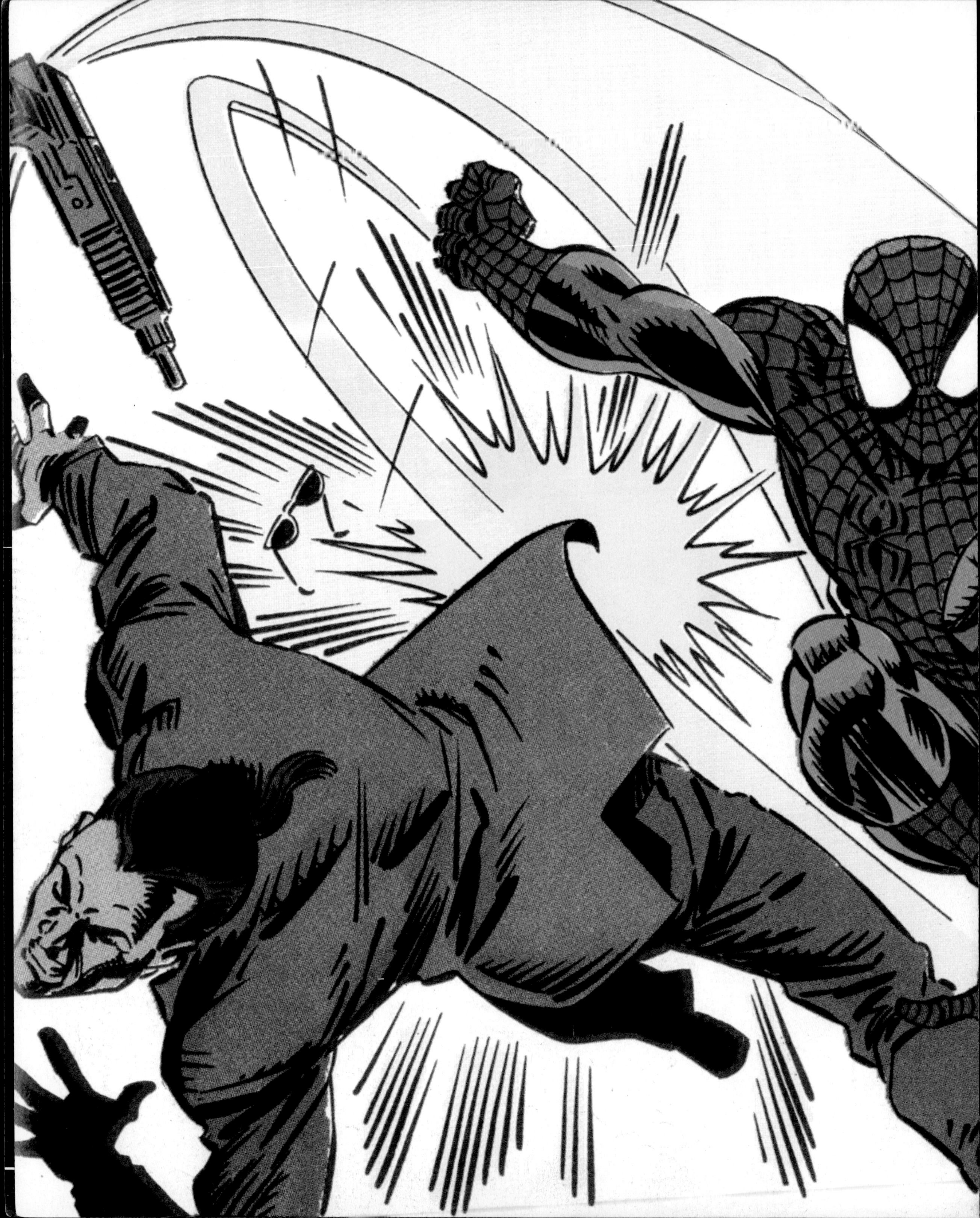

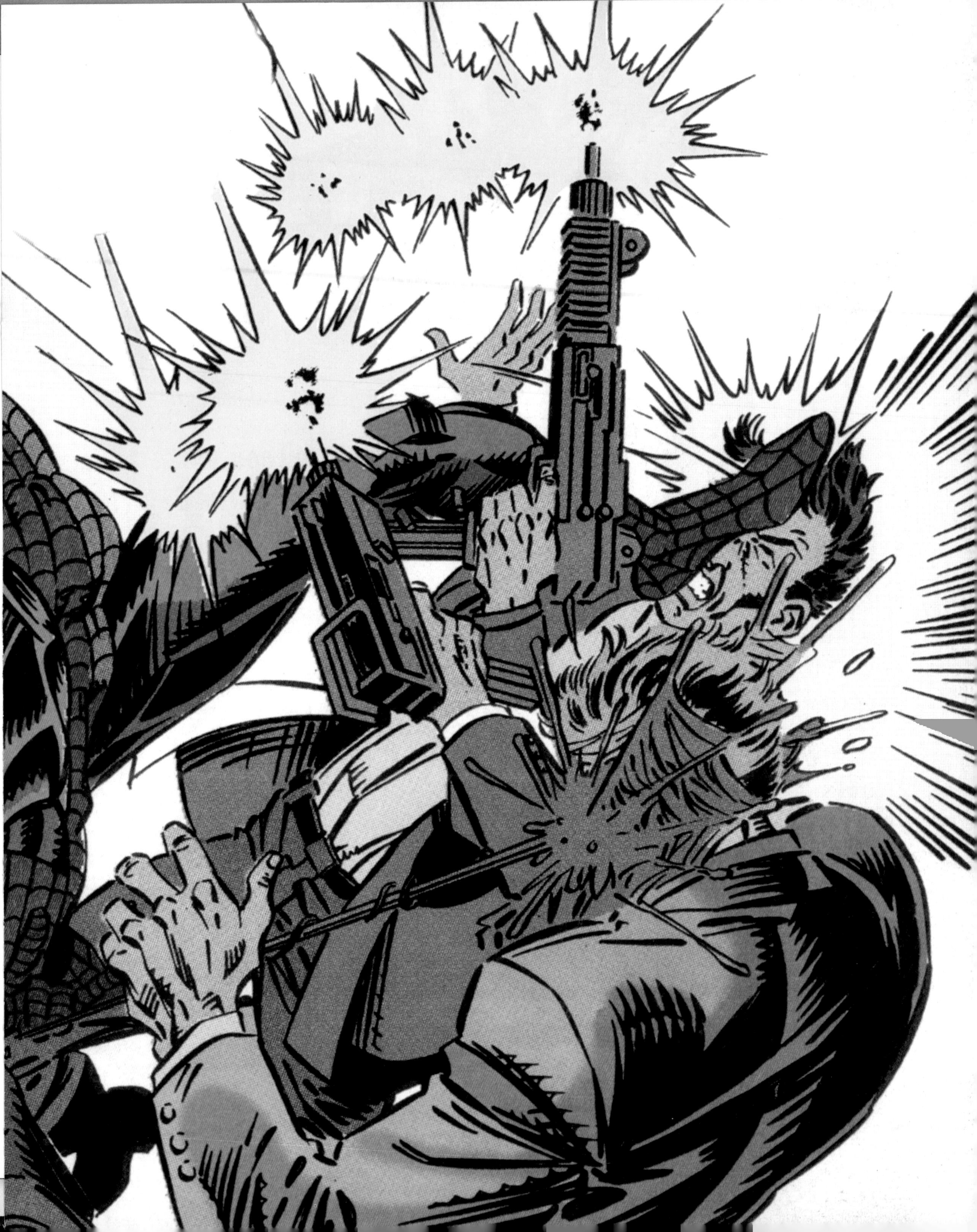

CARNAGE

Deranged and twisted beyond any hope of reformation, Cletus Kasady was probably the worst person to merge with a ferocious alien symbiote. Together, they are the bloodthirsty monster Carnage, one of Spider-Man's most dangerous foes.

ORIGIN

Cletus Kasady was a notorious serial killer even before he became Carnage. His first victim was his father, and he claims to have murdered his mother, too. Cletus was raised as an orphan at the St. Estes Home For Boys in Brooklyn. A small and shy child, Cletus was often terrorized by the older residents. He was transferred to another establishment when a fire burned St. Estes to the ground, killing many of his classmates as well as the home's dean of discipline.

As Cletus grew older, an alarming number of his acquaintances seemed to die under mysterious circumstances. A girl, who laughed at him when he asked her on a date, was pushed in front of a bus, and an alcoholic foster father was found beaten to death in a neighborhood alley.

By the time he reached his early twenties, Cletus Kasady had been convicted of 11 murders, but bragged of dozens more. He was sentenced to life imprisonment at Ravencroft penitentiary, where he found himself sharing a cell with Eddie Brock. Eddie, who had once been the man known as Venom, had recently been separated from his alien symbiote. One night, the symbiote returned to bond with and free Eddie, and Cletus was left in shock at what he had just witnessed. However, a small part of the alien symbiote had been left behind and merged with Kasady. The combination of the alien symbiote and Cletus's dangerous mind formed the psychopathic killer the world would come to know as Carnage.

Cletus Kasady watched in amazement as the alien symbiote merged with and freed his cellmate, Eddie Brock.

When a fraction of an alien symbiote dripped onto Kasady's arm, it merged with his bloodstream and became part of him. While surprised at first, Kasady has since welcomed the creature.

Carnage is stronger than Spider-Man and Venom combined. He can lift over 50 tons, and he never seems to tire due to the constant supply of energy from his symbiote.

When Carnage spawned a symbiote child, he condemned police officer Pat Mulligan to a life bonded with the symbiote. Mulligan adopted the name Toxin and attempted to use his new powers for good.

> ### "You didn't stop me. The tide just went out."
>
> Carnage

Dr. Tanis Nieves became Scorn when she bonded with another of Carnage's symbiote offspring to stop the villain Shriek.

Carnage was seemingly destroyed when the hero known as the Sentry ripped him in two in outer space. But the beast returned and promptly made life difficult for Spider-Man and Iron Man.

As Carnage, Kasady has pointed teeth and dagger-sharp talons, which are actually part of his alien symbiote.

Carnage's hands and feet can adhere to almost any surface.

Because the alien symbiote was once linked to Spider-Man, Carnage can generate and project a web-like substance from any part of his body.

KEY DATA

FIRST APPEARANCE: *The Amazing Spider-Man* #344 (February 1991)

REAL NAME: Cletus Kasady

AFFILIATIONS: None

POWERS/ABILITIES: Carnage has enhanced strength and speed. He can stick to most surfaces, generate and fire his own webbing, and circumvent Spider-Man's spider-sense. He possesses regenerative abilities and is immune to most gunfire. Carnage can also manipulate his form—he can generate "tendrils," elongate his body, and dislodge parts of his body to use as powerful weapons.

TOTAL CARNAGE

Carnage's alien symbiote suit appears to have gained several powers that Venom's doesn't possess, including the ability to turn extensions of the costume into powerful stabbing weapons. Similar to Venom, however, the alien symbiote was once joined with Spider-Man. Thus its presence doesn't set off the wall-crawler's spider-sense, allowing Carnage to sneak up on Spidey. But when the two first met, at a rock concert, Spidey discovered the symbiote's apparent only weakness—sound. The wall-crawler turned the stage's sound system against the criminal, blasting Carnage with a sound frequency that was high enough to knock the alien symbiote unconscious.

May 1993

THE SPECTACULAR SPIDER-MAN #200

*"Let's **face** it... people like you and me... we're better off **dead**."*

THE GREEN GOBLIN (HARRY OSBORN)

EDITOR-IN-CHIEF
Tom DeFalco

COVER ARTIST
Sal Buscema

WRITER
J.M. DeMatteis

PENCILER
Sal Buscema

INKER
Sal Buscema

COLORIST
Bob Sharen

LETTERER
Joe Rosen

MAIN CHARACTERS: Spider-Man; the Green Goblin (Harry Osborn); Mary Jane Watson-Parker; Liz Osborn
MAIN SUPPORTING CHARACTERS: Norman Osborn Jr.; J. Jonah Jameson
MAIN LOCATIONS: Harry Osborn's apartment; The Brooklyn Bridge; Peter Parker's apartment; the *Daily Bugle* office; Tony's Italian Kitchen; The Osborn Foundation building

BACKGROUND

Anniversary issues are a longtime tradition in the comic book world. Fans have grown accustomed to finding the payoffs to big stories in an issue #50 or #100 of their favorite titles.

The Spectacular Spider-Man #200 focused on the climax to Harry Osborn's long-running story. Lapsing in and out of drug-induced bouts of insanity since the death of his father, Norman Osborn (the original Green Goblin), Harry's mental illness took center stage in this issue, in what was intended to be the final chapter in his life. And while the 2008 Brand New Day storyline would bring Harry back from the supposed dead, writer J.M. DeMatteis's powerful tale alongside Sal Buscema's unflinching imagery capitalized on the use of silent comic panels to add to the impact of the story they were concocting. The overall effect was an issue truly worthy of the benchmark #200 that graced its cover.

THE STORY

Harry Osborn finally loses his battle with sanity and relapses into the Green Goblin for one seemingly final face off with Spider-Man.

It all started when Harry Osborn witnessed the death of his father. In what would be a traumatic event for any person to go through, the scene that played out in front of Harry Osborn's eyes was much more bizarre and twisted than anything he should have been forced to witness. Because Harry Osborn's father was Norman Osborn, the original Green Goblin. And the person Harry blamed for his death was his best friend, Peter Parker, the amazing Spider-Man.

Since that day, Harry had been in and out of his mind, his insanity growing stronger and stronger over time. Finally, he seemingly gave in to the Goblin inside him, and did what his father before him had done: kidnapped the love of Spider-Man's life, and brought her to the top of the Brooklyn Bridge.

This time it was Spider-Man's wife, Mary Jane Watson-Parker, who found herself the kidnapped victim of the Goblin (**1**). But instead of hurling the woman off the bridge, as his father had done to Gwen Stacy years before, this Green Goblin removed his mask to reveal that Harry Osborn wasn't as far gone as Mary Jane had believed (**2**). True, he blamed Spider-Man for the atrocities committed by his own father, but he had taken Mary Jane there just to let her know that no matter what happened between the Goblin and Spider-Man, he would make sure that she was safe.

Norman then returned Mary Jane to her SoHo loft, a gesture that Spider-Man wasn't pleased with. When the hero returned home after searching the city for any sign of MJ and discovered the Green Goblin there waiting for him, his first reaction was to lash out in anger at Harry (**3**). Mary Jane stopped her husband from his misguided attempt at protecting her, letting Peter know that Harry wasn't there for a fight. After pulling Spider-Man's mask off to look his old friend directly in the eye (**4**), Harry again reassured Mary Jane that she had nothing to fear from him, although he didn't say the same for Peter. Without another word, the Green Goblin flew off into the night, and returned to his own apartment and to Harry Osborn's seemingly normal life with his wife, Liz, and their son, Normie. But even as Harry prepared to open the charitable Osborn Foundation, he plotted the death of Peter Parker (**5**).

Days later, the Green Goblin would finally have the confrontation he was hoping for. Meeting Spider-Man on the rooftop of his Foundation, the two fought it out (**6**), until the Goblin drugged the wall-crawler and then activated a remote timer that would cause the building to explode in the next two minutes (**7**). Not only would Spider-Man die, but the Green Goblin would die with him. But then the unexpected happened, and Harry Osborn's personality once more emerged inside of the Green Goblin. He realized that Mary Jane and his son, Norman Jr., were still in the building that was rigged to blow. So he jumped onto his glider and took Mary Jane and Normie in his arms, flying them to safety (**8**). But the sedated Spider-Man was still on the rooftop (**9**). Until, once again, the Green Goblin surprised everyone by racing back into the building and saving his best friend (**10**). As the Foundation building exploded into a mess of smoke and fire (**11**), the Green Goblin had indeed saved the life of Spider-Man.

Outside on the street, Harry Osborn collapsed. The experimental Goblin formula he had injected himself with was too much for the young man. So like his father before him, Harry seemingly died (**12**), clad in his Green Goblin uniform and with his son present to bare witness. And just like that, Harry became yet another lost life that would weigh on the already burdened conscience of Spider-Man (**13**).

> "I did it, Peter. Just the way... you would've done it. A real hero."
>
> **HARRY OSBORN**

WHOOOM!

"TOO LATE, CARNAGE!"
SPIDER-MAN

> ## "HAPPY HOUR IS OVER!"
> VENOM

MAXIMUM CARNAGE

Spider-Man's world had just gotten a little darker. With the recent apparent death of his former best friend Harry Osborn, Peter thought the worst was behind him. But upstate at the Ravencroft Maximum Security Institution, the serial killer Cletus Kasady was about to prove the wall-crawler dead wrong. Changing into his Carnage alter ego, Kasady escaped the institution for the criminally insane, but not before freeing his fellow inmate—the emotion-altering Shriek. Soon joined by the monstrous, other-worldly Spider-Man Doppelganger, the trio set out at first to hunt down Spider-Man and Venom, and then simply to instigate chaos throughout the city of Manhattan. As his campaign of terror continued, Carnage recruited other powerful allies to his cause of murder and mayhem, including Demogoblin and Carrion. Meanwhile, Spider-Man found himself aided by Black Cat, Cloak, Dagger, Firestar, and even unlikely partners like Morbius and Venom. As the body count of innocent bystanders increased, other heroes like Deathlok, Iron Fist, Captain America, and Nightwatch joined the fray, until a battling Carnage and Venom were caught in a climactic explosion that rendered Carnage unconscious.

Carnage's murder spree caught Spidey off guard because his acts of violence were often random and unpredictable.

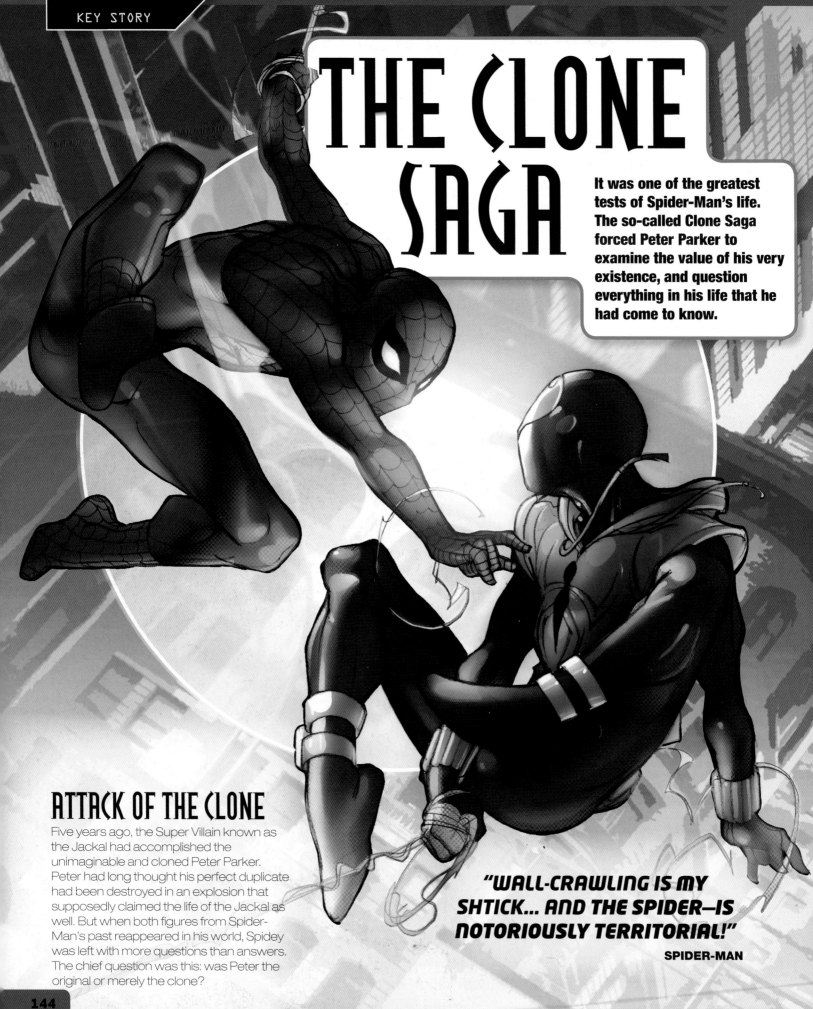

THE CLONE SAGA

It was one of the greatest tests of Spider-Man's life. The so-called Clone Saga forced Peter Parker to examine the value of his very existence, and question everything in his life that he had come to know.

ATTACK OF THE CLONE

Five years ago, the Super Villain known as the Jackal had accomplished the unimaginable and cloned Peter Parker. Peter had long thought his perfect duplicate had been destroyed in an explosion that supposedly claimed the life of the Jackal as well. But when both figures from Spider-Man's past reappeared in his world, Spidey was left with more questions than answers. The chief question was this: was Peter the original or merely the clone?

"WALL-CRAWLING IS MY SHTICK... AND THE SPIDER—IS NOTORIOUSLY TERRITORIAL!"

SPIDER-MAN

CARBON COPY

When Peter's Aunt May fell into a coma and her life seemed to be close to its end, Peter's clone returned to New York City to visit her where he encountered the real Spider-Man. Possessing all the original memories and feelings of Peter Parker, the clone felt a strong bond with May and couldn't live with himself if he never spoke to her again.

Now going by the name Ben Reilly, the clone shared Peter's sense of responsibility. So while he knew Peter possessed the right to call himself Spider-Man, Ben decided to adopt a similar costumed appearance and became the hero dubbed the Scarlet Spider by the press.

DYNAMIC DUO

While it took Peter some time to get used to Ben's presence in his life, the two soon became quite the team, and grew to think of each other as a brother. This bond proved very helpful when the Jackal reemerged in their lives and began to play with their minds.

GAMES OF THE JACKAL

Professor Warren aka the Jackal was sure that he could repopulate the world with clones, and had created dozens of Peter Parker doppelgängers to achieve his goal. While Ben and Peter managed to defeat the villain, it wasn't long before the Jackal managed to convince them that Peter was the clone and Ben was the original Spider-Man.

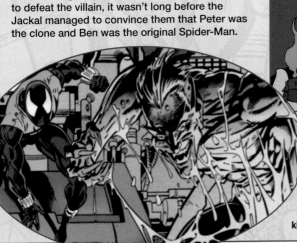

After hearing this revelation, Peter retired and Ben adopted the role of Spider-Man. Shockingly, Norman Osborn was revealed to be the mastermind behind the Clone Saga. Peter was revealed to be the true Spidey when Ben was killed and dissolved to ash.

KAINE

To the world at large, he is a cold-blooded killer, a remorseless assassin-for-hire who leaves his distinctive brand on the faces of his victims. But few know the truth about Kaine. He is actually a clone of Peter Parker, the first of Professor Warren's recreations to reach maturity. However, since Professor Warren was still perfecting his cloning technique, Kaine soon developed a condition called clone degeneration, the symptoms of which have left him horribly scarred.

Kaine believed that Ben Reilly was the original Parker and stalked him across America. He hated Ben, and did all he could to spoil the quality of his life. Kaine thought Peter was a clone like himself, and wanted to protect the life Peter had carved out for himself. With an ever-shifting moral code, Kaine still lurks in the shadows of Spidey's life, walking the line between hero and villain.

SCARLET SPIDER

He was Spider-Man's clone, and after five years away from New York City, Ben Reilly had come to terms with who and what he was. He had created a new identity for himself as Ben Reilly, and a second one to continue his mission: the Scarlet Spider.

During a memorable battle with Carnage, the alien symbiote attempted to bond with Reilly, temporarily becoming Spider-Carnage.

> "I'm no hero. This is just something I have to do."
> The Scarlet Spider

ORIGIN

When Peter Parker and his clone first met, they were both dressed as Spider-Man. Professor Warren as the Super Villain known as the Jackal had cloned Peter, and tricked his new creation into thinking that he was the one true Spider-Man. After he was seemingly killed in an explosion during their battle, Peter assumed that his clone was gone for good.

In an attempt to distance himself from Peter Parker, Ben later dyed his hair blond.

But the Spider-Clone hadn't been killed in the explosion that had seemingly taken the life of the Jackal. Instead, the clone had regained consciousness in the smokestack where Peter had left him, and he went off to make a new life for himself. Armed with Peter's memories and spider-like powers, he took the name Ben Reilly; Ben, after the uncle who had taught Peter so much about responsibility, and Reilly because it was Aunt May's maiden name. For five years, he wandered the country, using his powers to help people whenever needed. But when he returned to New York City to visit a sickly May Parker, Ben realized that he could no longer deny the responsibility that came with his powers, and he donned the costume of the Scarlet Spider.

When Peter and Ben first fought, each thought he was the original, raising the question of whether the true clone had actually died that day.

Ben made his costume partially out of a spider hoody he saw in a museum gift shop, altering it to make it sleeveless.

Ben Reilly's greatest enemy was Kaine. An imperfect Spider-Man clone with a grudge against anyone who could potentially ruin Peter Parker's life, Kaine had obsessively stalked Ben Reilly for several years.

Ben met his untimely demise when he intercepted the Green Goblin's glider before it impaled Spider-Man. As he died, Reilly crumbled to dust, proving without a doubt that he had been Peter's clone.

On one of his first outings as the Scarlet Spider, Ben managed to capture Venom and turn him over to the authorities, succeeding where Spider-Man had so often failed.

Recently, Kaine has adopted the identity of the Scarlet Spider, claiming the mantle of his longtime foe.

THE SECOND SPIDER-MAN

After his return to New York, Ben had been manipulated time and time again by the Jackal into questioning whether he was the clone or the original Spider-Man. Finally, he and Peter conducted their own tests, and the results seemingly pointed towards Ben being the original. Peter soon realized that everything had worked out for the best. He voluntarily gave up his life as a costumed crime fighter. Meanwhile, Ben took on the role of Spider-Man for a time, only to later die in the line of fire.

Ben developed stingers—darts that fired from his web-shooters, as well as minidot tracers, which were smaller and faster than Spider-Man's spider-tracers.

The Scarlet Spider often used impact webbing that splattered into a large clump on contact, encasing his opponent.

Peter and Ben had developed very different personalities during the five years they had been separated.

KEY DATA

FIRST APPEARANCE: *The Amazing Spider-Man* #149 (October 1975)

REAL NAME: Benjamin Reilly

AFFILIATIONS: The New Warriors

POWERS/ABILITIES: Ben was a near perfect clone of Peter Parker and therefore possessed all of Spider-Man's abilities and powers. He could stick to walls and sense danger with a "spider-sense," as well as recover quickly from his injuries. He possessed enhanced strength, reflexes, agility, endurance, and speed, as well as the majority of Peter's memories. Ben redesigned Peter's web-shooters and added new weapons to his arsenal.

April 1995

THE AMAZING SPIDER-MAN #400

*"No doctors. No hospitals... This time is for **us**—to say our **good-byes**."*

AUNT MAY PARKER

EDITOR-IN-CHIEF
Bob Budiansky

COVER ARTISTS
Mark Bagley and Larry Mahlstedt

WRITER
J.M. DeMatteis

PENCILER
Mark Bagley

INKER
Larry Mahlstedt with Randy Emberlin

COLORIST
Bob Sharen

LETTERER
Bill Oakley and NJQ

MAIN CHARACTERS: Spider-Man; Aunt May Parker; the Scarlet Spider; Mary Jane Watson-Parker
MAIN SUPPORTING CHARACTERS: Dr. Julia Caputo; Anna Watson; J. Jonah Jameson; Marla Jameson; Liz Osborn; Norman Osborn Jr.; Flash Thompson; Black Cat; Joe Robertson; Detective Connor Trevane; Lieutenant Jacob Raven
MAIN LOCATIONS: A hospital, New York; Ravencroft Institute; the Parker residence; the Empire State Building; undisclosed cemetery, New York

BACKGROUND

Easily the most controversial storyline ever to shake up the so-called "Spiderverse," the Clone Saga, which was launched in *Web of Spider-Man* #117 (October 1994), had already turned the life of Peter Parker on its ear. It started as just another idea thrown out by writer Terry Kavanagh at a brainstorming summit about bringing back Spider-Man's clone. But when faced with the story potential that could spring out of that simple concept, the idea blossomed into an ambitious comic book event that strived to be something more than the means to nab increased sales.

The folks in the Spider-Man offices wanted a story with weight and long-lasting consequence. And while her death might not have lasted as long as originally intended, May Parker's final moments in *The Amazing Spider-Man* #400 were meant to be just the kind of weighty story the team set out to tell. Even though it is often hard for good characters to stay dead in the world of comic books, Aunt May's death can still be read as the end of an era it originally signified.

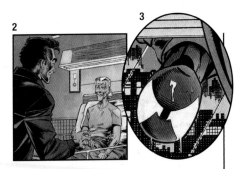

> "Let go. Fly.
> 'Second to
> the right—and
> straight on till
> morning.'"
>
> **PETER PARKER**

THE STORY

In "The Gift" story, Peter Parker spends his last treasured moments with Aunt May before she seemingly dies, while his clone watches on, unable to say goodbye.

It must have felt like a dream for Spider-Man. His Aunt May had been in a coma for days, and the doctors feared she might never wake up. So when Peter got a call from the hospital, he naturally assumed the worst (**1**). Swinging across town at a breakneck speed, the wall-crawler switched into his civilian identity with a heavy heart and entered the room of the woman who had been like a mother to him. A woman he wasn't ready to say goodbye to.

And luckily for Peter, he wouldn't have to. Because the woman who waited behind the door was as full of life as she'd ever been (**2**). She'd awoken from her coma, and would soon be ready to head home and resume her life. While Peter cried happy tears, he saw something else out of the corner of his eye. Ben Reilly, the Scarlet Spider, was watching the scene from outside (**3**). Although Spider-Man's clone might have been an outcast from the life he'd once thought was his, he couldn't help the fact that he loved Aunt May as if she was his aunt.

May returned to her familiar Forest Hills home to the delightful news that Peter and Mary Jane were expecting a baby (**4**). But just as Peter should have been enjoying this happy family time, the Scarlet Spider appeared from the shadows, intent on having a word with him. As the two talked, the Scarlet Spider revealed his plan. Now that he knew May was going to be OK, the Spider was going to leave the lives of the Parkers forever (**5**).

For a while, life at the Parker residence returned to normal. There was a lot of happy reminiscing about the past, and Aunt May and Peter even took a trip to the top of the Empire State Building to spend a little alone time together. It was there that May revealed to Peter that she'd known about his secret for years (**6**). She'd known he was Spider-Man and although his other life frightened her, she was proud of him just the same. The revelation was a weight off Peter's shoulders, even though it seemed to exhaust the elderly May. The two decided to head home, a new understanding now existing between them in the space where an unmentionable secret used to live.

What Peter didn't know at the time was that May had done what she set out to do. Now her fever had returned, but she wasn't fighting any longer (**7**). It was her time, and she knew it. Even though Peter still wasn't ready, May was. So he held her hand, and talked to her softly about a book she'd read to him as a child. May fell asleep and Peter and Mary Jane mourned her passing (**8**).

Outside May's window, another man was feeling her loss. A man who had sworn to leave the Parkers alone. A man dressed in a red and blue spider costume who was affected by Aunt May's death just as deeply as any of those lucky enough to be standing by her side (**9**).

It was cold on the day they buried May Parker. Peter and Mary Jane stood among a crowd of some of their closest friends and tried to keep their emotions in check (**10**). May's casket was lowered into the ground, and soon enough, the crowd dispersed and people went back to their daily lives. Peter and MJ were the last to leave. No words were spoken. Only an unsaid understanding passed between the two before they too left the cemetery.

And then another silent mourner arrived. Ben Reilly wasn't able to say goodbye to his "aunt," but still needed to pay his respects to the woman who had so influenced his life. Placing a single rose on the fresh earth before her tombstone, Reilly let himself cry, mourning not just May, but the life that he had never truly known (**11**).

IDENTITY CRISIS

"...THIS NEW IDENTITY IS GIVING US A CLEAN START, GIVING US OUR LIVES BACK!"

"...THIS NEW IDENTITY IS GIVING US A CLEAN START, GIVING US OUR LIVES BACK!"

SPIDER-MAN AS THE HORNET

After his resurrection, Norman Osborn proved that he wasn't the Green Goblin and cleared his own name. He also succeeded in framing Spidey, placing a $5 million reward on the hero's head. With every bounty hunter gunning for him, Peter Parker needed a new secret identity...

MULTIPLE PERSONALITY

Peter knew that other costumed heroes had temporarily adopted new identities in the past, but he also knew that they were always exposed. He wanted to beat the odds and decided to adopt more than one new alter ego. Realizing that it would be difficult to juggle different personas at the same time, he decided that each one would reflect some aspect of his real personality or powers.

RICOCHET

While searching through the used clothing section at a local thrift shop, Mary Jane discovered a leather jacket with a distinctive letter "R" on its back. Using that insignia as her starting point, she designed another new costume for her husband. Peter used his spiderlike agility to pretend that he was a super-athlete called Ricochet.

Ricochet was a wisecracking hero, annoyingly often in the middle of a battle.

Richochet seemed to be a less than law-abiding member of society.

Spider-Man wouldn't have been able to conceive of his new identities without Mary Jane's enthusiastic help.

DUSK

Spider-Man had visited an alternate dimension a few weeks earlier called the Negative Zone and had acquired a costume that allowed him to merge with shadows and become practically invisible. Peter decided to call this dark persona Dusk. The mysterious Dusk employed a utility belt that contained gas, smoke, and stun grenades.

As Dusk, Spider-Man spied on the underworld by pretending to be a criminal mercenary.

Dusk's ability to blend into shadows made him a monstrous creature of the night.

As Prodigy, Peter advocated strong morals.

PRODIGY

Conceived and designed entirely by Mary Jane, Prodigy was the consummate costumed hero. He possessed superhuman strength, a bulletproof costume, and could leap from one rooftop to the next with a single bound.

Protecting people from villains like Roughhouse, Prodigy was like the comic-book archetypes of Peter's youth. Prodigy became a media darling, achieving the fame and respect that had eluded Spidey.

HORNET

Peter went to visit his old friend Hobie Brown, an electronics wizard and inventor who was also the Prowler. Hobie had recently invented a cybernetically controlled jetpack and he gifted it to Spider-Man for his new Hornet identity.

Though the jetpack was far too heavy for a normal man to carry, Spider-Man had no trouble with it.

Not realizing who was wearing the costume, the Human Torch confronted the Hornet after hearing the "new" hero make a public statement about how Spidey was no longer a problem.

The Hornet could fly at nearly 50 mph (80 kph).

SLINGERS

A few months after Peter was able to prove Spider-Man's innocence and retire his four new identities, someone else reactivated them. Dan Lyons was an old man who had once been a costumed crime-fighter known as the Black Marvel. He gathered four young misfits and gave them Spidey's faux identities and powers, forming a new team of heroes called the Slingers.

"HANDS OFF THE GEEK, SCORPION! YOU AND I HAVE SOME UNFINISHED BUSINESS TO TAKE CARE OF!"

SPIDER-MAN IMPOSTER

When Peter crossed paths with the Scorpion, he discovered the villain had a new look, complete with a power upgrade.

EARLY RETIREMENT

Peter Parker was through with being Spider-Man. But unfortunately, Spider-Man wasn't quite finished with Peter Parker. After his latest battle with the Green Goblin, Spidey had hung up his webs to concentrate on his real life. But while at a job interview at the Tri Corp Research Foundation, not only did Peter run into the Super Villain Scorpion, but he also encountered a new Spider-Man.

A NEW CHAPTER

Spider-Man's life had been a chaotic mess of late. He'd been led through a maze of misdirection, where death and resurrection seemed to haunt him at every turn. It was time to finally get his life back on track. It was time to embark on a new chapter.

MAY'S RETURN

The reports of Aunt May's death were greatly exaggerated. As part of his master plan to toy with Peter Parker's life, Norman Osborn had hired an actress to portray May, while he had kidnapped the original. Peter had watched the actress die, not his beloved aunt, and he was now thrilled to have her back in his life.

During Spider-Man's retirement, a new Spider-Man appeared on the scene. Peter had no idea who this super-powered individual was, but when the imitator was bested by the villain Shadrac, Peter came to the novice's rescue, and realized that the new Spider-Man was in fact a teenage girl.

CALL OF DUTY

Though retirement seemed to agree with Peter, he eventually resumed his responsibilities and returned to the role that he was born to play. Spider-Man went back into action and fought new villains such as the Ranger, Shadrac, and Captain Power.

Peter returned to protecting the innocent from thugs, criminals, and Super Villains.

Spider-Man will always be haunted by his noble sense of responsibility.

After Peter reclaimed his Spider-Man mantle to battle Shadrac, his replacement decided to adopt her own Super Hero identity and became the new Spider-Woman. Revealed to secretly be teenager Mattie Franklin, she soon became a hero in her own right.

MOVING ON UP

While he still visited the old homestead once in a while, Peter Parker and Mary Jane had moved in to a deluxe condo in Manhattan, using the money Mary Jane earned in her modeling career. Aunt May even moved in with the young couple at their spacious penthouse duplex.

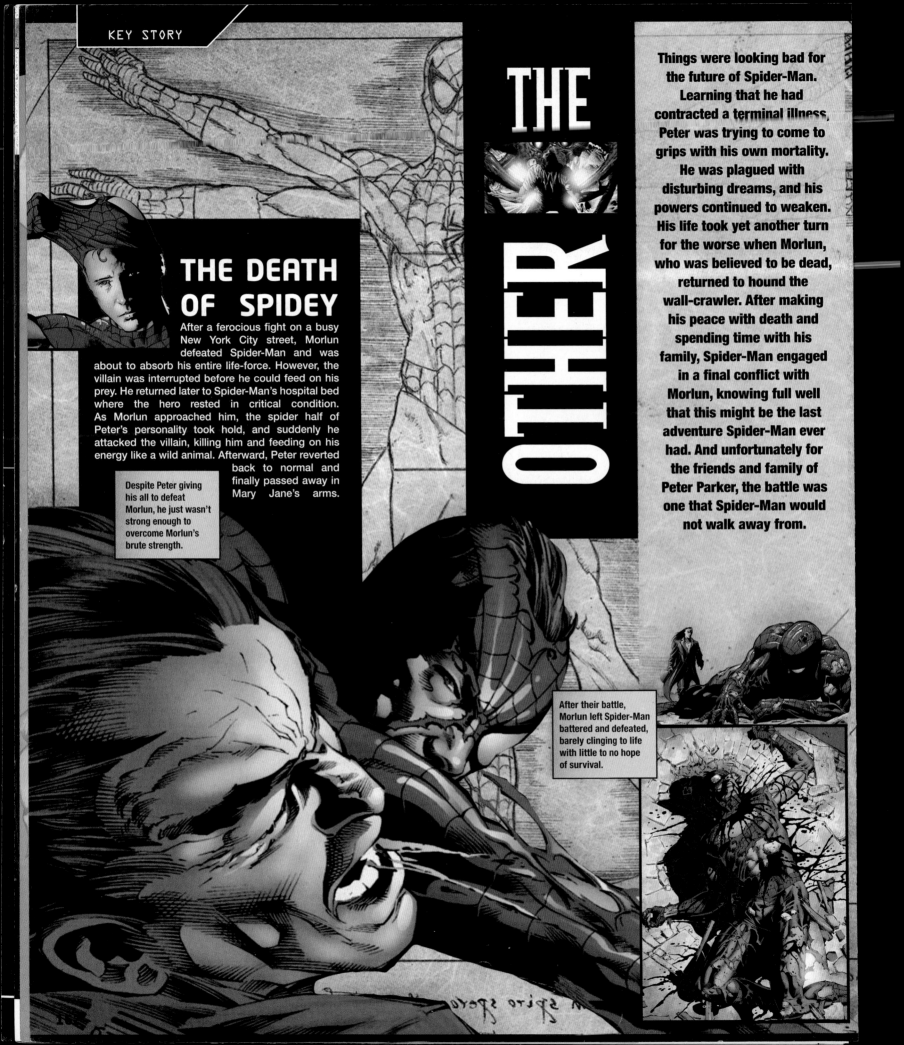

THE OTHER

THE DEATH OF SPIDEY

After a ferocious fight on a busy New York City street, Morlun defeated Spider-Man and was about to absorb his entire life-force. However, the villain was interrupted before he could feed on his prey. He returned later to Spider-Man's hospital bed where the hero rested in critical condition. As Morlun approached him, the spider half of Peter's personality took hold, and suddenly he attacked the villain, killing him and feeding on his energy like a wild animal. Afterward, Peter reverted back to normal and finally passed away in Mary Jane's arms.

Despite Peter giving his all to defeat Morlun, he just wasn't strong enough to overcome Morlun's brute strength.

Things were looking bad for the future of Spider-Man. Learning that he had contracted a terminal illness, Peter was trying to come to grips with his own mortality. He was plagued with disturbing dreams, and his powers continued to weaken. His life took yet another turn for the worse when Morlun, who was believed to be dead, returned to hound the wall-crawler. After making his peace with death and spending time with his family, Spider-Man engaged in a final conflict with Morlun, knowing full well that this might be the last adventure Spider-Man ever had. And unfortunately for the friends and family of Peter Parker, the battle was one that Spider-Man would not walk away from.

After their battle, Morlun left Spider-Man battered and defeated, barely clinging to life with little to no hope of survival.

REBIRTH

When a distraught Mary Jane returned home to Avengers Tower, she was shocked to find Peter's body reduced to a lifeless husk that had split open in two, as if something had hatched from inside it. Meanwhile, trapped in some sort of dream state, Peter had found his way beneath a New York City bridge, and somehow encased himself inside a giant cocoon. As he embraced a spider entity in his dream, giving in to his true self, his cocoon in the real world cracked open. Blood began to drip out into the water below, and like a natural birth, Peter's form emerged. Peter splashed into the water, and then dramatically surfaced, now a new man, reborn without a trace of his former injuries. Peter returned to Avengers Tower, and into the arms of Mary Jane and his Aunt May. As he underwent a barrage of scientific tests by his friends in the Super Hero community, and returned to his work as Spider-Man, Peter soon realized a strange new fact. He had not just been resurrected. When he exited his cocoon, Peter had evolved.

NEW SENSES

"EVOLVE OR DIE."

When he returned to the land of the living, Spider-Man discovered that he was much more in tune with his spider half than ever before. The hair on Spidey's arms was more sensitive, like that of a real spider, which in turn increased his ability to better perceive the world around him. Not only were his natural senses magnified, but he could also adhere objects to his back, a natural extension of his old wall-crawling ability.

STINGERS
After his resurrection, Spider-Man soon discovered his most startling new ability. When faced with danger, poisonous stingers would protrude out of his wrists as if by instinct. However, this new power appears to have gone away in the wake of recent events.

THE IRON SPIDER

When Peter Parker returned from the dead with his original costume in tatters, Tony Stark decided to take it upon himself to create a new uniform for his New Avengers teammate. Using the very same sophisticated nanotechnology that he employed in his own Iron Man suit, Stark developed a new look for Spider-Man to aid him in his war on crime.

NOW YOU SEE HIM...

One of the most practical features of the Stark-created costume was that it could blend in with a variety of backgrounds, rendering Spider-Man invisible to his opponents. Already well-versed in stealth techniques, Spidey used the uniform to take his abilities to a whole new level.

Spidey's new costume included lenses with enhanced visual capabilities, letting him see in the infrared and ultraviolet spectrums. This came in handy when stalking criminals and trying to locate their precise positioning.

QUICK CHANGE

Spider-Man adapted to his new costume quite easily. He could use its abilities to fight criminals in ways he wouldn't have been able to before. The new technology allowed him to keep the costume on in public at all times, as it could be made invisible to the naked eye. Using rapid response thought-control, the nanotechnology also let Spidey switch from his Iron Spider look to his street clothes, as well as to his traditional red and blue costume, and even his black uniform.

"I'VE TAKEN THE OPPORTUNITY TO MAKE SOME SLIGHT... IMPROVEMENTS." TONY STARK

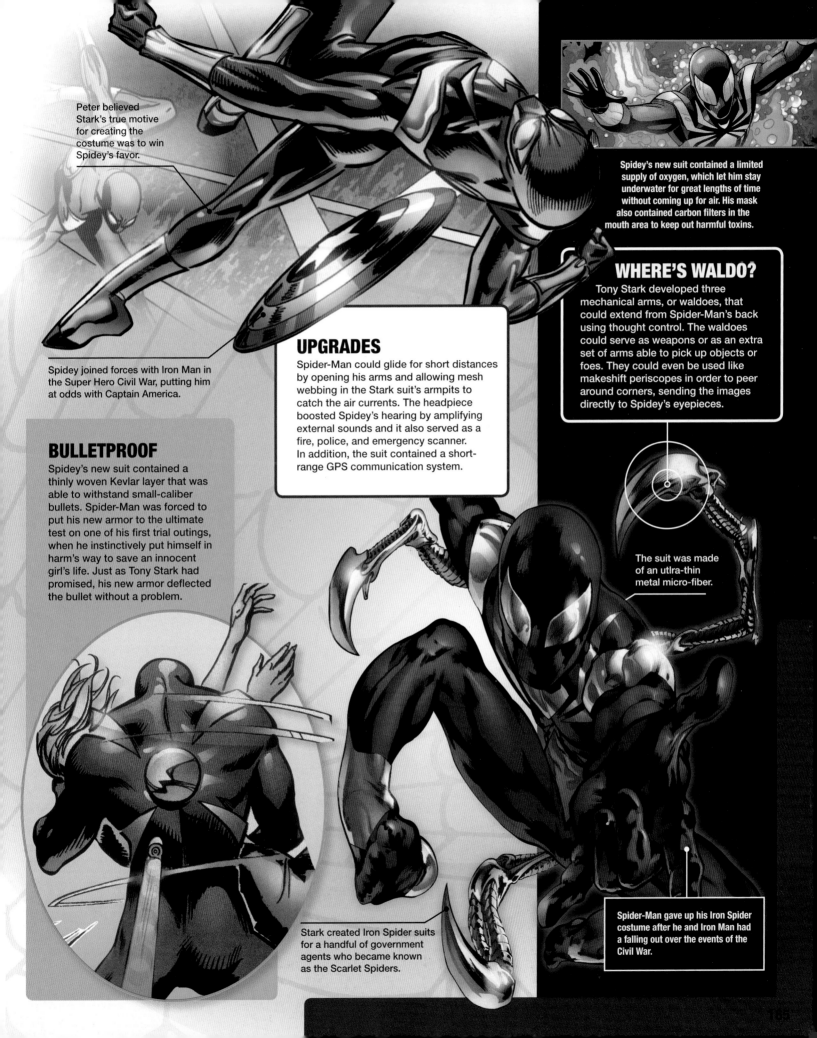

Peter believed Stark's true motive for creating the costume was to win Spidey's favor.

Spidey joined forces with Iron Man in the Super Hero Civil War, putting him at odds with Captain America.

Spidey's new suit contained a limited supply of oxygen, which let him stay underwater for great lengths of time without coming up for air. His mask also contained carbon filters in the mouth area to keep out harmful toxins.

WHERE'S WALDO?

Tony Stark developed three mechanical arms, or waldoes, that could extend from Spider-Man's back using thought control. The waldoes could serve as weapons or as an extra set of arms able to pick up objects or foes. They could even be used like makeshift periscopes in order to peer around corners, sending the images directly to Spidey's eyepieces.

UPGRADES

Spider-Man could glide for short distances by opening his arms and allowing mesh webbing in the Stark suit's armpits to catch the air currents. The headpiece boosted Spidey's hearing by amplifying external sounds and it also served as a fire, police, and emergency scanner. In addition, the suit contained a short-range GPS communication system.

BULLETPROOF

Spidey's new suit contained a thinly woven Kevlar layer that was able to withstand small-caliber bullets. Spider-Man was forced to put his new armor to the ultimate test on one of his first trial outings, when he instinctively put himself in harm's way to save an innocent girl's life. Just as Tony Stark had promised, his new armor deflected the bullet without a problem.

The suit was made of an utlra-thin metal micro-fiber.

Stark created Iron Spider suits for a handful of government agents who became known as the Scarlet Spiders.

Spider-Man gave up his Iron Spider costume after he and Iron Man had a falling out over the events of the Civil War.

CIVIL WAR

It turned brother against brother and friends into enemies. Triggered by the passing of the Super Hero Registration Act, the Super Hero Civil War shook the universe to its core, and created divisions that are still not fully mended to this day. And for Spider-Man, it changed everything.

THE STAMFORD TRAGEDY

When the latest incarnation of the Super Hero team known as the New Warriors engaged in a battle with a group of Super Villains, including the volatile criminal Nitro, their fight accidentally caused an explosion that destroyed a school and cost the lives of hundreds of innocents. Looking for a quick solution, the government rushed the Superhuman Registration Act through congress.

At a highly touted press conference, Spider-Man stood in front of the audience wearing his traditional costume. Then much to the public's shock and awe, he removed his mask, outing his identity to the world.

THE ACT

The Superhuman Registration Act meant that every hero and vigilante would be forced to register his or her identity with the government and placed on its payroll. Iron Man supported the Act, and asked Spider-Man to publicly endorse it. When Spider-Man revealed his secret identity to the world, Peter's friends and former employers, including J. Jonah Jameson, were floored by the news, and Peter Parker instantly became a household name.

THE RESISTANCE

Not everyone supported the Registration Act. Captain America considered it an invasion of privacy and a violation of civil rights. And with the Act's passing, the iconic hero became a fugitive merely by standing up for what he believed in. Hunted by Iron Man and other registered heroes, Captain America went underground, joining forces with other like-minded individuals.

Despite sticking by his mentor's side, Spider-Man began to regret his decision to register and make such a public stance. He and his family were hounded by the paparazzi and Super Villains with grudges. His attempt to protect his loved ones had backfired, and he was beginning to see how important his privacy had been. And after the hero Goliath was killed during a battle with Iron Man's forces, Spider-Man had had enough. He abandoned Iron Man and joined Captain America's rebels.

"I THINK THIS PLAN WILL SPLIT US DOWN THE MIDDLE."

CAPTAIN AMERICA

THE GOOD GUYS?

Iron Man wasn't above recruiting Super Villains to his cause. As a member of Captain America's underground resistance, Spider-Man was forced to confront nefarious criminals like Venom and Lady Deathstrike, Wolverine's murderous enemy. It was clear that Iron Man would stop at nothing to prove his point.

After so much bloody violence, Captain America finally looked around and took note of the devastation this war was causing. Like a true hero, he gave up the fight, and turned himself over to Iron Man's custody.

A NEGATIVE PLACE

The fights began to escalate, as Iron Man and company detained any and all unregistered heroes and villains in an other-dimensional prison complex located in the Negative Zone. Captain America's side invaded the stronghold, and directly confronted the registered heroes in yet another brutal battle.

ONE MORE DAY

It would be the ultimate test of their relationship, and one Mary Jane Watson and Peter Parker would pass with flying colors. Ironically enough, by proving their love for one another, their reward would be to spend the rest of their lives apart. All they had left was one last day together, before a dark force destroyed the relationship that had taken them so long to build.

> " JUST A FEW SECONDS MORE... LISTEN TO ME, PETER **LISTEN** TO ME "
> Mary Jane

Peter registered his aunt at the hospital under the name May Morgan to avoid attention.

AUNT MAY

Peter Parker's secret identity became public knowledge in the events leading up to the Super Hero Civil War. Due to the fact that Peter decided to disobey the law and join a group of underground rebels in the fight for Super Hero rights, he had become a fugitive. He was forced to hide his family in a seedy motel in order to avoid attention. But unfortunately, while Iron Man and his forces didn't find Peter's location, the Kingpin did. The crime boss sent an assassin to kill Spider-Man, but the bullet missed its mark and struck Aunt May instead. Clinging to life in a hospital bed, Aunt May's situation looked bleak indeed. The only saving grace was that her bills were paid for by Iron Man Tony Stark. Despite viewing Peter as a fugitive from the law, Tony realized May was an innocent victim, and knew she didn't deserve her fate.

Dr. Strange erased the world's memory of Spidey's alter ego.

> **" I WANT YOUR MARRIAGE. "**
>
> Mephisto

MEPHISTO

After asking nearly every person he could think of for help to save Aunt May, including Doctor Strange, Spider-Man was out of options. It seemed that no matter what he did, the woman who was like a mother to him was going to die, and it was going to be his fault. But then the devil came to call.

The demon Mephisto was more than a little interested in Peter Parker's situation. He understood the complex destinies of humankind, and knew that even the smallest brushstrokes of a person's life could be altered with dramatic consequences. Mephisto would allow Aunt May a full recovery, but for a price. He wanted to end Peter's relationship with MJ and make it as if their marriage had never happened. Seeing no other choice, Peter and Mary Jane gave in to the demon's terms, after spending one more day together, remembering everything they'd gone through as a couple. As Mephisto changed the world around them, MJ promised Peter that no matter what changed, they would find each other again.

DOCTOR STRANGE

When the doctors first told Peter that there was nothing they could do to help May, he turned to a doctor of a different sort, the master magician Dr. Strange. Although the mage couldn't heal May, he did help Peter visit other heroes and villains all over the planet in a search for aid. Later, Peter visited Dr. Strange again, this time begging the sorcerer to erase the world's knowledge of Spidey's true identity in order to protect his family.

THE NEW STATUS QUO

In the new reality Mephisto concocted, Mary Jane and Peter had never married, but had remained a couple. When May was shot, she recovered, and Spidey had Dr. Strange arrange for the world to forget that he was Spider-Man, with only Mary Jane remembering. Nevertheless the couple broke up when Mary Jane decided she could no longer deal with the dangerous world of Spider-Man.

BRAND NEW DAY

There had been a lot of magic in Spider-Man's life, and to Peter Parker, that wasn't necessarily a good thing. With all his recent encounters with mystical animal spirits and otherworldly demons, Spider-Man was ready to go back to a life more ordinary. But for Peter Parker, that meant the daily life and death struggles of everyone's favorite friendly neighborhood arachnid. Same old power. Same old responsibility. Brand new day.

In the wake of his new status quo, Spidey no longer possessed organic webbing, and once again had to use his artificial web-fluid.

AUNT MAY

Aunt May's health troubles were finally over. Recovering completely from being shot by one of the Kingpin's snipers, May was determined to utilize her renewed lease on life to the fullest and began volunteering at a soup kitchen. However, she still found time to worry about her nephew Peter, even though she no longer remembered that he was also Spider-Man.

With his new fresh start, Peter returned to the work he knew best: news photography.

AT THE *BUGLE*

With the glamorous life of living in Avengers Tower and working for Tony Stark now behind him, Peter was back to barely making ends meet. He lived in his aunt's house, and attempted to restart his photography career. Meanwhile, *Daily Bugle* publisher J. Jonah Jameson suffered a heart attack, and his wife Marla sold his paper out from under him, worried about the stress it caused him.

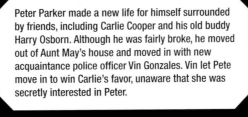

Peter Parker made a new life for himself surrounded by friends, including Carlie Cooper and his old buddy Harry Osborn. Although he was fairly broke, he moved out of Aunt May's house and moved in with new acquaintance police officer Vin Gonzales. Vin let Pete move in to win Carlie's favor, unaware that she was secretly interested in Peter.

CARLIE COOPER

Peter met forensic scientist Carlie Cooper through his old friend Harry Osborn. While he instantly liked Carlie, it took Peter a while to realize the extent of his feelings for her.

HARRY OSBORN

While the world believed him dead, Harry Osborn was actually in Europe, as part of an elaborate ruse concocted by his father, Norman. Back in New York, Harry became the owner of the Coffee Bean.

JACKPOT

The new Super Hero Jackpot was a legally registered hero working in Manhattan. Her more than passing resemblance to Mary Jane Watson continually confused Spider-Man.

MEANWHILE...

As Peter struggled to get his life together, Spider-Man was faced with his own set of problems. In the wake of the Super Hero Civil War, many vigilantes were considered outlaws, and could be arrested at any time. Peter had not registered with the government, so he fell into that unfortunate group. While heroes like the newly debuted Jackpot could fight crime without any fear of reprisals, Spidey had to constantly watch his back, knowing that the authorities were looking for an opportunity to take him down.

The situation only worsened when J. Jonah Jameson, having recovered from his heart attack, was elected Mayor of New York City. With the *Daily Bugle* no longer his responsibility, Jameson tried his hand at politics, and used his new power to cause Spider-Man more headaches than ever before. Jameson hired special task forces to take Spidey down, but fortunately Peter stayed one step ahead of the game. Spider-Man constantly made Jameson look foolish by eluding his costly high-tech forces in public, and the newly elected Mayor was eventually forced to call off his relentless war against the web-slinger.

"WE'VE MET. IN ANOTHER LIFE."
MARY JANE

MARY JANE...

Adjusting to the single life was difficult for both Peter and Mary Jane. While Peter spent most of the time alone, Mary Jane had a fling with actor Bobby Carr, before returning to Peter's circle of friends and attempting life on her own.

BRAND NEW THREATS

With his life's new direction and a renewed sense of self, Spider-Man had set out into a Brand New Day. Unfortunately, the so-called Parker Luck came with him, and soon a new breed of Super Villain was appearing all over Manhattan. Spidey's new status quo would come complete with plenty of additions to his rogues gallery.

SCREWBALL

INTERNET SENSATION

The very first live-blogging Super Villain, Screwball set out to gain millions of hits on her website by staging a crime wave and using a webcam to capture the results. With a live feed showcasing her every move, her first encounter with Spider-Man gained her so many extra viewers, she never shied away from crossing his path in the future. A glory hound with the desire to be the next extreme reality star, Screwball is an excellent thief and a master of gymnastics and aerial maneuvers, keeping Spider-Man on his toes and in her camera's sights.

THE ROSE

CRIMINAL LEGACY

When Sara Ehret accidentally injected herself with a virus used in her study of gene therapy, her boss, Dr. Phillip Hayes, was left to deal with the financial fallout from her laboratory accident. While Sara inherited powers and became the Super Hero Jackpot, Dr. Hayes turned to less noble pursuits, and became the newest criminal to adopt the moniker of the Rose in order to regain financial stability. Hayes ordered the criminal Boomerang to murder Sara Ehret's husband, as a message to Jackpot.

MR. NEGATIVE

SPLIT PERSONALITY

By day, Martin Li was an apparent philanthropist and the founder of the soup kitchen where Peter's Aunt May worked. But behind closed doors, he was the new boss of Chinatown's criminal underground. Mr. Negative used his super-power of influence and his army of Inner Demons to create a criminal empire that was eventually exposed by Spider-Man and the second vigilante to take the name Wraith.

MENACE

DEVOTED DAUGHTER

In an attempt to get her father elected as Mayor, Peter's friend and Harry Osborn's fiancée Lily Hollister used the equipment and Goblin Formula that once belonged to Norman Osborn to transform herself into the Super Villain Menace. As Menace, she terrorized her father's campaign, drawing sympathy and support from voters. However, when she was defeated by Spider-Man, her double life ended her father's political career. She later gave birth to Harry's second son before leaving for a life on the run.

FREAK

BEAST OF BURDEN
An addict who would do anything to score his next fix, Freak was born when he stole the donation box from the homeless center where May Parker worked. Tracking down the criminal, Spider-Man webbed him to a rooftop, but the thief got away by shedding his clothes. As he continued to flee, the criminal fell through a glass sunroof, and stumbled upon an experiment in progress by Dr. Curt Connors. Mistaking syringes he discovered for more commonplace illegal drugs, the thief injected himself and became the monstrous being called the Freak.

OVERDRIVE

FAST AND FURIOUS
A thief with the uncanny ability to instantly fuse with and customize any automobile, Overdrive has led Spider-Man on many chases. With just a touch, Overdrive can transform any vehicle to a sleek hotrod capable of near impossible maneuvers. At one point, Overdrive's antics ran him afoul of crime boss Mr. Negative, but the quick-witted thief was able to escape when Mr. Negative's men made the mistake of throwing the villain into the trunk of a car. Overdrive transformed the vehicle into his newest ride, and sped away from the scene.

PAPER DOLL

KILLER CUT-OUT
Paper Doll can flatten her body to razor-thin extremes, possessing the thickness of her namesake. With fingertips so sharp they can even cut Spider-Man's webs to ribbons, Paper Doll stalked the Hollywood actor Bobby Carr, killing those she thought were detrimental to his career. When she targeted Carr's then-girlfriend Mary Jane Watson, Spidey rushed to his ex's rescue, and was able to subdue Doll when she fell in a swimming pool and was forced to regain her three-dimensional shape in a desperate bid for air.

RAPTOR

IN THE WRONG
The former employer of Peter Parker clone Ben Reilly, Dr. Damon Ryder became completely unhinged when he injected himself with dinosaur DNA and killed his wife and children. Ryder adopted the name and costume of the villainous Raptor, and unjustly blamed Ben for the death of his family, even manipulating Ben's old enemy Kaine into helping him achieve his "revenge." Mistaking Peter Parker for his clone, Raptor attacked the innocent Parker several times before Spider-Man was finally able to stop his attacks and bring the criminal to justice.

IRON PATRIOT

Following the events of the Civil War, Spider-Man was now the villain. And Norman Osborn was getting ready to become the hero. With money and power on his side, Osborn geared up to end the menace of his archenemy.

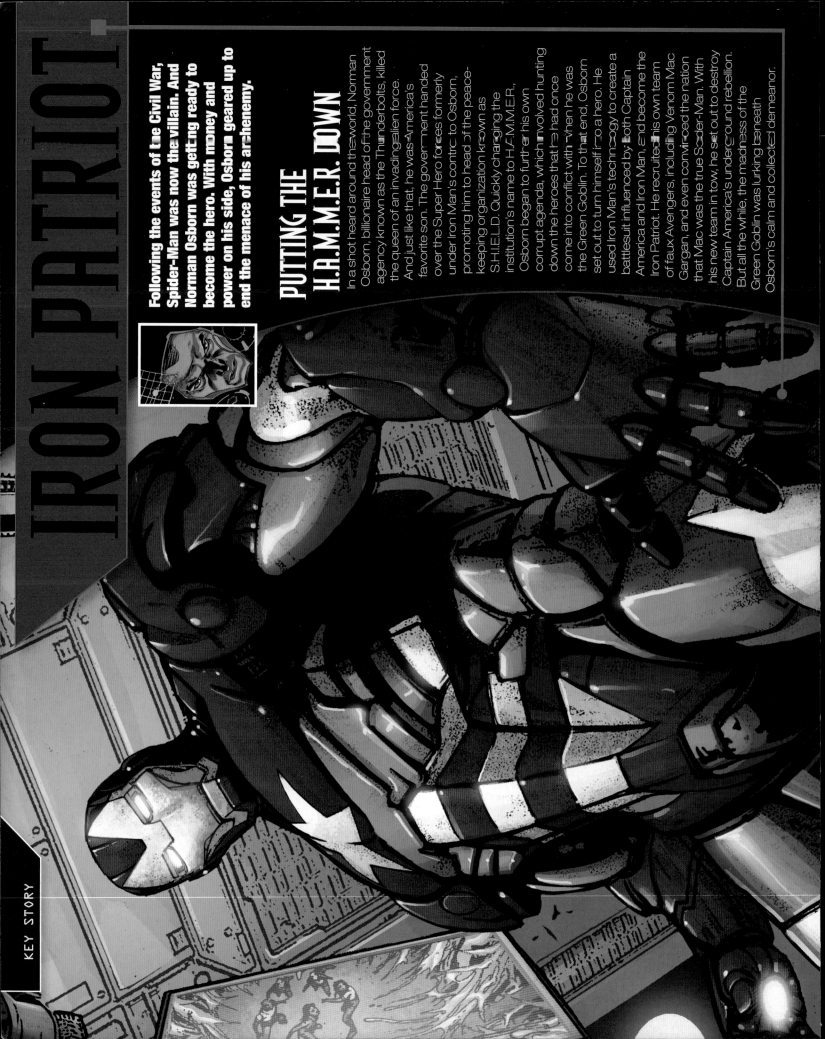

PUTTING THE H.A.M.M.E.R. DOWN

In a shot heard around the world, Norman Osborn, billionaire head of the government agency known as the Thunderbolts, killed the queen of an invading alien force. And just like that, he was America's favorite son. The government handed over the Super Hero forces formerly under Iron Man's control to Osborn, promoting him to head of the peace-keeping organization known as S.H.I.E.L.D. Quickly changing the institution's name to H.A.M.M.E.R., Osborn began to further his own corrupt agenda, which involved hunting down the heroes that had once come into conflict with when he was the Green Goblin. To that end, Osborn set out to turn himself into a hero. He used Iron Man's technology to create a battlesuit influenced by both Captain America and Iron Man, and become the Iron Patriot. He recruited his own team of faux Avengers, including Venom Mac Gargan, and even convinced the nation that Mac was the true Spider-Man. With his new team in tow, he set out to destroy Captain America's underground rebellion. But all the while, the madness of the Green Goblin was lurking beneath Osborn's calm and collected demeanor.

> **"THE SHEEP WANTED HEROES, AND I PROVIDED, GOOD SHEPHERD THAT I AM..."**
> NORMAN OSBORN

AMERICAN SON

It wasn't long before Norman Osborn decided that he wanted to recruit his son Harry into the family business. Using Harry's former fiancée, the heavily pregnant Lily Hollister, as a pawn in his game, Osborn was able to convince Harry to take up the mantle of the armored American Son as he believed Lily's child was his. However when Norman captured and was about to kill Spider-Man, Harry saw his father for the true monster that he was. He geared up in his American Son armor and bested his father in a violent clash. But rather than kill Norman and become as bad as his father, Harry decided to walk away and Norman was left without a son. However, he had won the heart of Lily Hollister, and planned to raise her son as the new heir to his twisted throne.

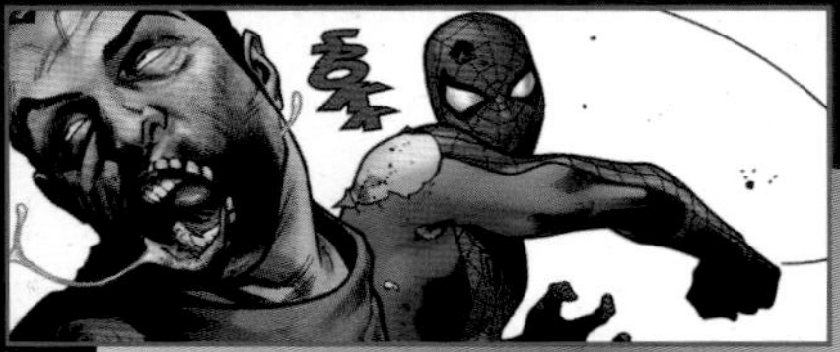

When Norman used government forces to storm Asgard, claiming it was a security threat, the world saw the extent of his madness and corruption. He was jailed and the Superhuman Registration Act was lifted, but only after Spidey got a little payback.

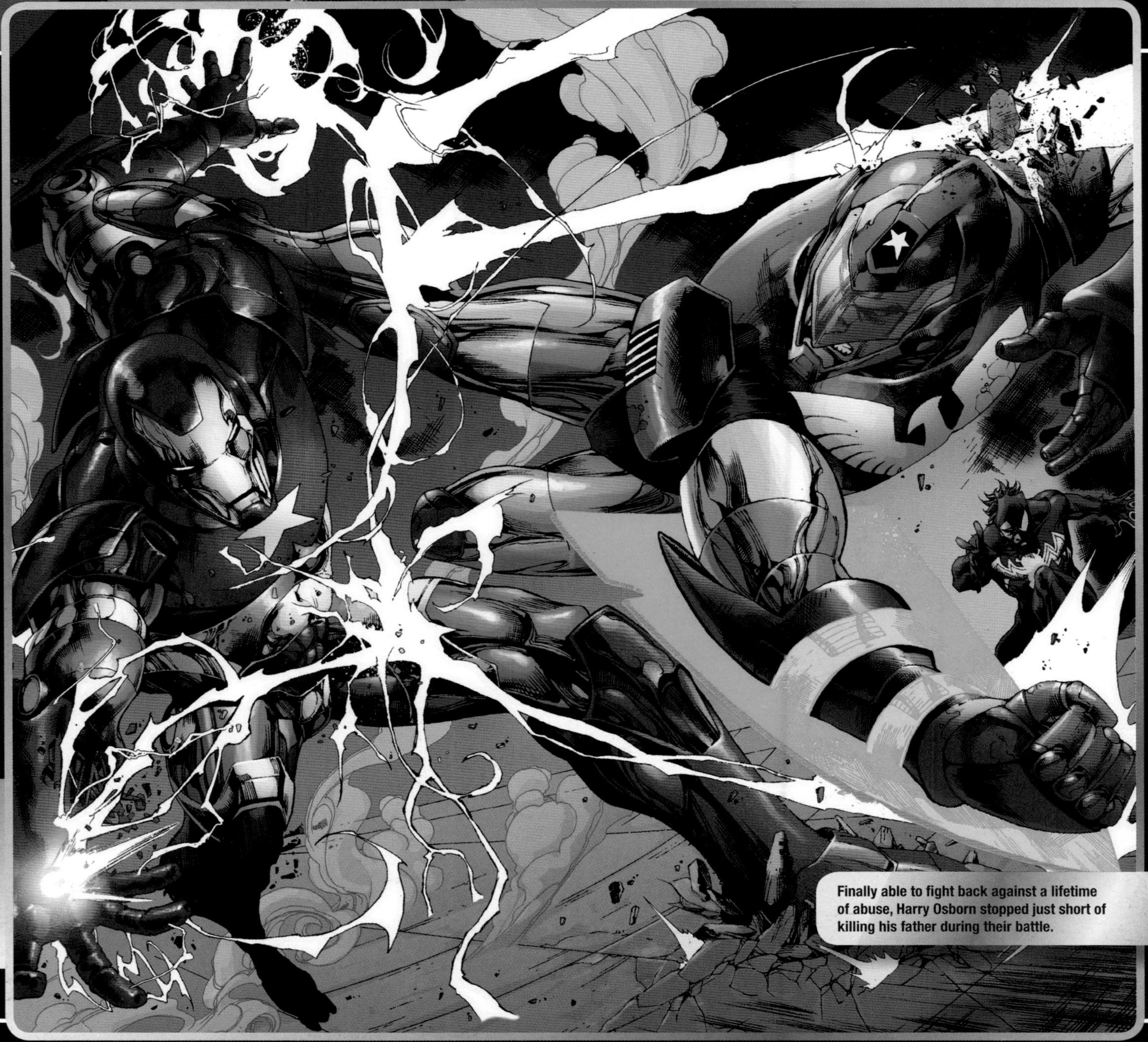

Finally able to fight back against a lifetime of abuse, Harry Osborn stopped just short of killing his father during their battle.

THE GAUNTLET

The villains were crawling out of the woodwork. Several of Spider-Man's old foes like Electro and the Lizard were getting power upgrades while dangerous faces like the new Vulture and Rhino were trying to replace other familiar rogues. Spider-Man was running a gauntlet of sorts, and was quickly reaching the point of exhaustion.

THE GRIM HUNT

Kraven the Hunter had died years ago by his own hand. But his family wasn't quite so ready to give up on the violent Kravinoff legacy. So they watched Spider-Man from the shadows, and slowly planned his death.

> "THEY'RE HUNTING US... THEY'RE HUNTING SPIDERS."
>
> KAINE

Kaine weakly made his way to Peter Parker's apartment, covered in his own blood and barely alive. He had to warn Peter of the coming danger.

WAR ON SPIDERS

Spider-Man felt as weak as a kitten. Running a gauntlet of his old foes and battling one almost immediately after the next had caught up with him. He was sick in bed with swine flu when he was surprised by his clone Kaine, close to death, but there to warn him that someone was hunting "spiders."

Spider-Man was then called into action when he heard an explosion nearby, and chanced upon Arachne being hunted by Kraven's children Ana and Alyosha. Spider-Man succeeded in saving Arachne's life, and the two fled to the nearest safe house Arachne could think of, the ransacked apartment of former Spider-Woman Mattie Franklin. There they encountered Spider-Man's old spider-powered mentor Ezekiel, apparently back from the dead. Ezekiel told the heroes of a prophesized war between Hunters and Spiders. The Kravens' next target would be Araña. Arachne and Spider-Man tracked down Araña, but they were overpowered by the Kravens, and Arachne and Araña were kidnapped. Ezekiel and Spider-Man traveled north of the city to pursue the Kravens, but it was a trap. Ezekiel was actually the Chameleon, Kraven's half-brother, in disguise.

Spider-Man thought the deceased Ezekiel was magically drawn to the fray due to being a fellow "spider," but he was the Chameleon in disguise.

The Kravens had kidnapped Mattie Franklin and Madame Web. Kraven's wife Sasha stabbed Mattie in the chest, and used her blood in an arcane ritual to resurrect Kraven's son, Vladimir, the Grim Hunter.

Led into a trap by the Chameleon, Spider-Man was ambushed by the Kraven family, falling into an open grave before being stabbed on Kraven's altar.

KRAVEN REBORN

A second chance at life was the last thing that Kraven wanted, having felt he had achieved the ultimate victory in defeating Spider-Man before taking his own life. However, he had no choice in the matter. When Spider-Man was lured to the Kraven estate, stabbed, and apparently killed, his blood triggered an alchemical spell, and the original Kraven the Hunter was returned to the living. Unlike Kraven's son Vladimir, who had returned to life as a hideous man-lion mutation due to the use of Mattie Franklin's "impure" blood, Kraven was in perfect health, seemingly from the pure essence of the spider that Peter Parker's body contained. But despite his physical condition, Kraven knew that the ritual was an abomination of nature, and something about it wasn't right.

Examining Spider-Man's body, Kraven realized that it wasn't the true spider that had brought him back. It was Spider-Man's clone, Kaine. When Peter Parker had fallen into the empty grave during his battle with Kraven's family, Kaine had buried Spider-Man to ensure that he would stay out of harm's way, and had taken his place in the grave.

Later, Peter regained his senses and climbed his way out of the earth. After discovering Kaine's body beside his old black costume and a note that read "Hunt me," Spider-Man complied with Kraven's wishes, angrily taking his fight directly to Kraven's family. He took the Kravens down one at a time, but was too late to save Madame Web from Sasha Kraven's wrath. Sasha killed the fortune teller, and Web passed her prophetic gift on to Arachne. And after the dust settled, and the casualties were counted, a familiar face emerged from the ground. It seemed that even death couldn't stop the force of nature that was Kaine.

Kraven was disgusted by his resurrection, and believed his wife Sasha had made a mockery of his accomplishments.

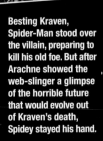

Besting Kraven, Spider-Man stood over the villain, preparing to kill his old foe. But after Arachne showed the web-slinger a glimpse of the horrible future that would evolve out of Kraven's death, Spidey stayed his hand.

ALTERNATE REALITIES

The Multiverse is populated with infinite Earths, each with its own timeline. But with an infinite number of alternate realities and futures exists an equally infinite number of possible Spider-Men.

2099

In an alternate future in the year 2099, Miguel O'Hara was a geneticist who worked in the bioengineering division of Alchemax, one of the world's largest corporations. He was assigned the task of enhancing human performance in order to produce the ultimate superspy. Inspired by the legend of the original Spider-Man, Miguel devised a procedure to rewrite a subject's DNA, giving him the proportionate strength, speed, and agility of a spider.

Miguel was ordered by his boss to test his new procedure on a human guinea pig. But the geneticist was sickened by the result and tried to resign. To force Miguel to stay, his boss gave him a farewell drink laced with Rapture, a highly addictive and expensive drug. Since Rapture bonds with its victims on a genetic level, Miguel attempted to cure his addiction using a different experimental procedure, hoping to restore his original DNA. But at the last moment, a jealous coworker changed the imprint sequence, and Miguel received the spider process instead. Miguel's DNA was written with the powers that turned him into the Spider-Man for a new generation.

Miguel was willing to risk his life in a desperate attempt to free himself from his addiction to Rapture.

BRAVE NEW HEROES

Many things have changed in the New York of 2099. Governments have given way to multinational corporations that now rule the Earth. People with jobs and money live in the upper levels of the inner city, where they are constantly watched by the Public Eye, a private police force hired to enforce corporate laws. To combat this unjust world, Spider-Man isn't the only hero who has donned a costume and placed himself in harm's way. Ravage is a former garbage man who gained superhuman strength along with a beast-like appearance. This era also has its own version of the Punisher, Dr. Doom, the Fantastic Four, and a virtual reality Ghost Rider. It even has a new team of X-Men.

HOUSE OF M

When the former Avenger known as the Scarlet Witch lost her grip on reality, she remade the world into a place where mutants like herself were no longer the hated and feared minority. In this new reality ruled by mutantkind, Peter Parker was a famous professional wrestler, married to Gwen Stacy, and frequently celebrated in the press. And Spider-Man was a celebrity in his own right. It was a perfect life Peter had never even dared to dream of—and one he knew deep down couldn't be true.

Realizing that his happy life somehow wasn't right, Peter began to lose his grip on reality. He even donned the costume of the villainous Green Goblin. Luckily, Peter soon joined a group of outlaws led by Wolverine, and helped restore the world back to normal by participating in an attack against the Scarlet Witch and the world's evil ruler, Magneto.

The Spider-Man of 2211 was forced to arrest his daughter Robin for crimes she had not yet committed. However, it was the act of breaking out of prison that caused Robin to go insane and adopt her role as the Hobgoblin in the first place.

2211

In the future of yet another alternate universe, the Spider-Man legacy endured even longer than 2099. In the year 2211, Dr. Max Borne adopted the mantle of Spider-Man. Armed with two pairs of artificial arms not unlike the Dr Octopus of today, Borne led an organization of time-traveling protectors known as the Timespinners. Dedicated to his service of this advanced temporal police force, Borne was forced to combat his own daughter, Hobgoblin, who was obsessed with killing every version of Spider-Man to ever exist in the timeline. Her time-traveling quest put her in conflict not just with Peter Parker, but also with the Spider-Man of 2099, forcing the Spider-Man of 2211 to travel to our reality on more than one occasion.

SPIDER-GIRL

In an alternate timeline in which Spider-Man and Mary Jane Watson are still happily married, their daughter May grew up to be the legacy hero known as Spider-Girl, proving that with great genetics came great responsibility.

Unlike the high school career of her bookworm father, May was the star of her school's basketball team.

ORIGIN

In a future that might have been, the wedding of Peter Parker and Mary Jane Watson went uninterrupted, and the happy couple went on to have a daughter named May. Unlike Spider-Man's reality today, Peter and Mary Jane's daughter not only survived the ramifications of the Clone Saga, but she grew up to be a thriving, amazing young woman. In this world, Peter retired from crime-fighting after a final battle with the Green Goblin cost him his right leg, and the Goblin his very life. Peter became a forensic scientist for the New York Police Department, which allowed him to contribute to the war on crime without having to place himself constantly in harm's way. The family moved back into Aunt May's house in Forest Hills, and May grew up without learning that her dad had once been the friendly neighborhood web-slinger.

May "Mayday" Parker was already a teenager in high school when her powers first began to manifest themselves. Their timing couldn't have been better, as Normie Osborn, the son of Harry and grandson of Norman, had recently taken over the family business and become the newest incarnation of the Green Goblin. Blaming Peter for the deaths of his father and grandfather, the new Goblin tried to goad Peter into resuming his costumed identity so that he could have the honor of killing Spider-Man. Reacting to the news, Mary Jane took May into the family attic and told her about Peter's past. In true Parker fashion, May donned her "Uncle" Ben Reilly's old costume, which Ben—a clone of Peter Parker— had worn during his brief time as Spider-Man. In that moment, a Spider-Girl was born. After fighting the Green Goblin, and saving Peter's life in the process, May promised to give up being Spider-Girl. To this end, she burnt Ben's old costume, promising that she'd never adopt the Super Hero lifestyle again. It was a vow that was not to last.

Unable to convince his daughter not to follow in his footsteps, Peter eventually accepted May's choice of becoming the teenage Spider-Girl. He couldn't deny the fact that she was simply born to be a heroine.

Possessing spider powers similar to those of her father, May honed her abilities on the street in civilian clothing. She also studied with Phil Urich, the one-time heroic Green Goblin. Phil missed the action of vigilante life, and gladly helped the young hero.

May's reality features the Fantastic Five—the Human Torch, his wife Ms. Fantastic, the brain of Reed Richards, Psi-Lord, and the Thing.

While Normie Osborn originally had set his sights on destroying Peter Parker, May later convinced him to give up his corrupt ways. The two went on to become extremely close friends, mending the Parker/Osborn rift.

Though she only possesses about half the super-strength of her father, Spider-Girl can easily match him when it comes to acrobatics and agility. These talents come in handy when facing the technologically advanced foes of the future.

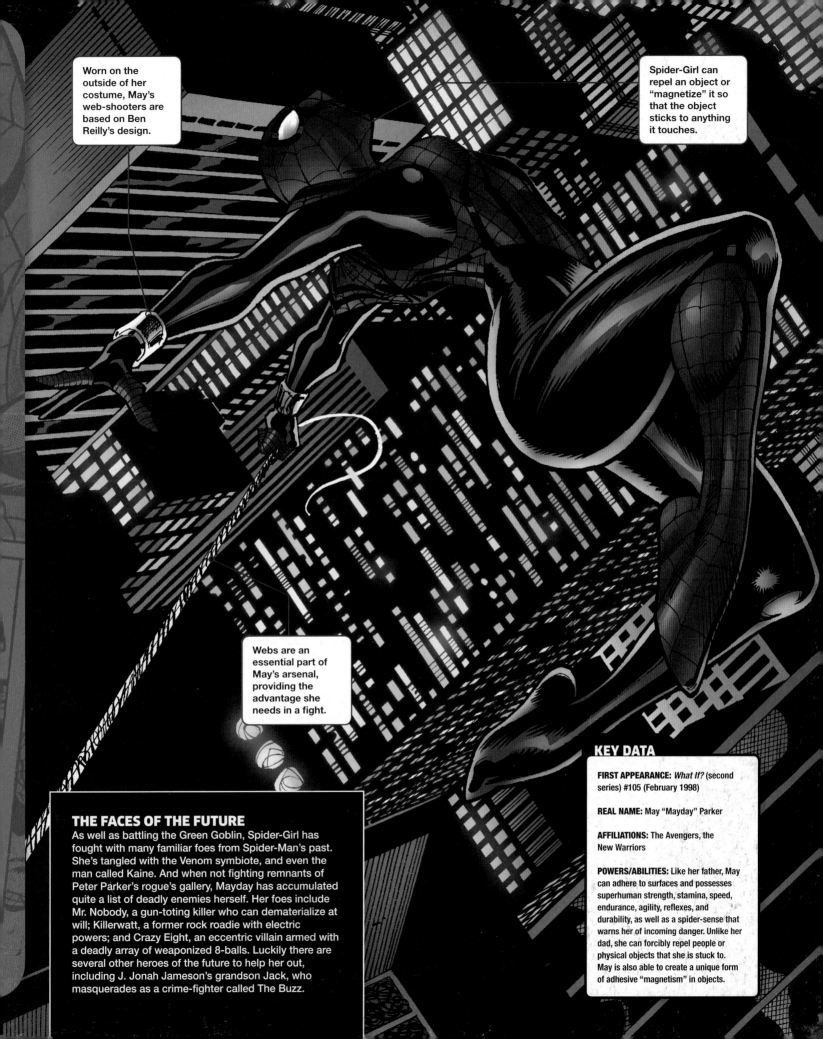

Worn on the outside of her costume, May's web-shooters are based on Ben Reilly's design.

Spider-Girl can repel an object or "magnetize" it so that the object sticks to anything it touches.

Webs are an essential part of May's arsenal, providing the advantage she needs in a fight.

THE FACES OF THE FUTURE

As well as battling the Green Goblin, Spider-Girl has fought with many familiar foes from Spider-Man's past. She's tangled with the Venom symbiote, and even the man called Kaine. And when not fighting remnants of Peter Parker's rogue's gallery, Mayday has accumulated quite a list of deadly enemies herself. Her foes include Mr. Nobody, a gun-toting killer who can dematerialize at will; Killerwatt, a former rock roadie with electric powers; and Crazy Eight, an eccentric villain armed with a deadly array of weaponized 8-balls. Luckily there are several other heroes of the future to help her out, including J. Jonah Jameson's grandson Jack, who masquerades as a crime-fighter called The Buzz.

KEY DATA

FIRST APPEARANCE: *What If?* (second series) #105 (February 1998)

REAL NAME: May "Mayday" Parker

AFFILIATIONS: The Avengers, the New Warriors

POWERS/ABILITIES: Like her father, May can adhere to surfaces and possesses superhuman strength, stamina, speed, endurance, agility, reflexes, and durability, as well as a spider-sense that warns her of incoming danger. Unlike her dad, she can forcibly repel people or physical objects that she is stuck to. May is also able to create a unique form of adhesive "magnetism" in objects.

ULTIMATE SPIDER-MAN

In a dimension similar to that of the normal Marvel Universe, a Spider-Man for a new generation was born. With a more fleshed-out and contemporary origin, a different version of a teenaged Peter Parker was bitten by a spider enhanced by Oz, a revolutionary drug developed by Osborn Industries. However, the result was the same as the spider's bite in classic Spider-Man, and the heroic web-slinger swung into the world of the Ultimate Universe.

PETER PARKER

Ultimate Peter Parker was a clumsy 15-year-old, who spent his days dreading being humiliated by Flash Thompson and his friends. After gaining his spider powers, Peter's confidence grew, and he began to speak up for himself. But perhaps the greatest boon to his self-esteem was his best friend and on-off girlfriend, Mary Jane Watson.

An honor student with a close relationship to his Aunt May and Uncle Ben, Peter was devastated when a burglar killed his beloved Uncle.

MARY JANE

With an interest in journalism and a mature outlook on life, it made sense that Mary Jane was attracted to the brilliant mind of Peter Parker. Unlike the normal Marvel Universe, the Ultimate version of Peter disclosed his dual identity to Mary Jane almost at the very start of his career. While the two went through their share of romantic turmoil, Mary Jane never stopped loving Peter.

NORMAN OSBORN

Norman Osborn was a ruthless entrepreneur. His company, Osborn Industries, was a world leader in scientific research, employing the greatest scientific minds that money could buy. After Peter was accidentally bitten by one of Osborn's test subject spiders while on a class trip to his facility, Osborn Industries lawyers feared a lawsuit from the Parker family and advised Norman to accept no responsibility for the accident. But Osborn shocked the legal minds by opting to play a more dangerous game. He ordered them to pay Peter's medical bill and to keep a close eye on the teenager.

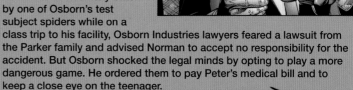

SPIDER-MAN BEGINS

With the simple bite of a spider, Peter Parker became Spider-Man. Not just content with his new spider powers, Peter designed a web formula based on the scientific innovations that his father had achieved before his untimely death. After his Uncle Ben was murdered, Peter focused his life on crime-fighting, and slowly began to adjust to his new role. He snapped some pictures of himself as Spider-Man and sent them to the *Daily Bugle*. While he didn't become an ace photographer as he had hoped, he was able to land a job there working on the paper's website. It wasn't long before Peter put the newspaper's resources to use in his career as Spider-Man, researching the city's criminals.

Though he originally felt sick from the spider's bite, Peter Parker would soon feel better than he had in his entire life due to his new powers.

GET PARKER

Norman Osborn gave Peter a second, "apology" tour of Osborn Industries, where he secured a sample of Peter's blood and discovered that Peter had gained fantastic powers as a direct result of his spider's bite. Norman then used the Oz serum on himself. The businessman was transformed into a demonic monster that destroyed the Osborn Industries building and then went on to burn down his own home. Not content with this destruction, Norman hunted down Peter, and the two battled for the first time as Spider-Man and the Green Goblin. Unfortunately for Peter, that fight was just the first of many.

Ultimate Spider-Man was more youthful than the Spider-Man of the regular Marvel Universe, but he retained his characteristic wit, humor, and acrobatic style.

KINGPIN

When researching the man who shot his Uncle Ben, Peter discovered that most of the city's crime was under the control of the Kingpin. So naturally, the crime boss became his first target. Although he wasn't an easy criminal to bring to justice, Spidey found condemning evidence of the villain, forcing the Kingpin to flee the country.

ICEMAN AND THE HUMAN TORCH

As his crime-fighting career continued, Spidey developed some real friendships with a few like-minded Super Heroes. Among those were the Human Torch of the extremely popular Fantastic Four, and Iceman, a member of the not-so-popular mutant team the X-Men. Both heroes even became Peter's roommates when Aunt May took them in after the tragic events of the world-shattering Ultimatum.

GWEN STACY

Gwen eventually ended her relationship with Peter because she was not really sure how she felt about him.

When the street-smart Gwen Stacy transferred to Midtown High, Mary Jane discovered that she had a rival for Peter's affections. That jealousy only got worse when Aunt May offered to let Gwen live in the Parker home after her father, Captain Stacy, was killed. Later, when a combination of Peter's DNA and that of the Lizard was formed into a vampiric monster called Carnage, the creature traveled to the Parkers' home in search of Spider-Man. Instead, it found the unsuspecting Gwen Stacy and fed on her, forcing Peter to deal with yet another tragic death. When Gwen later returned, now an exact duplicate created by the Carnage entity, Peter welcomed her back into his world, and the two even dated for a time.

KITTY PRYDE

During a temporary breakup with Mary Jane, the X-Men's Kitty Pryde called Peter out of the blue. The two met for a date and instantly hit it off. Because Kitty also has superpowers, Peter felt that he could pursue a relationship with her, without having to constantly worry about her safety, as he had done with Mary Jane. However, when Mary Jane was nearly killed when she was injected with the Oz formula by a clone of Peter Parker, the real Peter came to her rescue. The two kissed, reigniting their old flame and putting an end to the relationship that Kitty and Peter had been building. Kitty later began dating Peter's classmate and former bully, Kenny "Kong" McFarlane.

HARRY OSBORN

Despite being one of the coolest kids in school, Harry Osborn was always kind to Peter. But when the mysterious Mr. Shaw unlocked Harry's powers and he was transformed into the Hobgoblin, Harry was drafted as an unwilling pawn into his father's double life. Spider-Man defeated the Hobgoblin in their first fight, but Harry was later killed by his own father during an epic Green Goblin/Hobgoblin clash.

ULTIMATE TALES

Life for the Ultimate version of Peter Parker proved just as trying as Peter's life in the regular Marvel Universe. But with the events of Ultimatum and the Green Goblin's escape from prison, Spider-Man's world would change forever.

ULTIMATUM

The mutant Magneto had had enough of the human race. Manipulating the planet's magnetic fields on a scale he'd never attempted before, the villain succeeded in causing a horrific flood in New York City, among other disasters. These events became known as Ultimatum. With many of their own forces now dead, the Super Heroes of the Ultimate Universe stormed Magneto's lair and forced him to undo the damage he'd done to the globe. During the chaos, Spider-Man went missing and was presumed dead. The *Daily Bugle* publisher J. Jonah Jameson even wrote a glowing obituary for the young hero, having a change of heart after seeing Peter's heroism up close and personal. But fortunately for the city, Peter survived, living to fight another day.

The Ultimate heroes took the battle directly to its source and stormed Magneto's citadel. Wolverine unleashed his full fury, stabbing Magneto in the chest and sacrificing his own life to mortally wound the mutant. Seeing the error of his ways, Magneto righted the world before he was killed by Cyclops.

When Mary Jane discovered Peter's mask in the wreckage of Manhattan, she wrongly assumed the worst.

SINISTER SPIDEY

In the Ultimate Universe, the government agency called S.H.I.E.L.D., led by Nick Fury, keeps a diligent watch on the super-powered community. After seeing the need for super soldiers on their payroll, Fury helped establish the Ultimates, a team of heroes operating out of the Triskelion, a base that also housed the prison cells of many of the world's most dangerous criminals. But when the Super Villain Dr. Octopus staged a prison breakout and freed fellow villains, the Green Goblin, Sandman, Electro, and Kraven, Spider-Man and the heroic Ultimates came head to head.

The Green Goblin blackmailed Peter into joining their criminal team, telling him that he would kill his Aunt May unless he helped the villains storm the White House. Now the unlikely sixth member of the band of criminals known as the Sinister Six, Spider-Man helped attack the President of the United States, until Captain America assured Peter that his Aunt May was safe in government custody. Free to fight his foes, Spider-Man joined forces with the Ultimates and helped to defeat the villains.

THE DEATH OF SPIDER-MAN

Deep down, all of Peter Parker's loved ones knew the day was coming. By putting his life on the line day in and day out, Spider-Man had been tempting fate since the beginning of his vigilante career. Even a Spider-Man can't live forever, but he did prove notoriously hard to kill. During a large-scale Super Hero skirmish that happened just as the Green Goblin was escaping from his prison cell yet again, Spidey was shot in the midsection while saving the life of Captain America. Slowly bleeding to death, Spider-Man survived long enough to save his aunt from the Goblin's wrath, defeating the villain before dying a true hero.

After Peter died in Mary Jane's arms, she started to point fingers at those involved in Spider-Man's death, rather than allowing herself to mourn her loss.

THE NEW SPIDER-MAN

Eleven months before Peter Parker died, Norman Osborn was working on his Oz formula in an attempt to recreate the same accident that gave Peter his spider powers. However, test spider number 42 crawled out of its containment box and found its way into the bag of a burglar raiding the Osborn Industries facility. That burglar was Aaron Morales, uncle to Miles Morales, an intelligent young charter school student. While visiting his uncle, Miles was bitten by the spider, and soon developed strange powers like the ability to stick to walls and to camouflage himself to appear invisible. Despite rescuing a little girl and her dog from a blazing fire, Miles decided to continue on with his life as usual, not wanting to become a Super Hero. However, when he learned that the real Spider-Man had been shot and killed, Miles realized that with great power came responsibility, and later embarked on a career as the new Spider-Man.

KANGAROO BOXING

One of the first Super Villains the new Spider-Man faced was the Kangaroo, who proved to be a much tougher opponent than his name implied. While Spidey was surprised how difficult it was to beat this new foe, he was more disturbed by how the public found his own costume to be in bad taste, and he soon changed his costume.

While it took him a while to get used to his new strange powers and abilities, Miles Morales has finally come into his own as the current Spider-Man of the Ultimate Universe.

191

AMAZING ARTWORK

There is perhaps no image of Spider-Man more famous than artist Jack Kirby's iconic cover of Spider-Man's first appearance in *Amazing Fantasy* #15 (August 1962). In fact, the cover is so well known that many artists have chosen to pay homage to it by creating a similar image with their own personal twist. The cover has been rendered in media ranging from paint to a computer-generated hologram, and has featured subjects as diverse as zombies, villains, and Comedy Central TV star Stephen Colbert (in *The Amazing Spider-Man* #573). In fact, as a celebration of the cover, Marvel even offered comic book retailers an opportunity to be immortalized on a variant edition of *The Amazing Spider-Man* #669. Also of note is Steve Ditko's original unpublished cover for *Amazing Fantasy* #15 (second row, third from left), which didn't have quite the dynamic appeal that editor Stan Lee was looking for.

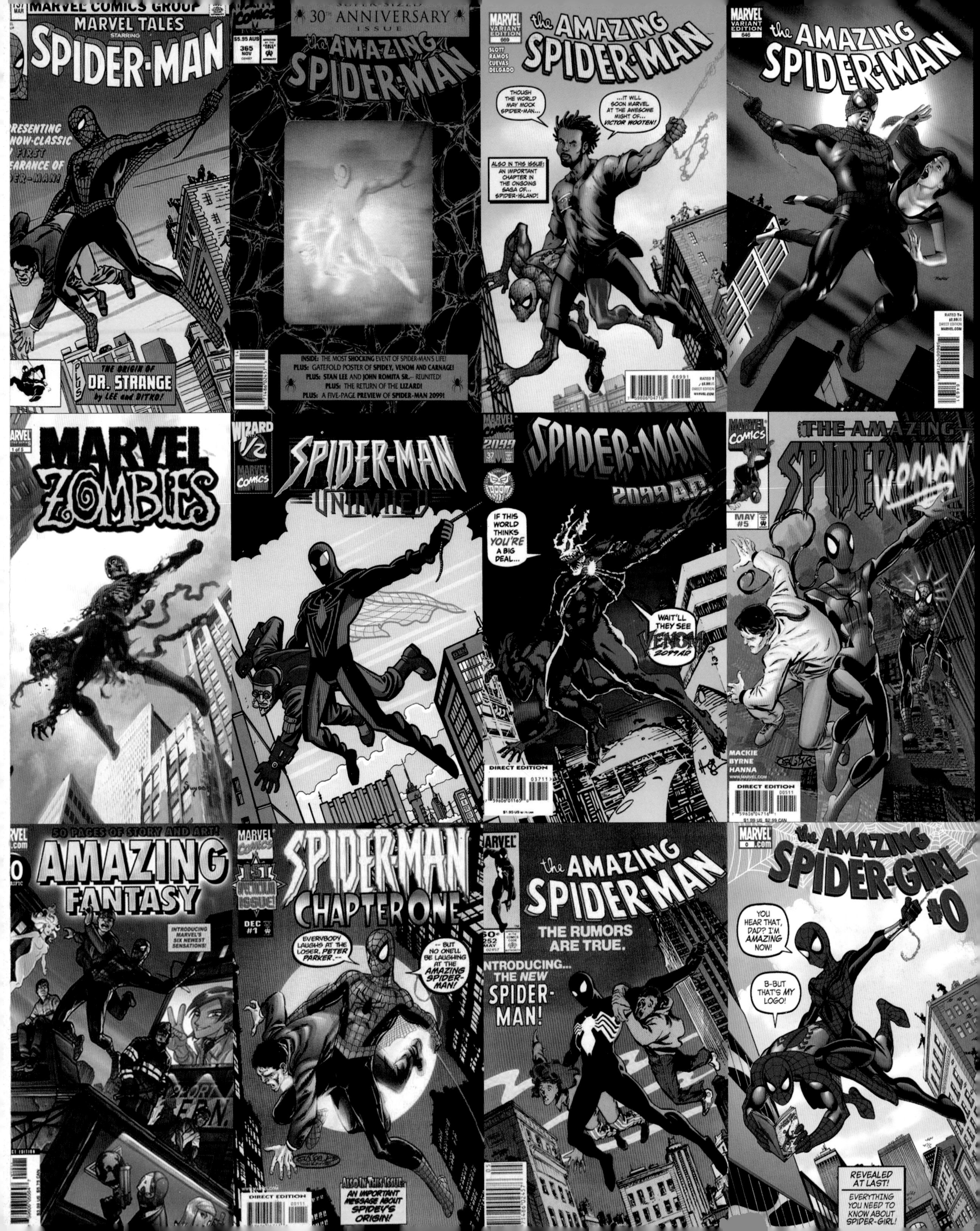
MARVEL COMICS GROUP
MARVEL TALES STARRING SPIDER-MAN
THE ORIGIN OF DR. STRANGE by LEE and DITKO!
30TH ANNIVERSARY ISSUE
the AMAZING SPIDER-MAN
INSIDE: THE MOST SHOCKING EVENT OF SPIDER-MAN'S LIFE!
PLUS: GATEFOLD POSTER OF SPIDEY, VENOM AND CARNAGE!
PLUS: STAN LEE AND JOHN ROMITA SR.-- REUNITED!
PLUS: THE RETURN OF THE LIZARD!
PLUS: A FIVE-PAGE PREVIEW OF SPIDER-MAN 2099!
MARVEL VARIANT EDITION
the AMAZING SPIDER-MAN
SLOTT RAMOS CUEVAS DELGADO
THOUGH THE WORLD MAY MOCK SPIDER-MAN...
...IT WILL SOON MARVEL AT THE AWESOME MIGHT OF... VICTOR WOOTEN!
ALSO IN THIS ISSUE: AN IMPORTANT CHAPTER IN THE ONGOING SAGA OF... SPIDER-ISLAND!
MARVEL VARIANT EDITION
the AMAZING SPIDER-MAN
MARVEL ZOMBIES
SPIDER-MAN UNLIMITED
SPIDER-MAN 2099 A.D.
IF THIS WORLD THINKS YOU'RE A BIG DEAL...
WAIT'LL THEY SEE VENOM 2099 AD
DIRECT EDITION
THE AMAZING SPIDER-WOMAN
MAY #5
MACKIE BYRNE HANNA
DIRECT EDITION
50 PAGES OF STORY AND ART!
AMAZING FANTASY
INTRODUCING MARVEL'S SIX NEWEST SENSATIONS!
SPIDER-MAN CHAPTER ONE
DEC #1
EVERYBODY LAUGHS AT THE LOSER, PETER PARKER,--
--BUT NO ONE'LL BE LAUGHING AT THE AMAZING SPIDER-MAN!
ALSO IN THIS ISSUE: AN IMPORTANT MESSAGE ABOUT SPIDEY'S ORIGIN!
DIRECT EDITION
the AMAZING SPIDER-MAN
THE RUMORS ARE TRUE.
INTRODUCING... THE NEW SPIDER-MAN!
the AMAZING SPIDER-GIRL #0
YOU HEAR THAT, DAD? I'M AMAZING NOW!
B-BUT THAT'S MY LOGO!
REVEALED AT LAST!
EVERYTHING YOU NEED TO KNOW ABOUT SPIDER-GIRL!

Index

Bold indicates main entry.

A

Acme warehouse 12-13, 116
A.I.M. 161
Alchemax 184
Alias the Spider 194
alien symbiote
  Anti-Venom 16
  Carnage 35, 42, 53-55, 138-139, 146
  Spider-Man 17, 52, 107, 109, 119
  Venom 34-35, 40, 54, 127-129
Allan, Liz 32, 44, 48-49, 52, 101
Alonso, Axel 180
Amazing Bag-Man costume 17
Amazing Fantasy #15 10, **12-13**, 60, 192
Amazing Spider-Man, The 12, 57-59, 60-61,
  63-64, 66, 68, 70, 73, 75-76, 80, 84, 86-87,
  89-90, 92-95, 100, 102-104, 116-117, 132,
  139, 147-149, 154, 158-159, 168-169,
  180-181, 192, 194
Amazing Spider-Man Annual, The 83
American Son 44, 55, 177
Andru, Ross 102
Answer 52
Anti-Venom 16, 35, 55
Ant-Man 37
Arachne 34, 55, 107, 178-179
Araña 54-55, 107, 178
armored costume 16, 168
Austin, Terry 116
Avengers 7, 28, 34-36, **37**, 40, 42, 46, 50, 52,
  54-55, 68-69, 79, 82, 106-107, 160-161,
  176, 182, 187
Avengers, The 37
Avengers Academy 28
Avengers Mansion 37
Avengers Tower 37, 163, 172
Aunt May Parker *see* Parker, Aunt May

B

Bagley, Mark 148
Banner, Dr. Bruce *see* Hulk
Bannon, Lance 27
bat-glider (Hobgoblin) 113
Batman 56, 194
Battleworld 17, 52, 108, 118
Batwing 49
Baxter Building 36, 60-61, 168
Beacher, Jalome *see* Slyde
Beck, Quentin *see* Mysterio
Beetle 44, 49, 83, 88
Bench, Morris *see* Hydro-Man
Bendis, Brian Michael 154
Bennett, Dexter 26-27, 54
Berkhart, Daniel *see* Mysterio
Bestman, Gregory 65
Beyonder 118

Big Man 27, 45, 49
Black, Carmilla *see* Scorpion
Black Cat 17, 33, 35, 51, **104-105**, 143, 148
Black Fox 28, 52
Black Marvel 151
Black Tom Cassidy 114
Boomerang 44, 51, 83, 88, 174
Borne, Robin *see* Hobgoblin
Borne, Dr. Max 185 *see also* Spider-Man
Bradhaus, Ray 74
Brand New Day 54, 140, 154, 174, 180
Brant, Bennett 86
Brant, Betty 24, 27, 32, 49, 83, 86, 102, 129,
  180
Brock, Eddie 35, 41, 52, 54-55, 126-128, 138
  see also Venom
Brooklyn Bridge 33, 102, 140-141
Brown, Hobie 35, 151 *see also* Prowler
Budiansky, Bob 148
bulletproof costume 16, 55, 151
Burglar, the 12-13, 45, 60, 116-117, 181,
  188
Buscema, John 92
Buscema, Sal 140
Buzz 187
Byrne, John 168

C

Cabal 76
Caesar, Jonathan 91
Cage, Luke 37, 160-161
Calypso 81, 136-137
Captain America 22, 37-38, 51, 54, 143,
  160-161, 165, 167, 169, 176, 190-191
Captain Atom 11
Captain Power 153
Captain Universe 16, 52, 114, 131
Caputo, Dr. Julia 148
Caramagna, Joe *see* VC's Joe Caramagna
Cardiac 53
Carnage 35, 38, 39, 42, 53-55, 127, 133,
  138-139, 142-143, 146, 181, 189
Carpenter, Julia 107 *see also* Spider-Woman
Carr, Bobby 173, 175
Carrion 47, 51, 143
Carter, Sergeant Stan *see* Sin-Eater
Castle, Frank *see* Punisher
Central Park 98, 115, 118
Chameleon 41, 45, 48-49, 53, 60-61, **62-63**,
  80, 82-83, 178-179, 183
Champions, the 45, 51
Chance 52
CIA 24, 45, 48
Circus of Crime 49
Civil War 17, 28, 37, 54, 161, **166-167**,
  168, 170, 173, 176
Cloak 45 *see also* Cloak & Dagger
Cloak & Dagger 39, 51, 143
Clone Saga 53, 102, 132, **144-145**, 148,
  186
Cohen, Janice 102
Colbert, Stephen 192
Connors, Billy 71
Connors, Dr. Curt 17, 86, 175 *see also* Lizard
Connors, Martha 71

Conover, Jacob 27, 116-117
Contraxia 32
Conway, Gerry 92, 102
Cooper, Carlie 25, 33, 54-55, 173, 180
Corazon, Anya 35, 107 *see also* Spider-Girl
Cosmic Spider-Man 16, **130-131**
Crime-Master 49
Crazy Eight 187
Creeper 11
Cyclops 190

D

Daily Bugle 25, **26-27**, 28, 32, 46-50, 54, 56,
  61-63, 65, 74, 83, 85-87, 89, 101-102, 112,
  117, 121, 127, 140, 168-169, 172-173,
  180-181, 188, 190
Daily Globe 28
Dagger *see* Cloak & Dagger
Daredevil 7, 27, 39, 42, 49, 74, 98, 121, 161
Dark Avengers 55, 76, 84
DB, The 26-27, 54
DC Comics 11, 56, 132, 136, 194
Deathlok 143
Dee, Johnny 60
DeFalco, Tom 136, 140
Defenders 46
De'Lila 36
DeMatteis, J. M. 140, 148
Demogoblin 47, 52, 143
DeWolff, Jean 52, **120-121**, 181
Dex 159
Dill, Ralph 136-137
Dillon, Anita 72
Dillon, Jonathan 72
Dillon, Maxwell *see* Electro
Ditko, Steve 10-12, 60, 86, 92, 192
Doc Ock *see* Doctor Octopus
Donovan, Arnold "Lefty" 112-113 *see also*
  Hobgoblin
Doppelgänger 53, 143
Dove 11
Dr. Doom 48, 82, 130, 183-184
Doctor Octopus 40, 48-51, 53, 56, **66-67**,
  82-83, 86-87, 96, 107, 169, 185, 190
Doctor Strange 11, 54, 170-171
Drago, Blackie 64, 65 *see also* Vulture
Drew, Jessica 106 *see also* Spider-Woman
Duffi, John 60
Dusk 151

E

Echo 161
Ehret, Sara *see* Jackpot
Eisner, Will 116
Electro 11, 27, 41, 49, **72-73**, 82-83, 160,
  178, 190
Emberlin, Randy 148
Emissaries of Evil 73, 89
Empire State University 16, 23, 25, 28, 32, 43,
  49, 51, 64, 102, 105, 130
Enforcers, the 45, 49
Enigma Force 16, 131
Esposito, Mike 102
Exterminators 63
Ezekiel 54, **158**, 159, 178, 181

F

Fancy Dan 44
Fantastic Four 7, 11, 16-17, 36, 39, 48, 56,
  60-61, 82, 119, 161, 169, 182-184, 189
Fantastic Four, The 36
Fantastic Five 186
Fester, Norton G. 47
FF uniform 16
Fireheart, Thomas *see* Puma
Firestar 38
Fishbach, Bella 29
Fisk, Wilson *see* Kingpin
Fly 51
Force Works 34
Foreigner 52
Forest Hills 7, 13, 91, 149
Fortunato, Don 128
Fortunato, Angelo *see* Venom
Foswell, Frederick 27, 86, 181
Franklin, Mattie 55, 107, 179 *see also*
  Spider-Woman
Freak 55, 175
Frenz, Ron 116
Frightful Four 68, 73
Front Line 26-27, 55
Frog-Man 51-52
Fury, Nick 7, 24, 190
Future Foundation 16, 36, 55, **182-183**
Future-Future Foundation 183

G

Gargan, MacDonald "Mac" 84, 128 *see also*
  Venom; Scorpion
Garney, Ron 168
Gathering of Five 107
George Washington Bridge 50, 96-97, 181
Ghost Rider 36, 184
Gibbon 50
Goblin Formula 53, 76-77, 100, 113, 174
Goblin-Glider 50, 76-77, 97, 100, 146
Gog 83, 93
Goliath 167
Gonzales, Michele 33
Gonzales, Vin 25, 33, 54, 173
Grandmaster 46
Grant, Glory 27, 51, 180
Gray Goblin 44, 54-55
Green Goblin
  Barton Hamilton 51, 101
  Harry Osborn 42, 51, 90-91, **100-101**,
    140-141, 173, 186, 188-189
  Norman Osborn 23, 25, 33, 40, 42, 49-50,
    52-53, 56, **76-77**, 78, 82-83, 86, 96-97,
    101-103, 113, 140-141, 146, 150, 152,
    176, 181, 185, 190-191
  Normie Osborn 186-187
  Phil Urich 53, 101, 186
Grim Hunt 35, 55, 107, **178-179**
Grim Hunter 53, 107, 178
Grimm, Benjamin *see* Thing, the
Grizzly 47, 51, 103

H

H.A.M.M.E.R. 55, 76, 161, 176
Hammerhead 47, 50, 63, 83

Hamilton, Dr. Barton 101
Hand, the 161
Hardy, Felicia *see* Black Cat
Hardy, Walter 105
Harrison, Timothy 116-117
Harrow, Jonah *see* Hammerhead
Hawk 11
Hawkeye 36, 161
Hayes, Dr. Phillip 174
Headsman 49, 76
Heroes for Hire 104
Hill, George 113
Hobgoblin 52, 82-83, **112-113**
  Harry Osborn 189
  Jason Macendale 44
  Ned Leeds 27
  Phil Urich 27, 55
  Robin Borne 185
  Roderick Kingsley 42
Hogan, Crusher 12-13, 16
Hollister, Lily 33, 54-55, 174, 177 *see also*
  Menace
Horizon Labs 16, **29**, 55
Hornet 150-151
Howling Commandos 7
Hudak, Steven 46
Hulk 7, 11, 18, 20, 36-37, 49, **78-79**, 107,
  131, 159
Human Torch 17, 36, 39, 44, 49, 55, 60, 151,
  182-183, 186, 189
Hydra 35, 106, 160-161
Hydro-Man 43, 51, 69, 83, 88

I

Iceman 38, 189
Iguana 51
Image Comics 136
Incredible Hulk 136
Infinity Inc. 136
Inner Demons 174
Invisible Girl 60
Invisible Woman 36, 168, 182
Iron Fist 143
Iron Man 7, 28, 37, 54, 138, 160-161,
  164-170, 176
Iron Patriot 55, **176-177**
Iron Spider 17, 54, **164-165**
ISO-36 serum 86

J

Jackal 43, 45, 47, 50-51, 53, 99, 102-103,
  144-145, 147
Jack O'Lantern 44, 51, 113
Jack-O'Lanterns 76, 96, 112
Jackpot 35, 54-55, 173-174
Jackson, Uatu 29
Jaffrey, Sajani 29
Jameson, Aunt May *see* Parker, Aunt May
Jameson, Jack *see* Buzz
Jameson, John 48, 50, 60-61, 89 *see also*
  Man-Wolf
Jameson, J. Jonah 25-29, 43, 48-49, 54-56,
  60-63, 85-87, 89, 102, 117, 121, 124, 140,
  148, 166, 168-169, 172-173, 180-181, 187,
  190

Jameson, J. Jonah, Sr. (Jay) 24, 25, 55, 180
Jameson, Marla 26, 55, 148, 172, 180-181
Jenkins, Abner *see* Beetle; Mach-V
Jobson, Alana *see* Jackpot
Jones, Jessica 160
Juggernaut 51, **114-115**

K

Kaine 53, 145-146, 175, 178-179, 187
Kane, Gil 92, 102
Kane, Marcy *see* Contraxia
Kangaroo 50, 191
Kasady, Cletus *see* Carnage
Kavanagh, Terry 148
Kawecki, Annette 102
Ka-Zar 51, 93
Kelly, Joe 180
Killerwatt 187
Kingpin 39, 42, 45, 50, 63, 130, 170, 172, 189
Kingsley, Roderick *see* Hobgoblin
Kirby, Jack 10-12, 60, 86, 192
Klum, Francis 74
Kraven, Alyosha 53, 81, 178-179
Kraven, Ana 55, 81, 178-179
Kraven the Hunter 14, 35, 41, 49, 52-53, 55,
  62, **80-81**, 82-83, 86, 107, **122-123**, 137,
  178-179, 181, 190
Kraven, Sasha 81, 178-179
Kraven, Vladimir 81, 178-179 *see also* Grim
  Hunter
Kravinoff, Dmitri 80, 81 *see also* Chameleon
Kravinoff, Sergei *see* Kraven

L

Lady Deathstrike 167
Lady Octopus 67
Lee, Stan 7, 10-12, 56, 60, 86, 92, 192, 194
Leeds, Ned 49, 102-103 *see also* Hobgoblin
Li, Martin 174
Lincoln, Lonnie *see* Tombstone
Lizard 14, 42, 49-50, **70-71**, 83, 87, 136-137,
  155, 178, 189
Loki 130, 131
Loners 112
Looter 47, 49
Lubensky, Nathan 181
Lubisch, Professor 130
Lyons, Dan *see* Black Marvel

M

Macendale, Jason 47, 52, 112-113 *see also*
  Hobgoblin; Jack O'Lantern
Mach-V 44
Madame Web 34, 51, 55, 107, 114, 178-179
Mad Thinker 72
Maggia 46-47
Magneto 130, 185, 190
Magnum, Moses 99
Mahlstedt, Larry 148
Man-Wolf 50
Mandarin 130
Manfredi, Silvio *see* Silvermane
Manhattan 38, 40, 51, 53, 64, 67, 73,
  102-103, 120, 122, 131, 137, 143, 153,
  173-174, 181, 190

Mann, Sylvester *see* Sandman
Markham, Maxwell 47
Marko, Cain 114
Marko, Flint *see* Sandman
Marrow 32
Martin, Marcos 180
Marvel 7-8, 10-11, 56, 60, 86, 92, 108, 132, 136, 154, 168, 184, 188-190, 192, 194
Mason, Phineas *see* Tinkerer
Massacre 181
Masters of Evil 66, 84
Master Planner 86-87
McFarlane, Kenny "Kong" 189
McFarlane, Todd 132, 136
McPherson, Pierce 168
Menace 54, 174
Mephisto 54, 125, 171
Michelinie, David 136
Midtown High School 12-14, 20, 23, 25, 28, 32, 48, 189
Mighty Avengers 37
Milla, Matt 168
Miller, Frank 108
Mockingbird 161
Modell, Max 29, 180
Molten Man 44, 49
Montana 45
Moore, Alan 108
Morales, Aaron 191
Morales, Miles *see* Spider-Man (Ultimate Universe)
Morbius 34, 50, 143
Morlun 54, 158, **159**, 162
Mr. Fantastic 36, 60, 119, 168, 183
Mr. Negative 35, 47, 54-55, 174-175
Mr. Nobody 187
Mr. Shaw 189
Ms. Fantastic 186
Ms. Marvel 33, 37, 161
Mulligan, Patrick *see* Toxin
Multiverse 184
Murdock, Matt *see* Daredevil
Mutant Growth Hormone 35, 99, 107
Myers, Fred *see* Boomerang
Mysterio 41, 48-49, **74-75**, 82-83, 103, 183
    Daniel Berkhart 51

N

Natale, Jimmy *see* Vulture
Negative Zone 151, 167, 182
New Avengers 36, 37, 54, **160-161**, 164
New Avengers 37
New Enforcers 16, 53
New Fantastic Four 36
New Warriors 38, 147, 166, 187
New York City 7, 12-13, 24-26, 33-37, 42, 45-46, 50, 53-55, 60, 67, 73, 86-87, 98, 102, 114-117, 121, 136-137, 145-148, 159-160, 162-163, 169, 173, 180-181, 183-184, 190
New York Globe 127
Newton, Professor 60
Nguyen, William *see* Captain Universe
Nieves, Dr. Tanis *see* Scorn
Nightwatch 143

Nitro 166
Norse Gods 161
Now Magazine 26
NJQ 148

O

O'Hara, Miguel 184 *see also* Spider-Man (alternative realities)
Oakley, Bill 148
Octavius, Otto *see* Doctor Octopus
Ohnn, Jonathan *see* Spot
Omega Flight 34
Osborn, Amberson 77
Osborn, Harry 25, 32, 33, 40, 49-55, 75, 77, 96, 100-101, 140-141, 143, 173-174, 177, 186, 189 *see also* American Son; Green Goblin
Osborn, Liz 140-141, 148
Osborn, Norman 21, 25, 42, 44, 46, 49-50, 54-55, 76-77, 96-97, 100-101, 113, 128, 140, 145, 150, 153, 173-174, 176-177, 186, 188 *see also* Green Goblin
Osborn, Normie (Norman, Jr.) 32, 52, 101, 140-141, 148 *see also* Green Goblin
Osborn, Stanley 55
Osborn Foundation 140-141
Osborn Industries 188, 191
Our Lady of Saints Church 119, 127
Outlaws 68
Overdrive 17, 54, 175
Owl 39
Ox 45
Oz 188-189, 191

P

Paper Doll 55, 175
Parker, Aunt May 12-13, 22, 24, 28, 31-32, 40, 48, 50-51, 53-55, 60-61, 66, 75, 83, 86-87, 116, 125, 145-146, 148-149, 153, 163, 168-175, 180, 186, 188-190
Parker, Mary 22, 24, 31, 48, 181
Parker, May "Mayday" *see* Spider-Girl
Parker, Peter **22-23**, **30-31** *see also* Spider-Man
Parker, Richard 22, 24, 31, 48, 181, 188
Parker, Rick 136
Parker, Uncle Ben 12-13, 22, 24, 31, 45, 48, 50, 83, 87, 91, 116, 146, 181, 188-189
Peter Parker, the Spectacular Spider-Man 92, 112
Petit, Corey 168
Prodigy 151
Prowler 35, 50
Pryde, Kitty 189
Psi-Lord 186
Puma 27, 35, 52, 119
Punisher 46, 50, **98-99**, 181, 184

Q

Quality Comics 194
Queen 21, 54
Quesada, Joe 154, 168
Question 11

R

radiation 10, 13, 20, 48, 67, 69, 87-88, 159

Raft 160
Ranger 153
Raptor 55, 175
Rapture 184
Ravage 184
Raven, Lieutenant Jacob 148
Ravencroft Institute 53, 143, 148
Raxton, Mark *see* Molten Man
Red Skull 130
Reilly, Ben 17, 34, 47, 51, 53, 145-147, 149, 175, 186-187 *see also* Scarlet Spider
Reinhold, Bill 168
Rhino 43, 50, 55, 82-83, **88-89**, 178
Richards, Franklin 183
Richards, Reed 169, 182, 186 *see also* Mr. Fantastic
Richards, Sue 169, 183 *see also* Invisible Woman
Richards, Valeria 183
Ricochet 150
Ringer 51
Ringmaster 39, 49
Robertson, Joe "Robbie" 25-27, 46, 50, 102, 148, 168, 180
Robertson, Martha 180
Robertson, Patricia 127
Robertson, Randy 25, 50, 180
Rocket Racer 23, 51
Rodriguez, Anton Miguel *see* Tarantula
Rogue Scholars 38
Romita, John Sr. 92
Romita, John Jr. 116, 168
Ronin 160-161
Rose, the 27, 52, 55, 174
Rosen, Joe 116, 140
Rosenthal, Judge Horace 121
Roughhouse 151
Rushman, Sarah *see* Marrow
Ryder, Dr. Damon *see* Raptor

S

Sanders, James *see* Speed Demon; Whizzer
Sandman 40, 48-49, **68-69**, 82-83, 190
Savage Land 93, 160, 179
Scarlet Spider 17, 34, 53, 67, 145, **146-147**, 148-149, 180
Scarlet Spiders 17, 165
Scarlet Witch 185
Scheele, Christie 116
Schultz, Herman *see* Shocker
Scorcher 46, 49, 76
Scorn 55, 138
Scorpia 53, 83
Scorpion 53, **84-85**, 152
    Carmilla Black 54
    Mac Gargan 43, 49, 54, 128
Scourge 181
Scraps, Grady 29
Screwball 55, 174
Scrier 53
Secret Empire 44
Sentinels 131
Sentry 42, 138, 160, 181
Serba, Anthony 102-103
Shadrac 153

Shallot, Clifton 64 *see also* Vulture
Sharen, Bob 136, 140, 148
S.H.I.E.L.D. 32, 35, 54-55, 85, 121, 161, 176, 190
Shocker 25, 43, 50, 83
Shooter, Jim 116
Shriek 53, 138, 143
Silver Sable 34-35, 52
Silver Surfer 7
Silvermane 46, 50
Simek, Art 12, 86
Sims, Ezekiel *see* Ezekiel
Sin-Eater 52, 121, 127
Sinister Seven 83
Sinister Six 49, 52, 63-64, 66, 68, 70, 73-74, 80, **82-83**, 89, 112, 126, 183, 190
Sinister Syndicate 43-44, 46, 52, 89
Sinister Twelve 63-64, 68, 70, 73, 76, 82-84
six-armed Spider-Man 17, 92
Skrulls 36, 55, 161
Slingers, the 151
Slott, Dan 180
Slyde 46, 52
Smythe, Alistair 47, 52, 85 *see also* Ultimate Spider-Slayer
Smythe, Spencer 44, 47, 49, 52
Solo 52
Spectacular Spider-Man, The 132, **140-141**
Speed Demon 46, 51
Spider-Carnage 146
Spider-Girl 35, 55, 106-107
    May Parker **186-187**
Spider-Island 55
Spider-Man
    alternative realities 184-185
    belt 14-15, 20, 48
    clone 45, 51, 53, 102-103, 132, 144-147, 175, 178-179, 186
    costume 13, **14-15**, **16-17**, 20, 48, 61, 108, 118-119, 164-165, 182-183
    family **24-25**
    friends **24-25**, **34-35**
    impostor 152-153
    in love **32-33**
    powers **18-19**
    team-ups **38-39**
    teams **36-37**
    TV appearance 117, 181
    see also Cosmic Spider-Man; Spider-Man (Ultimate Universe); Ultimate Spider-Man
Spider-Man (Ultimate Universe) 191
Spider-Man 132, **136-137**
Spider-Mobile 51, 103
spider-sense 15-16, 19, 55, 61, 63, 75, 77, 85, 96-97, 103, 126-127, 139, 147, 158, 187
spider-signal 15, 20, 48
spider-strength 130
Spider-Slayer 47, 49, 55 *see also* Ultimate Spider-Slayer
spider-tracers 15, 19, 49, 72, 147
Spider-Woman 37, **106-107**
    Jessica Drew 35, 51, 160
    Julia Carpenter 34, 52
    Mattie Franklin 54, 153, 178

Spidercide 45, 53
Spot 45, 52
Stacy, Captain George 49-50, **96-97**, 189
Stacy, Gwen 33, 40, 43-44, 49-51, 54, **96-97**, 100, 102-103, 125, 141, 168, 181, 185, 189
    clone 51, 102-103
Stacy, Gabriel *see* American Son; Gray Goblin
Standard High School 100
Stark, Tony 17, 28, 161, 164, 168-169, 172
    see also Iron Man
Stark Tower 28, 168-169
stealth suit 16, 55
Stegron the Dinosaur Man 51
Stern, Roger 116
Stillwell, Dr. Farley 43, 85
Storm, Johnny 16-17, 39, 182 183 *see also* Human Torch
St. Patrick's Cathedral 180-181
Straczynski, J. Michael 154, 168
Stromm, Professor Mendel 49, 77
Styx & Stone 52
Superego 183
Superhuman Registration Act 54-55, **166-167**, 169, 177
Superman 56, 194
Swarm 45, 51
symbiote *see* alien symbiote
Sytsevich, Aleksei *see* Rhino

T
Tarantula 46, 51, 102-103, 194
Thing, the 18, 36-37, 60, 161, 182, 186
Thompson, Eugene "Flash" 12, 25, 41, 48-49, 112, 127, 148, 168-169, 188 *see also* Venom
Thor 18, 36-37, 159
Thunderball 116
Thunderbolts 54, 76, 84, 176
Timespinners 185
Tinkerer 46, 48, 74
Titania 131
Tombstone 46, 52, 83, 90
Toomes, Adrian *see* Vulture
Toxin 35, 54, 138
Trainer, Carolyn *see* Lady Octopus
Traveller, Judas 53
Trevane, Detective Connor 148
Tri Corp Research Foundation 152
Tri-Sentinel 52, 131
Triskelion 190

U
Ultimate Spider-Man 154
Ultimate Spider-Man **188-189**
Ultimate Spider-Slayer 47, 52, 85 *see also* Spider-Slayer
Ultimates, the 190
Ultimatum 189-190
Uncle Ben Parker *see* Parker, Uncle Ben
Underworld 46
Uni-Power 16, 131
Urich, Ben 27, 101, 180
Urich, Phil 42, 100, 112-113 *see also* Green Goblin, Hobgoblin

V
Vault 37
VC's Joe Caramagna 180
Venom 40, 42, 53, 90, **128-129**, 133, 138-139, 143, 146, 167, 187
    Eddie Brock 35, 52, 83, **126-127**
    Flash Thompson 34, 55
    Mac Gargan 43, 54-55, 83, 85, 176
Venom: Lethal Protector #1 133-135
Vermin 51, 122-123
Vicente, Muntsa 180
Videoman 38
Von Meyer, Fritz *see* Swarm
Vulture 39, 48-49, 55, **64-65**, 82-83, 169, 178
    Adrian Toomes 40
    Blackie Drago 50
    Clifton Shallot 50
    Jimmy Natale 65

W
Waid, Mark 180
Warren, Professor Miles 49 *see also* Jackal
Wasp 37
Watanabe, Captain Yuri 180
Watson, Anna 32, 91, 148
Watson, Judge Spencer 125
Watson, Mary Jane 24, 31, 32, 35, 48, 50, 52-54, 62, **90-91**, 100, 102-103, 122-125, 136-137, 140-141, 148, 150-151, 153, 162-163, 168-171, 173, 175, 186, 188-191
webs 8, 13-17, **20-21**, 26, 64, 75, 85, 126-127, 131, 137, 139
    web cartridges 15, 20
    web fluid 15, 20-21, 48, 89, 172
    web formula 15, 188
    web-lines 61, 97, 117, 136-137
    web-shooters 14-15, 17, 20, 48, 54, 102, 117, 127, 147, 187
Web of Spider-Man 109-111, 126, 132, 148
Webs: Spider-Man in Action 28
West Coast Avengers 161
White Dragon 47, 51
White Rabbit 52
White Tiger 51
Whitman, Debra 32
Whizzer 46
Wild Pack 34, 68
Will-O'-the-Wisp 51
Winters, Norah 25, 27, 55
Witter, Charlotte 107 *see also* Spider-Woman
Wizard, the 130
Wolfman, Marv 102
Wolverine 24, 36-38, 98, 160-161, 167, 185, 190
World War II 46, 161
Wraith 174
Wrecking Crew 116
wrist-shooters 13, 16

X
X-Men 7, 11, 38, 51, 83, 114, 161, 184, 189

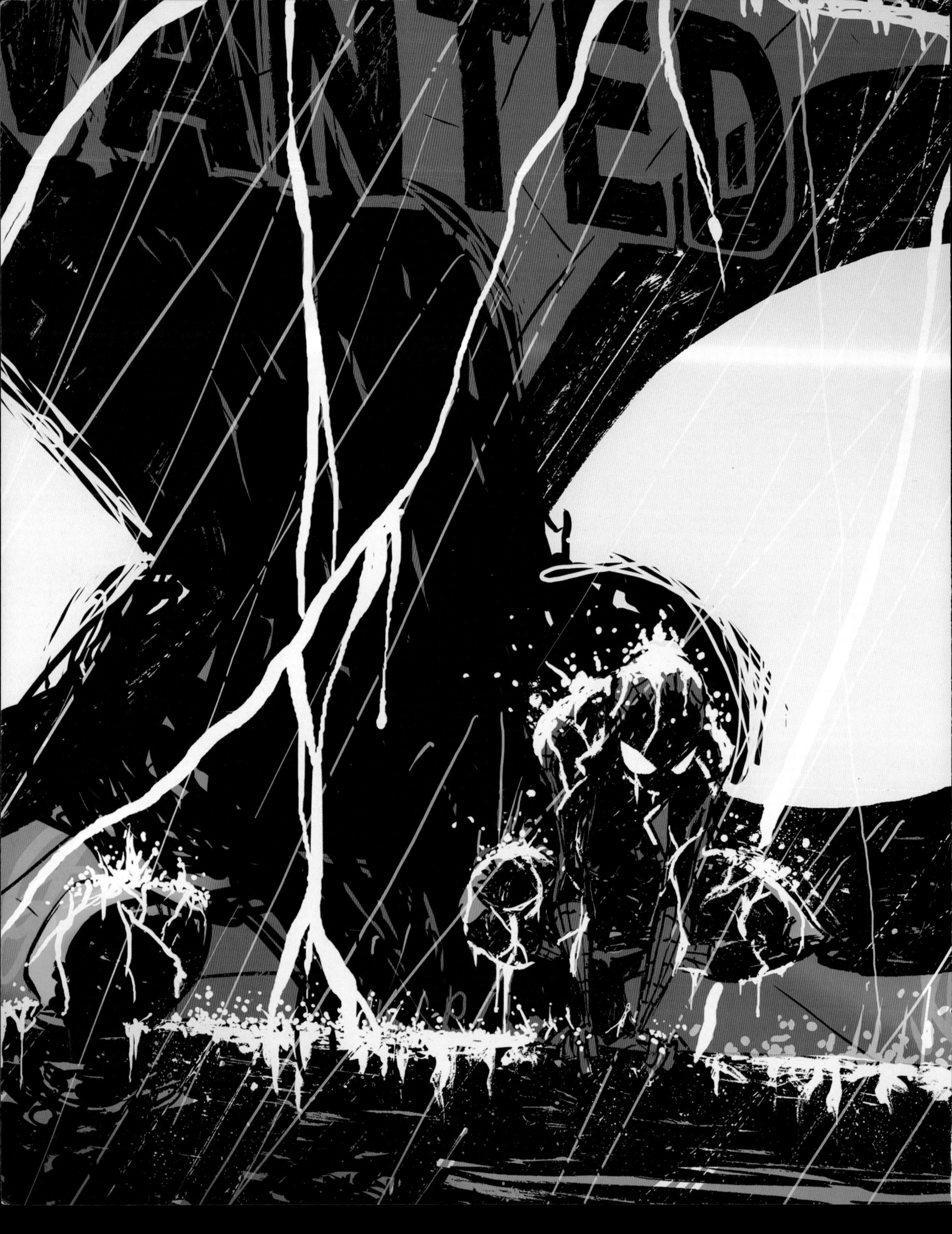